West Downs

A Portrait of an English Prep School

Lionel Helbert

Kenneth Tindall

Jerry Cornes

The Three Headmasters

West Downs

A Portrait of an English Prep School

Mark Hichens

The Pentland Press Limited
Edinburgh · Cambridge · Durham

First Published in 1992 by
The Pentland Press Ltd.
5 Hutton Close
South Church
Durham

ISBN 1   872795   76   5

Typeset by Elite Typesetting Techniques
Southampton.
Printed and bound by Antony Rowe Ltd.,
Chippenham.

Foreword
by
Lord Sherfield, G.C.B., G.C.M.G., F.R.S., D.L.

I do not know how many histories of British preparatory schools have been published. I would guess that there are not very many, and it certainly requires commitment and enthusiasm to sit down and write one.

Mr Mark Hichens has both qualities. But then West Downs was no ordinary run of the mill preparatory school. It was founded, if not by a genius, then at any rate by a man with a genius for teaching small boys and for managing them and their parents.

Lionel Helbert abandoned his career as a Clerk in the House of Commons to found West Downs on a hill above Winchester. He concentrated the whole of his tireless energy and fertile imagination and gave almost every minute of his waking hours to developing and improving the school, and to inspiring not only his pupils and his staff but also the parents. He was a bachelor, but found devoted women to back him in the development of the school as well as in covering and carrying out the tasks of a headmaster's wife. Some of his views and methods were unconventional, even controversial by the standards of the time, but he was a truly humane man, and the place was infused by his humanity and his devotion to the school.

He was twenty-seven when he founded it; he had burnt himself out before he was fifty. But he had, in that relatively short time, established a tradition and left an imprint on the school which it never lost.

There were only three headmasters between its foundation in 1897 and its closure in 1988, apart from masters who stood in during an interregnum, and Helbert's successors were very different sort of men from him, and indeed from one another. The mercurial Helbert was followed by the rather stolid Tindall. Cornes was in the Colonial Service and took to schoolmastering in later life. But partly, no doubt due to an unusual continuity of staff, the ethos of the place did not change much and the school flourished under all three regimes.

I went in March 1914 and left in July 1917, the difficult years of the First World War. No one who had known or been taught by Lionel Helbert could ever forget him. (Probably later generations felt the same about Tindall and Cornes.) As Mr Hichens relates, Helbert used to visit parents and boys in the school holidays. He came once to stay with my mother, myself and my younger brother who was also in the school. It was winter, in wartime, my brother and I were not particularly interesting little boys, and there was nothing to do. It must have been deadly dull, but Helbert illuminated the scene, and entered with apparent enthusiasm into our rather childish ways and pursuits.

This book will no doubt be read mainly by old boys and their sons and families, but it will, I hope, also be of interest to a wider audience. It portrays what most people nowadays would regard as a very old-fashioned sort of place. The central importance of Chapel, the adoption in 1914 of scouting as the basis of the school's structure, the Courts of Honour, the preoccupation with health, all represent in full measure the spirit of the old tag "Mens sana in corpore sano".

The narrative also leaves the impression that the boys were sheltered, not to say pampered, and with this went a certain naivety of outlook. But I suffered no great culture shock when I went on to Winchester, though there I was fortunate in going to a very humane house, compared with many of them at that time.

On the academic side, the concentration on the classics, the total absence of any science whatever in the curriculum right up to the mid sixties, certainly appears extreme, even if this was in part attributable to the narrowness of the Common Entrance requirements.

Quite apart from the policy and operations of the headmasters, there is some interesting characterisation of masters and boys, and some humorous moments; for example Mrs Tindall's sudden conversion to the virtues of cold air, resulting in what was known in the school as "The Little Ice Age".

The account of the vicissitudes of the school in the Second World War makes interesting, even dramatic reading. It brings out in full measure the strength of character of the Tindalls and the resourcefullness and endurance of the staff. They rose splendidly to the challenge and worked tirelessly to keep the school going. They survived the near nightmare of two moves in two years – from Winchester to Glenapp and then on to Blair Castle. Even worse was the move back in 1945 to a West Downs seriously vandalised by successive waves of soldiery. On top of all this the Tindalls suffered the loss of two sons killed during the war.

But the school settled down again in Winchester very much on the pre-war pattern. This achievement was partly due to the almost incredible devotion of the staff: two members of the teaching staff (Ledgard and Rose), and the music teacher (Miss Playsted) who were in place on my arrival in 1914 were still there in 1945; the legendary Miss Squilley had only retired in 1943; the matron had joined in 1930; and one master (Rawson) rejoined in 1948. Some changes of course took place. The old stalwarts finally retired and some successful appointments were made. More modern methods of teaching were gradually adopted. Maths teaching had always been good, but it seems extraordinary that science was not introduced until 1964!

When Tindall decided to retire after thirty years in office, he left the school in first class, if still rather old-fashioned condition with over a hundred pupils and a full order book. His own reputation in the prep school world, in which he had played a full part, was high, and his wife had given him invaluable support. He had been a dedicated and successful headmaster. If he had a fault, it was perhaps that he was rather too free with the cane!

Cornes, his successor, had been, like Lionel Helbert, a public servant with a consuming desire to own and run a private school. I never met him, so I cannot add anything of value to Mr Hichens' account, but he emerges from it as a man dedicated to his task and, again like Helbert, unconventional in his methods.

He did not hurry to make any major change in the way the school was run. He maintained and indeed, if scholarships are a fair measure, enhanced its academic standards. The school also maintained to the end nearly a hundred per cent success in Common Entrance at a time when the overall failure rate was thirty per cent. Cornes moved cautiously to adjust to the turmoil of youth in the sixties. He finally brought in science. He was much more easygoing in many ways than his predecessors, and this seems to have made the school a rather rougher ride for some of the boys. He bowed inevitably to the economic and social pressures which built up in the sixties and seventies by increasing numbers and admitting girls.

But all was well until he began to tire and decided to take "a back seat". Then danger signals began to appear. Cornes had retained only a minority share in the family company, into which he had turned the school in 1964. He was no longer in full control. A promising successor was found in his godson, Andrew Morrison, but Cornes stayed on as Bursar, and Morrison left after one year because of policy disagreements. In spite of valiant efforts by an acting head-master it appears that, owing to many uncertanties, something of a rot set in before the final curtain. So, like so many stories of real life, this one has an unhappy ending.

In 1988 Cornes decided to close the school and sell the property. Its value had risen dramatically. Some parents and old boys made the most vigorous and valiant efforts to acquire the school and carry it on. They were not successful. Cornes said he had a choice between the interest of the school and the interest of his family and must give preference to the latter. In doing so, he was of course acting within his rights.

The moral of the tale, if there is one, is that no school of the calibre and prestige of West Downs should be allowed to remain private property. It should be turned into an Educational Trust. A move to do this was made in the early 1950s, but it was not pushed through mainly because Tindall believed, probably wrongly, that it was not financially feasible. Andrew Morrison tried again in 1981, but was rebuffed and resigned on the issue. It was a great misfortune that these attempts and the prodigious final effort of 1987 ended in failure.

Mr Hichens has added a postscript identifying some of the more prominent among the 2,100 boys and the 100 girls who attended the school during its lifetime of ninety years. This may well not be exhaustive, but it is of considerable interest. There are a few well-known political figures (two in the Churchill cabinet) and a sprinkling in most other professions, but the list (based on *Who's Who*) reveals that nearly half of all those on it were in the Army or the Navy and reached the rank of Major General and Vice Admiral or better, up to one Field Marshal and one Admiral of the Fleet. OWDs of course served in the RAF, but none seems to have progressed beyond the rank of Group Captain, the senior of them being Group Captain Collingwood. What can be the reason for this extraordinary preponderance? Was it perhaps that the school was from 1914 based on scouting and, except for a short period in the seventies, on particularly strict discipline? Whatever the reason it is a remarkable statistic. It is perhaps less surprising that there is no engineer in the list at this level, and in science only one F.R.S., Edward Collingwood, and he was a mathematician rather than a scientist.

Preface

This book was conceived in Brooks's Club on the occasion of the OWD Society Dinner there in the summer of 1989. It was the first such occasion since the closure of the School and the prevailing feeling was the need to perpetuate the memory of West Downs. Various ideas were put forward and I was rash enough to suggest that a history ought to be written and fairly soon while the older OWDs were still alive. The reaction to this was prompt. Daniel Hodson (then Hon. Treasurer of the Society, now Chairman) said at once: "Well, why don't you write it?" This took me by surprise and I did not immediately jump at the idea. At the time I was thinking about writing another book and there were, I felt sure, those better qualified than I to write about West Downs. However, on thinking the idea over I became increasingly attracted by it. West Downs was certainly an unusual Prep School, in its way a great one. Its ninety-year history contained much that was noteworthy with many different elements – the admirable (even heroic), the mundane, the colourful and, certainly, the comic. It spanned the years from those of Victorian propriety to those of the so-called Permissive Society. It seemed to me that the story of West Downs was a slice of social history and should be recorded.

In taking on the assignment I was determined that the book should not be a conventional Prep School history – bland in tone, narrow in scope, and written from the point of view of one person only, usually a past or present headmaster. This history would contain many differing viewpoints – the affectionate, the ribald, the critical, even (within the laws of libel) the angry. For this it would be necessary to canvas past members of the School and try to obtain from them old memories and feelings. Fortunately this was possible as a register of OWDs and their addresses had been maintained. This was the work of Nicholas Hodson and my debt to him is considerable; not only did he provide me with a copy of the register but he also undertook the laborious task of circularising all OWDs urging them to write candidly of their time at the School. The response to this was encouraging; about a hundred OWDs replied with a varied assortment of memories and opinions.

This was a good start but it seemed to me that it could be extended as there were, I felt sure, many OWDs who would be more willing to talk than to write; and this proved to be the case. In the following months I imposed myself on some sixty or seventy OWDs and had many lively and agreeable conversations in the course of which some entertaining and sometimes surprising memories came to the surface.

Many people then have contributed to this book and I would like to record my gratitude to all of them. First, to Lord Sherfield for his admirable Foreword. It was very good of him to undertake this; it could not have given the book a better send-off.

My debt to Nicholas Hodson has already been mentioned. Certainly the book, in the form in which it has taken, would not have been possible without him. His brother, Daniel, has also played a key role: not only did he instigate the book in the first place, but also gave great support while it was being written and took upon himself the task of finding the necessary financial backing. David Howard (Hon. Secretary of the Society) has also given great help and support. Both he and Daniel will always be in the debt of OWDs for their great efforts to save West Downs from closure and subsequently to keep the memory of the School alive.

In the writing of the book I have had invaluable help from Sir Edward Ford who not only provided me with extensive memories but also read through the book in page proof and made many constructive suggestions as well as saving me from a number of errors. Lord Horder also read through the book in page proof and with his professional expertise made a great many corrections and improvements. Sir John Stephenson too has been generous with his help, allowing me to see a chapter on West Downs from a book he is writing, and reading parts of my book in typescript with helpful comments and amendments. I am grateful too for the help of Ann Bass (née Tindall) who made available to me the records of her father and provided a lively account of West Downs' odyssey in Scotland during the Second World War. Jerry and Ray Cornes also have been at great pains to help, letting me have all records and photographs I have asked for and submitting with great patience (and hospitality) to a barrage of questions. My thanks too to E.E. Knollys, A.W. Stephenson, H.J. Simpson and C.F.duM. Browning for providing photographs for the book.

Then there were the hundred or so OWDs who were kind enough to write to me. I hope they realise how vital their letters have been; they have made the book what it is. My only regret is that in order to avoid repetition it has not been possible to quote from them all, but the names of the writers should certainly be recorded:

J.L. Aldridge (1929), Sir Norman Arthur (1940), The Hon. David Astor (1921), D. Baring (1918), A.J. Barnett (1944), R.D.J. Bendall (1936), Sir Henry Beresford-Peirse (1943), S.H. Berthon (1959), Sir Alex Bethune (1918), C.C. Biggar (1941), P.D. Birchall, C.A.A. Black (1945), Sir Jack Boles (1934), T.C.P. Brooke (1947), J. Browne-Swinburne (1946), F.K. duM. Browning (1978), C.G. Burge (1919), The Revd. D.H. Buxton (1925), C.A.G. Campbell (1926), E.S.M. Cameron (1943), C.Clegg (1935), R.B. Cleminson (1953), J.A.P. Coates (1940), P.J. Colfox (1971), C.J. Collingwood (1909), P.R. Colville (1919), A.H.S.

Coombe-Tennant (1918), S.P. Courtauld (1948), C.W. Crawley (1909), M.W.P. Cripps (1939), B.D.B. Denison (1984), M.E. Denison (1981), A.W.S. Denton (1964), A.N.G. Duckworth-Chad (1951), G.L. Eddis (staff 1961–82), H.D.Y. Faulkner (1942), W.H. Fellowes (1912), The Earl Ferrers (1936), C.D. Forbes (1947), The Revd. A.E. Ford (1914), P.J.D. Forwood (1975), Lord Gainford (1930), B.C.P. Gething (1934), I.M. Graham (1929), J.D.T. Greenall (1946), W.E. Grenville-Grey (1939), P.L.J. Groves (1934), V. Guinness (1966), Miss V. Guy (matron 1930–64), A.J.C. Hawks (1948), Lord Hazlerigg (1918), J.A.C. Henley (1922), J.E. Holland-Hibbert (1975), Lord Horder (1919), S.M. Howard (1929), P.N.B. Howell (1928), R.H. King (1947), J.W. Kingstone (1931), C.E.J. Jerram (1962), M.C. Lloyd (1940), H.F. McCall (1948), A.D. McClintock (1952), D.C. McClintock (1922), A.G.M. McEwan (1961), D.F. MacQuaker (1941), R.W. Meynell (1932), The Revd J.A. Mitchell-Innes (1948), The Hon. J.S. Monck (1969), P.F. Morgan (1930), Sir Jeremy Morse (1937), Sir Anthony Mullens (1945), Sir John Nelson (1921), J.S.W. Passmore (1957), B.A. Pearson (1922), J.L.G. Pinhey (1945), T.A.G. Pocock (1934), R.S. Ponsonby (1961), D.S. Potter (1943), C.G.A.L. Potts (staff 1956–63), J.L.C. Pratt (1942), M.H. Priestley (1940), A.S.R. Pyper (staff 1941–43), P.F.I. Reid (1921), M.E. Rice (1942), Miss M. Richardson (staff 1943–80), C. Romer-Lee (1918), M.Q. Savege (1955), C.J. Scott (1930), G.M.B. Selous (1937), G.D.L. Selous (1962), A.E.A. Selous (1970), H.J. Simpson (1922), G.M. Singleton (staff 1936–38), M.R.F. Simson (staff 1938–40), J.H. Thornton (1937), J.R. Tillard (1933), A.G. Warrack (1953), P.S. Wilmot-Sitwell (1943), J.T.A. Wilson (1924), A.J. Wodehouse (1945), E.A. Wodehouse (1976), C.J.B. Wood (1932), P. Wrightson (1923), R. Wrightson (1925).

Finally the thanks of myself and all OWDs are due to those who made possible the publication of this book by generous financial assistance: Peter Wilmot-Sitwell, Michael Cripps, Sir James Spooner, Sir Jeremy Morse, Lt. Cdr. C. Marten, Lord Hazlerigg, J. Browne-Swinburne, P.D. Birchall, Lord Cochrane of Cults, A. Duckworth-Chad, D.S. Allhusen, Sir James Harvie-Watt, J.A.C. Henley, R.C. Allhusen, Sir Edward Ford, G.H. Mills, E.A.W. Williams, Sir Henry Warner, R.P. Norton, Mrs Ann Bass, David Dennison, Daniel Hodson, Lord Horder, C.F.duM. Browning, A. Drake-Brockman, Lord Falmouth, Sir John Nelson, H.J. Simpson, The Hon. David Astor, B.A. Pearson, Ivo Reid, J.F. Cornes, G. Thorne, P.R. Colville, The Hon. James Ogilvy, N.J. Hodson, S.P. Courtauld, C.A.G. Campbell.

It might be noted that in this Preface some 125 names have been mentioned which with those who agreed to be interviewed amount to nearly 200 names altogether – surely no mean tribute to West Downs.

Mark Hichens
63 Eccleston Square
London S.W.1.

Introduction

The boarding Preparatory School, or Prep School, is a peculiarly English institution. In no other country do the well-to-do send their sons at the age of eight or younger away from home to establishments often of considerable austerity. Foreigners look aghast at such a practice and many young parents in England vow they will never do such a thing, although, when it comes to the point, they usually find themselves obliged to comply with the system.

Some trace the origins of this system to the choir schools of the cathedrals; some go even further back to the practice of sending young boys into great households to begin their training as knights. But it was not until the nineteenth century, with the great growth of Public Schools, that Prep Schools, recognisable as such, began to appear. Before this boys of Prep School age had sometimes been taken into Public Schools, but there were great disadvantages to this, and in the 1830s Thomas Arnold barred them from Rugby and other headmasters followed suit. From then on there was a great demand for coaching establishments to prepare young boys for Public Schools, and it came to be recognised that an important part of this preparation was to acclimatise them to boarding school life at as early an age as possible.

In response to this need a variety of people came forward. Foremost among them were clergymen. With large rectories, inadequate stipends and often families of their own to be educated, the country clergy found an answer to some of their problems by taking in boarding pupils. Usually these establishments were of a temporary nature, but some of them developed into full-scale Prep Schools. Also to respond to this new demand were unmarried women, of whom in Victorian times there were a large number, and to whom there were few careers open apart from teaching. In consequence the so-called 'dame schools' began to increase in size and number, and some of these, notably Summer Fields in Oxford, developed into highly successful Prep Schools. Others in the field included assistant masters from Public Schools unlikely to obtain headmasterships there, retired serving officers, and miscellaneous others, not always of the highest character, who could not earn a living by any other means. But there were also a few genuine philanthropists who felt a call for work of that sort, and among these Lionel Helbert of West Downs was a notable example.

Of the early Prep Schools not all were of good repute: some notably the opposite. Stories abound of dilapidated and insanitary buildings, inadequate and inedible food and eccentric, sometimes barbarous, headmasters. As in Public Schools flogging was rife, often administered for little or no reason and with great brutality. One schoolboy later wrote that at his Prep School corporal punishment was not so much a punishment as a way of life. Another from a distinguished family wrote that his parents might as well have had him educated at a brothel for flagellants. And Lord Salisbury, the Prime Minister, wrote of his Prep School: 'My existence there was an existence among devils.' And yet, in spite of everything, more and more parents began sending their sons to Prep Schools, and more and more of these appeared on the scene – between 1875 and 1900 some 120. And some of these were not the bleak, inhuman places they were reputed to be – certainly not West Downs. Everything depended on the headmaster. For within the school he was all-powerful – a despot, benevolent or otherwise. It was he who set the tone of the school; more than that he imprinted his personality on it.

Few headmasters did this so distinctively and so lastingly as Lionel Helbert. He was, indeed, no ordinary Prep School headmaster, and this was reflected in the school he founded. Any history of West Downs, therefore, must first take a look at his life and personality.

Chapter 1

Lionel Helbert was born on 13th June 1870 in Brighton, the sixth child of Captain Frederic John Helbert and Sarah Magdalene Lane. On his father's side Lionel was of Jewish descent, his family being one of the first to have settled in England at the time of Cromwell when the ban on them was lifted. The family name then was Israel, and it is not known for certain how it came to be changed to Helbert, but it may have been from Helbertstadt, the town in Germany from which the family had come. It seems that the first Helberts worked as jewellers, but at the beginning of the nineteenth century one of them, John Helbert (Lionel's grandfather), joined with his brother-in-law to found the stockbroking firm of Helbert Wragg.[1] The business was successful and in building it up the partners were greatly helped by their association with another brother-in-law, Nathan Rothschild, for whom they did much business. However, it seems the firm was not large enough to contain all the members of John's family, and his son Frederic John (Lionel's father) had a career elsewhere. As a young man he joined the Indian Army in which he served for fifteen years but then had to retire early at the age of thirty-one because of ill health. By that time he had become converted to Christianity and had married a Christian lady, Sarah Lane, or Lena as she was known, who came from an old English family which included among its past members the Jane Lane who had helped Charles II, disguised as her servant, to escape after the Battle of Worcester.[2]

For the rest of his life Frederic seems to have engaged in various occupations – sometimes as a military correspondent, sometimes in short-lived business ventures. But although employment was sporadic and his family was growing rapidly – finally seven children – it does not appear that he was in financial straits. Perhaps there were private means emanating from Helbert Wagg; but for four years he was able to act as unpaid secretary to Mrs Gladstone, wife of the Prime Minister. This connection was to be of great importance to the Helbert family and especially to Lionel; for Mrs Gladstone's niece, Lucy Lyttelton, later Lady Frederick Cavendish, became Lionel's godmother. Lady Frederick was the most dedicated of Christians. After her husband had been assassinated by Fenians in Phoenix Park, Dublin, she sought out the assassins in prison to give them her forgiveness and made contact with their families to comfort them at the time of the executions. It is unlikely that such a person would have taken her god-

1

motherly duties lightly, and she must surely have been one of the people responsible for Lionel's deep Christian conviction.[3]

When Lionel was four his mother died, giving birth to a seventh child. Although hardly more than a baby at the time, Lionel was to retain a vivid memory of his mother; her warmth and piety made a deep impression on him, and he was always to have her photograph on his writing desk. Her death meant that he was never to have a proper family life. In childhood he was usually in the care of nurses and governesses, and with the other younger children spent much time with his maternal grandmother. But the one who especially took Lionel under her wing and was always very protective of him, even in adult life, was his elder sister, Amy, later Lady Goodrich. She was to play a prominent role in his life – and in that of West Downs.

At the age of eight Lionel was sent to a small private boarding school in Brighton. At that time such establishments were liable to be rigorous, not to say fearsome, but it seems that Lionel was fortunate. Two notable benefits came from his time there. In the first place it brought him into contact with a benevolent and exceptional schoolmaster, one Charles Harper. Unusually for that time, Mr Harper considered there was more to a schoolmaster's job than ramming home facts in the classroom. He was also interested in the welfare of the boys and the development of their talents, and continued to take an interest in them after they had left the school. It must be certain that Lionel's later strongly held views on the role of a schoolmaster owed much to Mr Harper. West Downs has reason to be grateful to him. The other benefit afforded to Lionel by his Prep School was that it helped him to gain the top scholarship to Winchester.

In 1883 Winchester College was hardly the august, beneficent seat of learning it is sometimes thought to be. It was in fact something of a rough-house. Conditions were, however, better than they had been at the beginning of the century. Then it had been almost complete bedlam. Boys were half-starved and neglected, were flogged brutally and often, and the general indiscipline made present day blackboard jungles seem pale in comparison. It was not unusual for open rebellion to break out, for the Riot Act to be read and, on one occasion, for troops with fixed bayonets to be called in to restore order. Today one can only marvel that parents at that time paid quite heavily to commit their sons to such a life, a life described by Lytton Strachey as one 'in which licensed barbarism was mingled with the daily and hourly study of the niceties of Ovidian verse.'

By 1883, however, Winchester had to some extent put its house in order. Taking a lead, like other Public Schools, from Dr Arnold of Rugby (himself a Wykehamist), schoolmasters came to realise that they were responsible for more than cramming Latin and Greek into their pupils. More attention was paid to the spiritual and physical needs of the boys, and games were introduced to absorb their energies. Nevertheless, when Helbert first went to Winchester conditions there, particularly in College where the scholars were housed, still left much to be desired. Nowell Smith, an exact contemporary of Helbert's, later wrote:

College at that particular moment was going through an unpleasant phase. There was a considerable gang of undesirables, some of them prefects, others 'inferiors' of some seniority and physical power. Discipline was lax and variable. There was not a little immorality and much more loose and low conversation.

It appears that the master in charge of College, a Mr Richardson, was totally ineffective:

Dear old Dick . . . 'Dick' he always was; and dear he became to all of us from the kindliness and simplicity of his character as well as from certain comfortable idiosyncrasies of voice and speech and manner. 'Dick', then, never came near us in College unless some altogether extraordinary yells or crash aroused him after we had gone bedwards: he would then appear with the ejaculation 'Arr-arr. Too much noise!' And after a moment or two of awkward silence return to his study.

In such a place there were clearly great dangers for a good looking and exceptionally gifted boy like Helbert. For exceptionally gifted he certainly was. According to Nowell Smith he had 'the divinest voice I ever heard in a boy.' He was also an outstanding pianist; almost entirely self-taught, he could read at sight and play by ear with equal facility. But it seems that he was not so much interested in playing the great classical pieces as in accompanying himself and others in lighthearted songs and musical jokes, this tallying with his other great gift which was for mimicry and acting. In development of these talents Helbert had much encouragement from the wife of the Master in College. Her husband might have had little interest in the boys in his charge, but not so Mrs Dick. Described, a little condescendingly, by Nowell Smith as 'jolly, stout, loud-voiced, free-spoken, free-jesting and infinitely loving', she assumed the role of mother to Helbert and became a powerful influence in his life. It was she who later on urged him strongly to start his own prep school. West Downs, maybe, is in Mrs Dick's debt.

Reading Nowell Smith's account of Lionel's career at Winchester, it is difficult to escape the conclusion that he was something of a dilettante with brilliant gifts which he was in danger of frittering. It seems that he made no great effort at his academic studies, and for the most part was content to 'get by'. However, before leaving he did pick up three top prizes for Historical Essay, Latin Essay and Reading. He also gained a scholarship to Oriel College, Oxford.

On the whole, then, Winchester served Helbert well: his academic excellence was maintained; he was allowed considerable freedom, possibly too much; he was not coerced into too many compulsory games at which he did not shine; and there was scope for his other interests, notably music and entertainment. But it is clear that, although he had some happy times there, Helbert had reservations about Winchester. As indicated by Nowell Smith, there was a darker side to the school, and this left a permanent impression on Helbert. In later years, when West Downs boys were about to pass on to Winchester or other Public Schools, he would warn them earnestly about the dangers that lay ahead and that only their Christian faith could see them through safely.

If Helbert had mixed feelings about Winchester, he had none about Oxford; his years there were blissfully happy. Oxford in the 1890s was, indeed, a place of great delights: the atmosphere was highly civilised, the pressures of work not insupportable, and opportunities for enjoyment abundant. Of these Helbert took full advantage, and it was not long before he had become a great social success. His vitality, wit and gift for friendship would have been enough for this, but he was, in addition, a superb entertainer, both on the stage with the OUDS and – more particularly, at parties – improvising on the piano and singing comic songs written by himself. Could he, one wonders, in different circumstances, have become another Ivor Novello or Noel Coward? Or could he, if he had put his mind to it, have become a professional musician? Hugo Wolf, the famous composer, once told Lady Goodrich that he was the finest amateur reader of music and accompanist that he had come across. Once again the suspicion occurs that he was squandering his talents. Should he perhaps be doing something more than singing light-hearted Music Hall songs? There was one event, however, of notable importance with which he was associated while at Oxford. This was the production of *The Frogs* of Aristophanes for which Sir Hubert Parry wrote the incidental music. This was significant not so much for Helbert's individual performance as Dionysus as for his achievement as co-producer. Here he showed for the first time exceptional powers of leadership which not only established harmony and good feeling among his fellow actors but also elicited from them performances of which they did not know they were capable. This was noted by his co-producer, Michael Furse, later Bishop of St Albans:

> As I think of him now the impression which comes uppermost in my mind is of that kind of transparent goodness and sincerity which is the most disarming and intriguing thing in all the world. It was that which was really at the bottom of it all, though at the time I don't suppose any of us would have said so. He was not a person that challenged analysis: he was obviously just himself, quick, clever, amusing, delightful, and as such we took him. But looking back, I can see that there was something very much bigger behind it all, and it was this which kept us all together, smoothed our difficulties and made us ashamed of the sort of petty jealousies which play-acting, I think, tends to foster, even in undergraduates.

In view of his diverse activities at Oxford there was a likelihood that Helbert's academic work would suffer, and when he sat for Mods, the first part of his degree course, he took only a second instead of the first of which he was certainly capable. This was the first set-back Helbert had known. Up to then success had been all too easy. It may have been disappointment at this result which prompted him rather suddenly not to complete his Degree but to leave Oxford and apply for a clerkship in the House of Commons. In this, backed by his godmother, Lady Frederick Cavendish, he was successful.

For a young man fresh from Oxford Helbert's job at the House of Commons must have been an enthralling one – very much at the centre of affairs and in contact with such parliamentary giants as Lord Randolph Churchill, Joseph

Chamberlain, Herbert Asquith, Arthur Balfour and the young Lloyd George. And towering over them all the titanic figure of W.E. Gladstone, then aged eighty-three and Prime Minister for the fourth time. Almost immediately after Helbert's arrival the House was thrown into a turmoil of excitement by the introduction of Gladstone's second Home Rule Bill for Ireland, to be passed amid great drama by thirty-four votes in the Commons, only to be rejected later by a large majority in the Lords.

Nor were Helbert's duties in the Commons unduly exacting; there were times when he was required to sit up all night, but there were others when business was slack. In particular there was a recess of four months in the summer when his time was his own, and he was free to pursue other interests. At that time his main interest was still the theatre. He became a friend of Sir Arthur Pinero and attended some of his first nights. He also mounted an amateur production of Pinero's *The Magistrate* to give performances in London and Oxford. The idea was to raise money for charity but, as was later to be seen at West Downs, Helbert had little sense of money. The production costs were much too lavish, including, as they did, a champagne dinner for the cast and others at the Randolph Hotel. It must be doubtful if the charity was much the richer for the venture.

The incident of *The Magistrate* was typical of Helbert's impulsiveness. He was always ready to embark on an attractive venture without counting the cost; to sit down and weigh this up beforehand was foreign to his nature. This impulsiveness with an irrepressible optimism was perhaps the root cause of a problem Helbert had to confront at this time, namely an addiction to gambling. According to his sister, Lady Goodrich, he was 'a born gambler'. He found a fatal fascination in attending race meetings and betting recklessly. On one occasion, when nearly cleaned out, he went off to Monte Carlo to chase his losses with a system 'that could not fail'. Miraculously he somehow managed to arrive back in England more or less solvent. A few years later he was to undertake his greatest gamble of all when he founded West Downs.

It seemed that in the House of Commons Helbert was set on a secure, congenial career which would have brought him distinction and perhaps in time a knighthood. But it was not to be. For during the long Parliamentary recesses he was to try his hand at tutoring boys for Common Entrance and to do some occasional teaching at St Andrew's School, Eastbourne. It was not long before he had decided that this was his vocation in life and he became resolved to found his own Prep School. To his friends and colleagues at the House of Commons this seemed foolhardy; he had hardly any capital and very limited teaching experience. But he was not to be put off. And there were some who gave him strong encouragement and were, indeed, prepared to back this with financial assistance. But at first there was not the money to buy a school outright; it would be necessary to take a lease. And when Helbert enquired at Messrs Gabbitas and Thring about school premises to rent, the opportunities were not encouraging; the

The original building in the days of The Winchester Modern School and Westfields.

only thing they had on their books was a rather bleak building on the outskirts of Winchester on the top of West Hill, just beyond the Hospital and Prison. This had been built some seventeen years previously for the Winchester Modern School, a day fee-paying school for 'the lower middle classes and respectable working classes' of Winchester and the surrounding district. It had been founded out of the philanthropy of Lord Northbrook, a local patrician landlord of considerable wealth who had once been Viceroy of India. It seems that he bore the entire cost of building the school himself. He was also Chairman of the Board of Governors which included the Dean of Winchester, the Mayor of the City and two members of the Corporation, one of whom was to represent 'the agricultural interests'. To add further lustre the Bishop of Winchester was installed as Visitor. But despite these august sponsors the Winchester Modern School did not thrive and after seven years had to be closed down. Its place was then taken by a Preparatory School known as Westfields, but this too failed, and for the last two years the building had been empty, or, as the Winchester Directory of 1896 more graphically described it: 'void'.

When Helbert first saw Westfields he could not but be disheartened; it was not at all what he was looking for. Lady Goodrich was horrified. 'I shall never forget my dismay,' she later wrote, 'when I saw the barrack of a place. As usual a high wind was blowing and I was nearly blown away when we finally arrived at the top of the Tower.' Unattractive and unsympathetic though the building may have been, however, it was available at a rent which Helbert could afford, and he decided to take it on. It was his great achievement that within only a few years he had transformed the run-down property into one of the most flourishing and fashionable Prep Schools in the country.

---

[1] Subsequently Schroder Wragg.
[2] It is an attractive thought that the founder of West Downs might be descended from 'The Merry Monarch' but Jane Lane was one of the few ladies with whom that sovereign came in contact by whom he did not have issue.
[3] Lady Frederick's religious devotions were considered extreme even by the standards of the time. Her sister-in-law, Katherine Lyttelton (coincidentally the grandmother of the present author), who reserved to herself the right to speak candidly of her near relations, once said of her: 'Church is Lucy's pub. You can't get her out of it.'

Chapter 2

When Helbert first arrived at West Downs the main building was about half the size it later became and was divided into two parts. A driveway ran through what later was the main entrance, on one side of which was the headmaster's quarters and on the other the main body of the school with classrooms, dining-hall and dormitory block. Later these two parts were joined together, another storey was added on top, and extensions were made at both ends of the building. But in 1897, when West Downs was founded, these had to wait. Money was limited and, as yet, there were only four pupils. There is some obscurity about the first beginnings. Lady Goodrich, writing much later, mentions a partnership, but does not spell out the details. She merely says that Helbert asked a man to join him, and that the partnership was not a success, and that after hours of painful indecision Helbert came to the conclusion that the partnership should be dissolved and the man paid off – something which nearly brought financial ruin to the whole undertaking. It is not certain who this unnamed man was, but in the first photograph of the founder members of West Downs there is one other man besides Helbert, one R.G.L. Austen, who disappears after 1898.

It is perhaps something of a miracle that West Downs remained intact financially, for not only did Helbert have limited capital but also very little sense of finance – strange in the grandson of the founder of Helbert Wragg. His ideas about money were, to say the least, unworldly; his instincts were generous even prodigal. He was never greatly concerned about the profitability of West Downs and sought to keep the fees as low as possible. When it became essential for these to be put up, he was always apologetic and added that if any parents of boys already at the School felt that the increased fee was likely to prove too great a strain on their resources, it would be 'a pleasure' to let the existing scale of charges remain unchanged.

Certainly West Downs would not have been possible without the financial backing of a number of Helbert's friends. Foremost among these was an Oxford friend, the Revd A. Pope, who for a time, until Helbert repaid him, was a sleeping partner. Just how widespread and numerous were these well-wishers is shown by the first prospectus which contained a formidable list of referees. These included Helbert's godmother, Lady Frederick Cavendish, her brother-in-law, the Right Hon. J.G. Talbot, MP and her brother, the Hon. and Revd Canon Edward

Lyttelton, then Master of Haileybury and soon to be a much loved but somewhat controversial Headmaster of Eton. Also included were the Headmaster and several housemasters from Winchester, two fellows of Oriel College and several members of the House of Commons staff. One rather unexpected name was that of H.H. Evans, headmaster of the recently founded and rival Prep School of Horris Hill.

That first prospectus was admirable in its brevity and clarity (and generous use of capital letters), very different from the glossy outpourings of today:

MR. LIONEL HELBERT, M.A.

(late scholar of Winchester College, and Scholar of Oriel College, Oxford)
Prepares pupils between the ages of 8 and 14, at the above address, for the Public Schools and the Royal Naval College, Osborne.

No day boys are taken.

The School is situated on the Downs outside Winchester, and stands over 350 feet above the level of the sea; the air is particularly bracing.

The cricket field, 9 acres in extent, adjoins the house; there is a gymnasium, swimming bath, and isolated sanatorium.

The whole system of ventilation has been carried out on the most modern lines, and is certified at regular intervals by a leading London Specialist.

The youngest boys are taught by a Governess, and every effort is made to secure individual attention in work, games, and physical development.

The Lady Housekeeper and Matrons have had a long experience of children, and the Senior Matron is a trained Hospital Sister. The Doctor visits the School every day: a fixed fee covers all normal Medical and Sanatorium expenses incurred during term-time.

The fee for board and tuition is 45 Guineas a term, payable in advance.

A term's notice, or the payment of the fee for the following term, is required before the removal of the boy.

With the dissolution of the partnership Helbert was free to run West Downs on his own lines and to mould it in his own image. Ideas he had in abundance – some brilliant, some far-fetched. At times members of staff were left stunned by some sudden whim; but more often they were carried along by Helbert's sheer exuberance. The exciting atmosphere of the early years of West Downs has been described by a near neighbour and great admirer of Helbert's, Teresa Rannie[1] who, with her husband, came to West Hayes, just up the Old Sarum Road, in order to run a pre-preparatory school. Later in a biographical study of her husband she included a tribute to Helbert:

> He was in fact an artist with a swift perception and a desire to give all that he had to the art of education. He was never a pedagogue, but always, to those in his charge, a sympathetic, fatherly and boyish friend, capable of great severity when that was required, yet succeeding in making West Downs a thoroughly happy and exciting place. Something was always happening there; the life was never dull and humdrum simply because of Mr Helbert's vitality and surprisingness.

Numerous as were Helbert's ideas about running a new school, central to them all was his profound Christian faith. Of this his close friend Nowell Smith (see above p. 2) wrote:

> Personal devotion to Jesus Christ as a living and ever-present friend was the faith by which he lived; and, when all allowance has been made for his sunny temperament, it must be allowed that probably nothing but this faith could have inspired the persistence of his selfless radiance through all the trials and temptations of his intense and adventurous life.

Like many headmasters of that time there was a strong Evangelical streak in Helbert. He had much in common with his greater predecessor at Winchester and Oriel, Thomas Arnold of Rugby, who did so much to introduce a new spirit into English Public Schools. He had more warmth and humour than Arnold and lacked his fanaticism, but he would have agreed with him that the principal task of a headmaster is 'to make the school a place of really Christian education'. Arnold had laid it down that what he looked for at Rugby was 'first religious and moral principle; secondly gentlemanly conduct; thirdly intellectual ability'. It is likely that Helbert would have agreed with this order of priorities. He would also have had great sympathy with Squire Brown of *Tom Brown's Schooldays* who, when asked why Tom had been sent away to school, replied: 'If he'll only turn out a brave, helpful, truth-telling Englishman and a Christian, that's all I want.'

When he went to West Downs Helbert was greatly concerned at the prospect of taking chapel and giving religious instruction. He felt he was unqualified for this. But he then took great pains to discover how it might be done most effectively, and here he found he had a great gift. Both boys and parents were struck by the beauty and simplicity of the services in West Downs chapel. They were also impressed by the simple and moving prayers Helbert himself wrote. As one of his pupils later said: 'I don't think there is anyone like L.H. for putting great thoughts into simple language.'[2]

Although Helbert felt it his duty to instil Christian values into his pupils and placed great emphasis on character development, he was always careful to let boys develop along their own lines and he went to great pains to get to know them. He would have been horrified at the idea he was 'moulding' a boy. This is emphasised in the following extract from a tribute to Helbert by a former pupil, Victor Montagu (formerly Lord Hinchingbrooke and Earl of Sandwich):

> Helbert came to the conclusion that lessons and games were not all that was needed to train mind and body. He considered that there was something wrong with a school in which the bell rings for work and play and for meals and bed. He had distressing visions of the boys all copying each other in a herd-like way in one occupation or the other, chewing their pencils and gazing at the master, or running like mad round the field so as not to be seen standing still by the referee, or swallowing their food against the clock and only discovering themselves and their personalities at the end of the day, after lights out, in a dreamy sleep.
>
> He decided, right at the beginning of his career as a schoolmaster, that boys dream during the day as well as at night, and he was determined to turn these dreams to good account . . .

Helbert reading aloud.

Sports Day 1909. Blindfolded fathers with wheelbarrows and sons take part in Navigation Race.

I remember watching this extraordinary man on several occasions. When all eyes were on the boys with school colours performing in the middle of a cricket field, he used to wander to a corner of the ground and sit down on the grass to talk to the boy who was looking for grubs or burning a daisy with a magnifying glass, or even doing nothing. What was he trying to find? Not fame, not success, not upmanship, not even conventional behaviour. Just individuality, originality, and the desire for experiment, the stuff of dreams. Helbert set the spark alight and encouraged it. I could tell you the names of half-a-dozen of those boys who are now at the head of great professions. They owe everything to him.

In his efforts to get to know the boys in his care Helbert began even before they arrived at the School. He was prepared to travel long distances in order to visit a pupil in his own home. On these occasions he was at his best; there was nothing about him of the stern unbending headmaster. Children were instantly beguiled by him. Philip Colville (1919–23) recalls how at first he had had a strong aversion to going to West Downs, and was determined to maintain an icy reserve during Helbert's visit; but Helbert broke this down at once and by the time he left Philip couldn't wait to be going. And Lady Rose Baring, whose brothers went to West Downs, remembers Helbert coming to the family home and delighting all the children with little conjuring tricks and by tearing up old copies of *The Times* to make palm trees and other objects.

When a new boy arrived at West Downs Helbert lost no time in getting to know him better. This has been described by Miss Hills:[3]

> Much of the influence which Mr Helbert had with his boys, not only at West Downs, but on into after-life, was due, no doubt, to the watchful care and sympathy that he gave to them from the very moment they were handed over to him and packed away into the 'Mush' train at Waterloo.[4]
>
> He held, and rightly, that those years before ten are times of lasting impression for good or ill. And so he set himself at once to find the key to each little new character. As a rule it was not difficult, because he really cared for them; and they knew it, in that mysterious way a child does know. A child's full confidence is only given to real affection, that is the special gift they bring with them from the Hand of God.
>
> In the busy first days of the term the little new boys were constantly with him. They might come to him whenever they liked. A little shy, in the first moments, sitting on the study floor perhaps with picture books, or wandering about looking at the endless treasures on that shelf running round the room.
>
> And they took walks together, just the new boys and Mr Helbert, no-one else. So in a very short time he knew far more of each little one than anyone else did, and in the later difficulties he could very often explain what turn or twist of character it was that was producing the trouble.

---

[1] Her son, Alan, was at West Downs. Later he taught there for a time and often played the organ in chapel.

[2] Some of these are included in the Appendix. See p. 187–188.

[3] For more than forty years a mistress at West Downs where, for some reason, she was known by everyone as Miss Squilley (see below p. 14).

[4] A corridor train chartered by Helbert to bring boys from London. All new boys were encouraged to come on it. For the occasion Helbert would be in full morning dress with shining top hat. The stationmaster, also in morning dress, would be in attendance.

Chapter 3

The speed with which West Downs became established was exceptional for a new Prep School. The four boys with whom Helbert had started in 1897 had by 1900 grown to thirty, by 1907 to sixty-five and two years later to over eighty. The growth might have continued but for lack of space. The original building was quite inadequate and, as soon as the success of the School was assured, additions and adaptations were undertaken. These needed capital which Helbert did not have, and once again he had to rely on friends and well-wishers which included an increasing number of parents.

First to be added was a swimming bath in 1903[1], and in the following year the Masters' Lodge was built where before there had been a tennis court. In 1909 an extra dormitory (West) was added above the private wing. Before this the top floor had ended with a small dormitory called the Crow's Nest which was very popular with its occupants. At the same time the playing fields were levelled and soon after took the form they have had ever since. According to Alan Rannie (1906–10) this involved transferring 'a large chunk of solid chalk bank from the upper side to the lower side, with the result that the lst XI football field now occupies the site of what used to be called The Wilderness, a happy haunt for dreamers or bug-hunters on Sunday afternoons.'

The most important additions to the School came in 1913 with the construction of Shakespeare, a large recreation room and the new chapel, but more of these later.

With the growth of the School came additions to the staff. One of the tests of a good headmaster is his ability to attract and to keep good teachers, and Helbert scores highly in this. At the turn of the century several notable personalities arrived at West Downs, but the one who was to play a special part in the establishment of the School was Walter Kirby. Helbert placed special reliance on him. For fourteen years he was his second-in-command until he went away to the War which he survived, only to die soon afterwards from a painful illness. Not much is known of Walter Kirby; it was, perhaps, his natural instinct to keep in the background. In some ways he was the antithesis of Helbert – shy, reserved, level-headed, commonsensical. But he complemented him perfectly, and, no doubt, did much to keep his feet on the ground. Alan Rannie wrote of him:

He was a singularly perfect example of an English gentleman, brave, loyal and unselfish in an exceptional degree. Without the natural optimism and enthusiasm of Helbert, he carried a heavy share of the burden of West Downs, and the high standard which he set was one of the most important elements in the success of the School. He made no bid for popularity but he won, from most of us, an admiration which increased rather than diminished as time went on.

In 1899, one year before Kirby, there had arrived at the School one of the great stalwarts of West Downs – D.L. Rose. With a break for war service he was to be at the School for the next forty-eight years. Kindly, patient, genial and no great disciplinarian ('Stop that nasty rude grinning noise!'), he was always popular. He was remembered later for his teaching qualities and beautiful copperplate handwriting, as well as for his errant false teeth which tended to come adrift in moments of stress, and for certain setpiece jokes ('Every time I open my mouth some fool speaks.'). He also had a fine tenor voice and in early days could always be relied on for a ballad at School concerts ('Ring the Bell, Watchman,' maybe or 'The White Light Shines Bright.'). Later he was best known for solos in Chapel, notably as the king in 'Good King Wenceslas'. It is recalled by Mike Singleton, who was a master at West Downs from 1936 to 1938, that in the Masters' Lodge Rose would give his reminiscences of the First World War and indicate sometimes that a little soldiering would not come amiss with some of his younger colleagues.[2] Among the boys, as is often the case with amiable, slightly quaint schoolmasters, there were usually a number of jokes in circulation, as well as some doggerel verse, usually beginning: 'Nobody knows except Mr Rose.' Mike Singleton remembers one of the more repeatable of these:

> Nobody knows except Mr Rose
> What was the length of Pythagoras' nose.

In 1901 there arrived another great West Downs institution, Miss S.M. Hills, the incomparable Miss Squilley.[3] In high collar, cravate and chestnut brown ensemble which never varied, she was to take the bottom form of the School for the next forty years. Her classroom, full of models, pictures and educational toys, had a special atmosphere, and new boys in her care soon forgot their homesickness. Her great gift was as a storyteller. In husky voice she would tell stories from the Bible, Shakespeare and Dickens and even on occasions, it is recorded, 'ripping Red Indian yarns,' and the class sat riveted. She took more senior classes for one period a week for English Literature, and to many this was the highlight of the week's work.

In 1907 there appeared on the scene someone else destined to become a legend in his own lifetime, W.H. Ledgard. Although not always evident to timid new boys, he was a man of charm and good humour. His humour, it is true, could have a sharp cutting edge, and he did not suffer fools gladly, but boys who got to know him appreciated his wit and inherent kindness. He is remembered for many idiosyncrasies – those races down the drive leading to Melbury[4] with a Late Mark for anyone arriving after him, the pronunciation of seven as 'sevving' and eleven as 'elevving', and at Christmas lunch, while boys were polishing up their sixpences from the Christmas pudding, he never failed by some sleight of hand to produce half a crown for himself. And then there was the rigmarole if an unfortunate boy, wanting to go to the lavatory, came to him and said: 'Please, sir, can I go to *foricas*?'[5] And he would reply flatly: 'I don't know.' Then, when the boy looked totally baffled, he would go on: 'How should I know if you *can* go to *foricas*?' Until it was borne in on the unfortunate boy that what he should have said was: 'May I go to *foricas*?' In class too there was plenty of barbed humour, and he could be severe: anyone transgressing his rules of gentlemanly behaviour would be dubbed a 'vulgarian' or in extreme cases a 'super-vulgarian.' Also he seldom failed to tell each successive class at the beginning of the year that it was the worst he had ever had, relenting later to concede that it was not quite as bad as he had expected. Although some boys found his wit rather mordant, many delighted in it. Barclay Pearson (1921–25) writes of him:

> A quite wonderful man, deserving of a book all to himself. Quiet and unassuming, yet a strict disciplinarian. He was in charge of the rather special little band of boys (6 or 7) who slept down at Melbury. I like to think that they were specially chosen, for we much enjoyed the privilege for about a year. He was no athlete and in any case by the 1920s was getting on in years:[6] but how pleased we were to be assigned to his cricket Net where he would bowl his off-breaks or googlies at us for hours, until in the end he would either scatter our stumps, or say with such conviction that we believed him: 'That was out – bound to have been caught.'[7] It was he with his neat handwriting who kept the entries up to date in our moneycards. He had an extensive knowledge of the English language – the spelling games we had at his table in the Dining Hall were great fun, as well as being a good way to widen our vocabularies. He was also no mean poet and at the end of each year would compose short doggerel verses about each school-leaver and then recite them to a piano accompaniment (he had no singing voice!) in true 'music-hall style'.

One of these was about Pearson himself who had just played the part of Ariel in *The Tempest*:

> His way now young Pearson is winging
> To Sherborne, like Ariel singing
> Where the bee sucks, suck I,
> But I hope he won't try,
> For bees have a habit of stinging!

On occasions W.H.L. could turn an impish sense of humour on to Authority. At staff meetings it was usually his habit to sit tucked away in a corner doing *The Times* crossword which he seldom failed to finish. But on one occasion he was moved to intervene when the headmaster, Helbert's successor, proposed a rule banning all whistling in the School. 'But, headmaster,' he is reputed to have said, 'Scout Law distinctly lays it down that a Scout smiles and whistles in all difficulties.' It must be doubtful if Kenneth Tindall thought this funny. With a break for war service Ledgard was to be at West Downs for forty-seven years until he was over eighty, the only member of staff to serve under four head-masters.

Another member of staff who came in the early years and was later to play a crucial role at a time of crisis was Wilfred Brymer. More outgoing than Kirby and less of a professional, he is remembered by OWDs for his geniality, style and occasional fierceness, as well as for a rather prominent nose.[8] Always very much the gentleman, he insisted on the highest standards of behaviour. 'We don't do that sort of thing at West Downs' was his usual rebuke and it seldom failed to find its mark. B.A. Pearson who knew him in his last years at West Downs has given this description of him:

> 'Bruin' was an imposing figure, tall and immaculately dressed, sporting across his waistcoat a massive gent's gold Albert watch chain. He was a particularly tidy-minded man and I remember so well being instructed by him how to fold my clothes on the little stool between our dormitory beds, a lesson that included rolling up one's tie on top of the chest of drawers, not only to be neat and tidy but also, in his view, to help preserve the material.

In time Brymer was to inherit a large country estate in Dorset from an uncle. Otherwise he might have become headmaster of West Downs.

There are two other faithful servants of West Downs who certainly deserve to be mentioned. Miss D.M. Playsted arrived at the School in 1904 and for the next forty-two years taught the piano and took music classes. These included a percussion class which, according to Kenneth Tindall, 'produced barbaric sounds but which obviously gave considerable pleasure and emotional outlet to the performers.' Many OWDs remember her with affection and gratitude. Lord Horder (1919–23) writes of her:

> Miss Playsted – sole support of a widowed mother in Stanmore – never spared herself on our behalf; she never used any printed course of tutorship, always wrote out ta-fa-tefe-tefe endlessly in pencil in a penny notebook for each one of her pupils. How any musician can bear to listen day after day to children playing their first exercises beats me; but I know how much I owe to her patience with me.

Madame Calviou did not arrive at West Downs until 1916 and only stayed nine years, but during that time she greatly enlivened the teaching of French, notably with the introduction of the French Play which was to become a regular feature of West Downs life. With rubicund complexion and a bun of black hair on top of her head, she was no beauty but had considerable personality. Charles Romer Lee remembers her well:

> She gave me as sound a grounding in French as anyone could have done. She was truly the salt of the earth. I remember her referring to an elderly friend of her mother's in a description which could equally be applied to herself: 'Voilà une femme qui est homme!'

There were others besides teachers who played indispensable roles in the running of the School. Most necessary to Lionel Helbert, who was a bachelor, was a lady who would undertake all the duties usually performed by the headmaster's wife – entertaining parents, coping with the domestic staff and supervising all matters relating to health. There were several who served Helbert in this capacity. The first was a Miss Manton, described a little coolly by Mrs Rannie[9] as a 'pleasing lady'. But the one who served longest and who was a crucial figure in West Downs life was Miss Dix who, until dying of a long and painful illness in 1917, devoted herself totally to the School. Life must have been difficult for her at times. She once recalled how Helbert used to come and consult her on certain matters, listen carefully and politely while she gave her views, and then go away and do exactly the opposite. Mrs Rannie wrote of her:

> Miss Florence Dix, guileless and single-minded, gave the best of her years and her whole physical strength to the School, acting with rare tact and discretion and carrying on with unflinching courage to within a few months of her death.

There were others too who served West Downs well. These were recalled by Alan Rannie in The West Downs Magazine (1949–57):

> Dr Richards ('Punch') who appeared daily on the elevated driving seat of a primeval motor car, to see if a red flag was flying from the sickroom window.[10] Russell, the groundsman and cricket coach (ex-Hampshire professional), who mowed the field with the help of a pony called Raspberry.[11] The redoubtable and bearded 'Bo-sun', who looked after our boots and had memories of the Bombardment of Alexandria in 1882. 'Sago', the drill instructor, a man of many wiles, whom L.H. used to send vast distances on a push-bike with messages that would now be telephoned. And Mrs Hudson, the very type of a substantial cook, who appeared dramatically in the hatch half-way through lunch every day, often behind a steaming battery of 'West Downs Puddings'.

---

[1]Said to have been the first indoor swimming bath in Winchester.

[2]All too soon to come about. Mike Singleton himself ended the Second World War as a colonel, wounded and with a Military Cross (see below p. 84).

[3]A semi-official nickname. The origins and reasons for it are obscure. The only explanation offered is that it came from Lionel Helbert because she reminded him of his quill pen. But this is not altogether convincing.

[4]An annexe to West Downs on the other side of the Romsey Road. See below p. 36.

[5]For reasons of propriety the Latin form of lavatory was always used. A notion imported from Winchester.

[6]He was to be at West Downs for another 30 years.

[7]Another of his ploys was to place his old and somewhat battered hat on a good length and defy any bowler to hit it.

[8]Lord Sherfield (1914–17) recalls a rhyme current in his time:

> I thought I saw an albatross sitting on my Latin primer;
> I looked again and saw it was the nose of Mr Brymer.

[9]Mrs Rannie kept in contact with West Downs long after her son had left. Like Miss Squilley and the late Queen Mary, Mrs Rannie did not feel it necessary to bow to the whims of fashion. In the late

1930s she would appear in chapel in full Edwardian dress with veils, ribbons and massively decorated hats, a formidable figure with a marked resemblance to Lady Bracknell.

[10]A means of attracting attention which was carried on for many years despite the prevalence of the telephone.

[11]With hooves well wrapped to prevent damage to the turf.

Chapter 4

When Helbert started at West Downs he said to his four founder members: 'Now, boys, this School is going to be what you yourselves make it. Will you join with me to make it the best Preparatory School in England?' If this help was to be forthcoming, he realised that he must have the boys' complete trust; there must be no question of 'us and them'. To gain their confidence he made a striking gesture. When he took the building over each classroom had a glass panel in the door. 'I suppose,' said a boy, 'you have those in order to peep in and see what we are doing?' Helbert was horrified at such an idea, and promptly ordered all the glass panels to be removed. His trust was not misplaced, and later he could be sure that, if a class was left on its own, it would carry on with what it was supposed to be doing. And if anyone did do anything wrong and was called on to own up, he seldom failed to do so. Certainly Helbert created a unique atmosphere at West Downs. In particular he tried to give it a family flavour. To this end he always kept in close contact with parents. Unlike some headmasters to whom parents are a necessary nuisance to be kept at a distance and seen as little as possible, Helbert was glad to see them and welcomed them warmly on their visits to West Downs. Not that he always found this easy with some parents, as Mrs Rannie noted:

> With a certain psychological blindness towards womanhood, he did not understand the deep respect and admiration with which the mothers viewed him . . . He loved to score off the too fashionable mother, he could show harshness from lack of sympathy with them. One of these ladies, a really charming woman, said to me in a moment of confidence, 'I have had a conversation with L.H. He made me feel a worm but he has promised to take the boy.'

As well as meeting parents Helbert also spent long hours at night writing to them and taking them fully into his confidence. This, although laborious and ultimately overtaxing of his strength, proved rewarding: through him parents often came to know their sons better. And the goodwill and practical assistance of parents were invaluable in the building up of the School.

The atmosphere at West Downs owed much to Helbert's personality. Humour played a part in this. Of all qualities sense of humour is for a Prep School headmaster the most necessary. Without it he can become pernickety and irascible. Fortunately Helbert had it in abundance. It kept breaking through at the most unlikely moments, and the boys laughed with him not at him, as is often the case with humorous schoolmasters. The one thing Helbert dreaded about West Downs was that it would lapse into a drab routine with the boys doing exactly the same thing in the same way day after day. He was, therefore, a great one for the unexpected. The boys never knew when a surprise might be sprung on them, as when a whole holiday was proclaimed because it was such a lovely spring day; and all work was put aside (sometimes to the dismay of the staff), and everyone went off the Crab Wood or Farley Mount to enjoy the countryside and the spring sunshine. This unpredictability was noted by a number of people including Alan Rannie:

> He was liable to appear at any moment in any place and he almost seemed to acquire the power of being in two places at once. He was also full of original suggestions, as when on a pouring wet night in February, when work in the class which he was taking was not going particularly well, he suddenly announced that we would go for a run. We all changed, including Helbert of course, and covered about two miles of country, returning wet through, but, after hot baths, none the worse for our unconventional lesson.

And Rolf Gardiner (1913–17):

> The activity of the school was intense and alive. Slackness was the sin. L.H., one felt, was determined to prevent any sort of perfunctoriness or sleepy habit. Consequently he was always inventing surprises, events, pranks to keep us on our toes, to prevent anyone from getting into a rut of mere routine. Some boys felt this intense animation too highly pitched ... Doing many things 'at the double', standing to attention, saluting, etc., in the military or naval cadet style, although they invoked smartness and *esprit de corps*, would today seem overdone. But they reflected L.H.'s own keen, 'post-showerbath' briskness and toned-up vigour of mind and body. Life was a race to be run, not slouched through.

It was inevitable that music should play a prominent part in West Downs life. Helbert himself took choir practice and organised school concerts; and these were never the routine hum-drum affairs they so often are. Helbert always managed to make them special occasions. They were recalled later by A.F.B. Broadhurst (1900–1904):

> An early picture comes to my mind: Mr Helbert seated at the grand piano in the Drawing Room, all of us sitting on the floor and joining in the choruses when a boy sang the Newbolt-Stanford Songs of the Fleet. Another memory is of an end of term concert (in the Dining Hall – no Shakespeare then). Stretched across the stage was a white sheet with large lines and the treble clef sign and ten holes big enough for a boy to put his head through, stretching across from middle C and top E. Ten of the more musical boys were alloted to the holes (mine was Violin A) and we first practised the scale. When we were sure of our own individual notes, Mr Helbert stood in front and pointed with his baton, playing tunes on us at will.

With his exceptional talent it might be expected that Lionel Helbert himself would have taken part in these concerts and sung some of the songs which had made him famous at Oxford. But it seems this was not the case and he could only very rarely be persuaded to perform.

Lionel Helbert's other great passion in his youth, besides music, had been drama, and one might have expected that this would have been a major feature at West Downs. But efforts here seem to have been rather modest.

Not many major occasions are reported in *Hesperid*.[1] Each dormitory (later patrol) gave its version (in its own language) of a Shakespeare play; and later, with the arrival of Madame Calviou, a French play was introduced. But generally it seems that drama did not play the same part in school life as it did under Helbert's successor. Of course it must be remembered that there was no Shakespeare until 1913 and no Melbury (see above p. 36) until 1916.

Something for which Helbert had a great love was special occasions. One of these was Trafalgar Day – for some reason he always felt a strong affinity with the Royal Navy. The *Hesperid* for 1911 reports:

> On 21st October, which, as every English boy knows, is Trafalgar Day, the whole school paraded in the gym at 1.15. Then Mr Helbert read an account of Nelson's death from Southey's Life of Nelson. At the words, 'he expired at thirty minutes past four, three hours and a half after he had received his wounds,' everybody came to attention, and the head of the school gave three cheers for Lord Nelson. The School responded heartily, then saluted the colour and passed out *(sic)*.

This would be followed by a procession headed by 'Bo'sun', bearing aloft the White Ensign, and later in the afternoon there would be a debate usually with a stridently patriotic motion such as 'That it is in the interests of England to declare war on Germany immediately' (1909). Or 'That the presence of Turkey in Europe is to be deplored.' It might be noted that both these motions were defeated. In the evening there would be a fireworks display:

> Then packets of fireworks were given out, and everyone went out into the field. First of all a maroon was let off, then everyone let off their own fireworks. After that there were two or three magnificent set-pieces, and then everybody assembled at the senior steps, in order to march to the bonfire and burn the 'Prize Rotter'. They then sang 'The British Grenadiers', 'Auld Lang Syne' and 'God Save the King'. After cheering Lord Nelson, they went in, had chapel, and went to bed.

Another notable occasion was Harvest Festival when chapel was decorated with prize specimens of fruit and vegetables which, after the service, would be carried in procession down to the Winchester Hospital. On a different note Lent was observed by everyone foregoing sugar on his porridge, the money saved going to some worthy but unnamed good cause. The main religious festival of the year was Advent Sunday; for this chapel was decked out in white flowers (perhaps because it sometimes coincided with Confirmation), and 'Advent Schemes' depicting some biblical scene, which boys had been painting for some weeks before, were put on display. Before the service Helbert gave the school a special talk on the foundation of West Downs and on the School motto of 'Honest Brave

French Play – L'Avare. The future leader of the British Union of Fascists (Oswald Mosley) is on the left of the picture.

Pure'.[2] He always took great trouble with this talk and for days beforehand would shut himself away in a remote room and would not be disturbed for anyone.[3] After the talk there was a special Advent Service and, as Mrs Rannie noted, everything was 'fraught with deep solemnity'.

The great social event of the year was Paters Match when two teams of fathers, some of them by no means in their first youth, put on ancient blazers and faded flannels (sometimes called 'creams') and measured up to the bowling and batting of their sons. This was a festive occasion for all the family with lavish refreshments and a band playing. In the evening a concert would be given by distinguished performers (on several occasions the well known singer Mr Plunket-Greene) for which the audience was requested to be 'more or less in evening dress'.

But the most popular occasion of all was the celebration of Lionel Helbert's birthday on 13th June. It seems that some boys became beside themselves with excitement as the day approached. One later recalled: 'I remember so well going to bed the night before his birthday and being seized with terror lest I might die in the night and so miss it. I used to lie and pray that I might live until tomorrow. I have never in my life looked forward to anything so much as his birthdays.' Miss Hills described one such occasion:

> This was a great event, and it usually began very early. A sort of raid seems to have been made on Mr Helbert at or before 6 o'clock in the morning, to wish 'Many Happy Returns of the Day', and the Raiding Party was driven off with wet sponges, soap in a frothy condition, and other damp objects.
>
> Then the real business of the birthday began. Oldest clothes having been got into, and a not too early breakfast dispatched, a great many offerings of flowers were placed on the table in the study, all grown in the school gardens, and picked according to the owners' views as to such matters; so that saucers and flat plates had to be provided for pansies or rosebuds without any stalks.
>
> The picnic party started as soon after breakfast as possible; it was before the days of motor charabancs. Brakes therefore arrived with three horses, and a scramble for the box-seats ensued.
>
> As a rule the second brake was the most interesting and varied, as it contained a change of clothes for everybody who might tumble into a river or pond; mid-morning lunch; provisions which had been left behind by the light cart, which had already started in charge of Russell; kettles, hampers, cameras, anything Mr Helbert thought might be nice to take at the last minute; rugs, sweets, Charlotte wedged in under a mountain of burberrys, Mrs Hudson carrying some specially magnificent cake, and all the boys who could balance on top of the load. Mr Helbert, several of the boys and some of the masters bicycled, and much entertainment was provided by the butterfly nets, which were always getting mixed up with overhanging boughs in the forest, and other people's heads in the open. Dinner was spread in a shady place. Later on, after the Scout Movement had been adopted, rations were served out, and those who liked cooked part of their own dinner. One menu was something of this sort: Omelette – a little hard, Sausages and potatoes (roasted), Jam puffs, Cake, Fruit, Lemonade, More jam puffs, Fried eggs and bacon.
>
> After a rest parties went off in different directions, some hunting butterflies, exploring, playing games, taking photographs, and other things. Tea gathered all the

'stray aways' together again, and after a grand scramble for sweets the brakes were filled and the long drive home was accomplished with much cheering and singing, in spite of which some of the little ones nearly always went to sleep wrapped up in rugs, and only awoke to join in the final cheer, as West Downs came in sight.

Then supper and to bed.

Another event keenly anticipated was 'Bread and Water', the heavily sarcastic name of an end-of-term feast, attended by parents of leaving boys, when plain school fare, such as brisket of beef and toad-in-the-hole, was replaced by luxury foods like turkey or salmon. This was an occasion for speeches and congratulations and a few surprises – maybe a Christmas present for each boy or a card with a message from Lady Goodrich.

It must not, of course, be imagined that life at West Downs was all play. Far from it. Along with Helbert's 'treats' and sense of fun went a deep seriousness and austerity. He always exerted himself to the utmost of his strength (and indeed beyond), and expected others to do the same. He made it clear to the boys at West Downs that they were there to work. And he could at times be severe and use the cane, which he regarded as being sometimes the kindest form of punishment. His ideas about corporal punishment were, perhaps, a little idiosyncratic. A.F.B. Broadhurst recalls:

> Another memory: I had told a lie and was in the Study. We had a long discussion about it, and it was eventually agreed between us that I should be caned. I may say that I almost invariably adopted this plan when I was a headmaster myself.

It is notable that Helbert reserved his greatest severity not for misdemeanours, or even dishonesty, but for slackness. To him the great crime was to waste time, to fritter away opportunities and to be at half-cock. It was significant that the 'Prize Rotter' who was burned in effigy on Trafalgar night had not committed some heinous crime but 'had made no effort'.

It was Helbert's great hope (often fulfilled) that boys at West Downs would continue to regard themselves as part of the West Downs family after they had left the School. He stressed this strongly in the leaving talk he had with each boy. Basically this was concerned with the facts of life, but it also contained a solemn warning about life at a Public School. Helbert's time at Winchester, although mainly happy, had left him with a deep-seated distrust of Public Schools. Rolf Gardiner wrote of this:

> He regarded the prevailing Public School customs as hard-bitten institutions which had somehow got to be endured, withstood and passed through unscathed. So he sought to endow small boys with an inner fund of inextinguishable faith and fervour.

It is possible that Helbert's warnings to leaving boys about the dangers that lay ahead of them at Public Schools were exaggerated and that they were no longer the sinks of iniquity they had once been. But Helbert felt strongly on the subject and urged boys to come to him if they found themselves in any kind of trouble.

He also gave them a little gold cross inscribed HBP to sustain them in times of crisis. These were gratefully received, and some OWDs became inseparable from them, some in the years ahead taking them into battle with them on the Western Front.[5]

It might be noted that Helbert's distrust of Public Schools was in some measure reciprocated, particularly at Winchester where some of the dons, steeped in the traditions of 400 years, looked askance at his unconventional methods. Although by no means free of eccentricity themselves, pillars of the Winchester establishment have always been disconcerted at the least sign of the unorthodox, and have been ready to write off new methods and ideas as 'crankiness'. Maybe they felt that discipline at West Downs was too lax and were shocked by the sight of Helbert striding across the Downs, arm in arm with a long line of boys listening eagerly to the stories he was telling. Maybe they thought academic standards were inadequate. Certainly they felt that boys at West Downs were pampered. And here, perhaps, there was an element of truth, for Helbert was, indeed, somewhat obsessed on the matter of health. He was haunted by the thought that a boy might die while in his care, and so medical supervision was, perhaps, somewhat excessive. Doctors, surgeons and nurses were always readily available. He himself would sit up through the night with any boy who was seriously ill. In sickness and in health all boys gargled daily with some pink fluid, and their bowel movements were closely monitored. C.J. Collingwood (1909–13) recalls Sister Drought making her evening rounds of the dormitories:

> Sister Drought, the matron, used to stalk the dormitories just before lights out with a large spoon and a bottle of Syrup of Figs. She would arrive in the doorway and sniff loudly and then announce: 'What a smell of the human body!' She would then administer a dose to her selected victims and wish us good night before repeating the performance in the next dormitory.

At the beginning of each term boys were required not only to bring with them a health certificate affirming they had not been in contact with any infectious diseases during the holiday, but were also put through 'Puffing Billy'. This has been described by Charles Romer Lee (1918–22):

> A small room into which some 12–15 boys at a time were herded. The room was then filled with steam laced with some kind of antiseptic which was supposed to ward off colds. The boys wore their burberrys and could not escape quickly enough after some 5 minutes worth of fumigation.

And by Lord Hazlerigg (1918–22):

> It was a dreadful experience on the first day of each term being 'sterilised' inside and out in a tiny, dark, airtight room with nasty smelling and suffocating steam. Did it do any good?

But although crusty Wiccamical figures might scoff and make jokes about 'the cotton wool shop', and boys from other schools make cracks about 'Wet Downs', the charge of cosseting cannot be sustained, as anyone who has slept in St Cross Dormitory during winter or been coerced into a cold bath first thing in the morning can testify.[6]

It should be realised too how great were the dangers of epidemics at Prep Schools in those days. These could sweep through a school, sometimes with fatal results. The incidence of scarlet fever or diphtheria usually meant that the school had to close down for a month or two. When diphtheria broke out in Twyford School in 1896 the school had to be evacuated completely and moved to other premises[7] while a major fumigation took place and the lethal drainage system replaced. Foul drains had been found to be the cause of many Prep Schools' troubles. That is why so many school prospectuses, including West Downs', emphasised strongly the modernity of the drains and the regularity with which they were inspected by experts.

One result of Helbert's preoccupation with health, which must have been welcome to many boys, was the dispensation with Eton suits.[8] In 1913 the following circular was despatched to parents:

> It will be noted that Eton suits and black trousers have been taken off the clothes lists for next term, and that dark grey suits have been substituted for them.
>
> The change had been made entirely on the score of health; after wearing a thick tweed suit all the week, the change to a short jacket like the Eton coat is a pretty severe one for a small boy in mid-winter, especially in a climate such as ours.
>
> It is only with great reluctance that Etons have been dropped: nothing will ever look quite so smart to those who have been used to them all their lives, but I hope that we may find that the change to the more sensible costume may prove to have been worthwhile.
>
> Messrs. Billings and Edmonds have agreed to supply the grey suits at the same price as the Etons. The change need only be made according as the boys outgrow the Eton suits and black trousers which they now have.

---

[1]The school magazine which came out twice a year. The name comes from the Greek, *hesperus*, meaning 'western'.

[2]Allusion was often made to the School motto in sermons preached in West Downs chapel. Once a visiting preacher likened the three words to the three stumps of a wicket at which the Devil was bowling and which a West Downs boy was stoutly defending.

[3]Not quite. Once, when thus closeted, the Duke of York (later George V) dropped in for an unofficial visit, and Helbert was prepared to come out of his seclusion for him.

[4]Honest Brave Pure, the motto of the School. See above p. 21–22.

[5]On a lighter note there was an occasion when two O.W.D.s met after a dinner where they had drunk not wisely but too well, and one of them showed the other his gold cross and expatiated at length on how much it meant to him and how it was always with him. For a time the other listened through a haze dreamily, and then at length when there was a pause in the conversation, leaned forward and said as clearly as he could, 'Old boy, I have to tell you that at this moment both of us are just a little short on P.'

[6]There is too the well known story of a West Downs mother who said that the only place where her hat had been blown off indoors was in the corridor at West Downs.

[7]Including for a time the empty buildings recently vacated by Westfields School before the arrival of West Downs.

[8]Commonly known as 'bum-freezers'.

Chapter 5

It is certain that Helbert made a profound impression on many of the boys in his charge. Frederick Browning (1905–8)[1] is recorded as saying that he had deeply affected his life. And Michael Culme-Seymour (1918–22)[2] recalls how when he was interviewed for the Royal Naval College, Dartmouth and was asked whom he regarded as the greatest man in history, he had replied without hesitation: Lionel Helbert.

Parents too were full of admiration. Some, it is true, were a little overawed by him, but most were overwhelmed with gratitude for what he was doing for their sons. A notable tribute came from Sir Robert Morant, an eminent educational administrator.[3]

> I have been bursting with things to say to you ever since I left the station and have been thinking back over those delightful, illuminating and inspiring three days . . . But I must not even try tonight to write one tithe of what it has made me feel and made me want to tell you. I must cram it all into one all-inadequate sentence by saying that I felt your work at West Downs to be of the *very* best; the best that *can* be done for England's rising generation, the best that *can* be given by one human being's whole-hearted, whole-souled, high-minded, and keen-brained personality for the good of the young fellows who have the good fortune to be served and moulded by such infinite devotion as you are giving.

To this Helbert replied with typical self-depreciation:

> And as for the teaching, Basil [Sir Robert's son] is in process of teaching me far more than I have ever taught him; and a very poor show his pupil makes.

Praise such as this from a man of the calibre of Sir Robert Morant is high praise indeed and makes any criticism of Helbert seem almost blasphemous. But as he himself would be the first to affirm, Helbert was no god, and if there are discordant voices it is the duty of the historian to record them. To many, like Rolf Gardiner, he may have been warm and human and 'rollicking with fun', and this is almost certainly a majority view, but it is not how some remember him. To them he was remote, unsmiling and austere. It is likely that the latter came mainly from Helbert's last years when illness was closing in on him and he was weighed down by all the hardships and tragedies of a World War. But some of the criticisms made of him in his prime do have validity and should be examined.

27

Helbert was a great experimenter, and he would be the first to admit that not all his experiments had been successful and had had to be abandoned. But some questionable ones had been retained: for example, the Court of Honour. Here boys were arraigned, usually before the whole school, for such offences as stealing a penknife or telling lies. It is recalled by Rolf Gardiner:

> A particularly long-drawn-out 'Court of Honour', comprising the entire school, held when a boy (today one of the leading commanders-in-chief of Her Majesty's Forces) and his friend were forced to admit plagiarism in a play ascribed to their authorship. The public confessional was not devoid of a little hysteria.

Public confessionals do, indeed, have ugly connotations in the twentieth century, and have, surely, no place in a Prep School. Patrols Leaders' (Prefects) Meetings could also turn ugly. Here boys were summoned before the Patrol Leaders, harangued for their misdeeds and then, perhaps, awarded a certain number of strokes with a fives bat. One OWD remembers that when this brought tears, he was given one more 'for having let down the honour of the school'. Another practice of dubious merit was that by which a boy could challenge another for some supposed insult. One such incident was recorded in a letter of Edward Wyndham Tennant (1907–10).[4] Edward was normally a boy of singular gentleness and charm, but an alleged insult to his mother brought out another side to him:

> First of all a boy called X called me names. So I said cuttingly, 'Billy from Auntie Cis.' At this he got angry and said something that I thought insulting about you. Now I am not going to stand my Mother being called names, so I asked Mr Helbert if I might challenge X, and he said I might. So the next day we were told to go to the gym, so we went, and Mr Helbert explained to everyone the whole story, not saying what we'd said, but telling them I thought X had insulted my Mother, and then he told us to take our coats and waistcoats off and put on the gloves. I had a chap called Davies for my second, and he had Purdey. I let fly at X for all that I was worth and very soon he began to give in. I took advantage of this, and hit him as hard as I could; I got him into a corner, and this was the end of the first round. By the end of the second round he was howling for mercy, and saying, 'Don't hit me any more,' and I think I am right in saying that Master X will not insult you again.

In the same letter in a strange mixture of piety and pugilism Edward continues:

> The Advent Service came off very well. The sermon was preached by the Bishop of Dorking, who is shortly going to Japan as a missionary. He *is* a dear man. He was *so, so* kind to me. He said he is a cousin of Aunt Annie's. His words were: Then we are relations; so shake hands!
> P.S. – Please tell everyone about my fight.

Another similar incident, recalled by an OWD, resulted in great injustice. He was challenged by another boy for some offensive remark he had made about his aunt. The challenge was allowed and in the ensuing fight he got much the better of the unfortunate challenger – a sad case of adding injury to insult.

But a more important charge against Helbert, and a controversial one, is that, like Arnold of Rugby, he overburdened the boys with too much piety – 'more than young minds or souls can stand'. Some religious practices of his time seem excessive, as for example encouraging boys to stay behind in Chapel after the evening service for solitary prayer in front of a blue light by the altar. As with Arnold's Rugbeians, one result of this 'overworking of boys' consciences' was that they became old before their time with perhaps a touch of priggishness. Rolf Gardiner noted: 'West Downs boys seemed often (to one of them at any rate) rather like a lot of little old men.' Moral earnestness was evident too in boys' letters home. Edward Wyndham Tennant was a lively correspondent and for the most part his letters were concerned with the usual schoolboy subjects – marks in class, thanks for a cake and requests for a new elastic for his model aeroplane. But on occasions he became pious, as when he wrote to his mother at the age of twelve:

> The tent and soldiers and cannon are lovely, I do hope you all will have a happy Easter. On Good Friday it was Sunday till dinner-time. A lovely service at 12 when Our Lord was put on the Cross, and another when He died. Then we changed into ordinary clothes, and taking string and baskets set out for Crab Wood where we were told what we mustn't do. Then we set out and picked primroses, then we joined forces with Tennant major, and with him got some lovely moss and more flowers. It seems so awful that it should have happened, and Christ's life on earth seems to have been such a failure; except for the Great Crowning Victory at the end. It nearly makes me cry to think about it.

When Edward later went on to Winchester his housemaster wrote: 'He strikes me as distinctly older than our ordinary new boys, both in manner and character.' Although a sensitive and imaginative boy, Edward does not seem to have been oppressed by the rigours of Prep School life. Later he looked back on his days at West Downs with pleasure and corresponded with Helbert from the Western Front.

Less enthusiastic was his namesake, but no relation, Christopher Tennant (1906–10),[5] who was even older for his age than Edward. When he was eleven his choice of reading was the poetry of Browning and Rossetti and the writings of Oliver Lodge – a well known writer on psychic and spiritualist matters. His letters to his mother have a solemn, almost pastoral note:

> Well, I hope you will have a very happy birthday, Mum, with the dear Darling,[6] God bless her, watching over you and with you ...
> I have determined to try and support the Prefects, but I don't seem to quite know how to do it? but there, I will do my best and cannot do more. Well, dear Mum, again wishing you a most EXQUISITE AND JOYFUL BIRTHDAY, and warm and sunny. Let it be 'the day that the Lord hath made'. Your loving and adoring,
> CHRISTOPHER

And later, at the age of thirteen, in similar vein:

> Many, many happy returns of your birthday. I hope and feel sure there is a very happy year in store for you, and that the Darling will bless you abundantly. You

know it says in Proverbs, 'Blessed is a virtuous woman, for all her children rise up and call her blessed.' And all your children do bless you and love you more than words can express. Your dear 'buffday' will always bring you the thought of an infinite store of happiness for future years.

Inevitably, perhaps, for one of his maturity, Christopher found the life of a Prep School restrictive and a little bleak; and he seems to have been one of those on whom Helbert made little impression. Later, when he had joined the army, he wrote some autobiographical notes and had this to say of West Downs:

In 1907 I went to West Downs, a preparatory school near Winchester. I was very unhappy and very homesick at first, but it all helped me to gain that *savoir-faire* that enables one to get on with men. That is the most that can be said of it. At first I was entirely out of my element. The boys just above me bullied me and the others of my lot. I found my feet as I got on, and liked the place eventually. It was a clean school, though full of intrigues and petty spite, as schools are. The masters were very nice men; Helbert was a good teacher, and made the school run well, and made his boys as happy as they might be under such circumstances.

Personally I have always been a lover of freedom, and have resented the control of all my actions by vengeful deities. That control is necessary, I know, but it can be done with wise love, and it can be done in a spirit of smug prudery; and it is very often done in the latter. Perhaps I misjudged authority and thought harshly of it in those days, but moments of freedom and leisure made up to a large extent for the constant supervision. There is a certain kind of old-maidishness which makes my blood boil and I have always thought it latent in most schoolmasters. However, I am now inclined to think they are more like ordinary people, and assume a role which they imagine to be suitable for dealing with the young.

I thought West Downs at first what I should call 'hard', perhaps owing to the absence of carpets and other amenities of civilised life. The place was bare, the people's minds were bare. I noted at the time, without being able to express it, a certain mental inelasticity and absence of imagination in the people there. I was intensely romantic by nature then, and found no corresponding chord in my superiors. They were nice, but unsympathetic.

Apart from this criticism, I had a pleasant time the last few years at West Downs – at least, I sometimes feel that it was rather a grey stretch of vague indefiniteness, with pleasant moments and incidents dotted here and there. But I do not think one minds so much at the time, as on looking back on it afterwards.

Christopher was obviously a very serious-minded boy – at home at the age of thirteen he declined the offer to come down to dinner twice a week because it prevented his Bible study sessions with his mother – and it was likely that he would be something of a 'fish out of water' at a Prep School, but there are few signs of unhappiness in the letters he wrote home at the time; on the contrary there was much that he enjoyed. But how strange that he established no rapport with Helbert who is damned with faint praise and associated with 'mental inelasticity', 'bare minds' and 'smug prudery'. Surely unjust!

If it is true that an intense moral climate in a school induces too early maturity in pupils, it may also be true that it has an adverse effect on academic standards. As Bertrand Russell put it, writing of English Public Schools, 'The intellect is sacrificed to virtue'. This is not, perhaps, the place to examine this idea in depth, but it is true that the academic record of West Downs in Helbert's time was not brilliant. Boys passed Common Entrance readily enough, but scholarships were not plentiful. It may have been this Helbert had in mind when he used to say later: 'We don't do particularly well in lots of ways'. At one point Helbert was even talking of giving up trying for Winchester scholarships as they seemed so unattainable. West Downs can, perhaps, be forgiven its lack of scholarships in view of its record of success with middle-of-the roaders. A more serious charge is that the academic curriculum was too narrow. As in most independent schools at that time the main fare was classics.[7] Certainly they were well taught, particularly by Helbert who made Latin grammar so absorbing that Philip Colville (1919–23) remembers taking his Latin primer to bed with him. The other main subjects were Maths and French – taught, as in other schools at that time, grammatically as if it were a dead language.[8] English subjects were treated lightly and Science not at all. It is strange that Helbert, who had so many advanced ideas, did not seem to be interested in expanding the range of subjects taught and stuck so closely to well worn paths. But it must be remembered that he was very restricted in this by the requirements of Common Entrance.

In extra-curricular activities he was more enterprising and strongly encouraged handicrafts (being acutely aware of the absence of them in himself). A special kind of carpentry known as Sloyd, using only a very few implements, was taught, as also later, with the coming of Scouting, were such things as basketwork and bookbinding. He was also a little ahead of his time in introducing dancing classes. A Miss Tuite, graceful and bewigged, put boys through their paces. It seems that her repertoire was somewhat limited – the Waltz, the Two-step and the Lancers. Such modern numbers as the Fox Trot, the Tango and the Bunny Hug were considered unsuitable. OWDs remember that her classes were conducted with great decorum,[9] although on one occasion excitement mounted and Miss Tuite was knocked flat – with dire consequences to the culprits.

There was another way too in which Helbert tried to expand boys' interests; he went to great trouble to find outside lecturers, and lantern slide lectures became a great feature of West Downs life. These were on a wide variety of subjects including The Grand Trunk Pacific Railway, the R.S.P.C.A, Nelson's victories (using boys to represent ships), the slums of Bermondsey and Joining the Navy as a Midshipman in 1850.

A department of school life in which Helbert took an interest, but a moderate one, was Games. Unlike many Prep School headmasters at that time he was not obsessed by these. He was no muscular Christian. It is unlikely that it ever occurred to him that evil thoughts could be worked out on the rugger field, nor would he ever have thanked God in Chapel for a win over another school.[10] He had never been a great games player himself and it is likely that he felt little enthusiasm for them, but realised he must give them full support and see to it that the boys, as in everything, played them to the utmost of their ability. Helbert's

No more exciting moment. The future commander at the Battle of Arnhem (Frederick Browning) watches the bails fly.

The future commander of XXX Corps on D-Day (Gerard Bucknall) in no danger of bowling a no-ball.

West Downs' contribution to the coronation of King George V – four pages.

attitude to games has been summed up by Nowell Smith:

> Though no great athlete, he thoroughly enjoyed physical exertion of almost any
> kind, and could enter with a boy's zest into his boys' games without regarding and
> discussing them with that earnest solemnity which makes so many schoolmasters
> ridiculous.

[1]See p. 182 & 186.

[2]Sir Michael Culme-Seymour, Bt.

[3]Sir Robert started life as a Prep School master, and then for a time found himself as tutor to the
nephew of the King of Siam. From this he went into educational administration and subsequently
became Permanent Secretary at the Board of Education and the chief architect of the 1902 Education
Act.

[4]A boy of exceptional promise, he was killed in the Battle of the Somme. Later his mother, Lady
Glenconner, published a book in his memory.

[5]He also was to be killed on the Western Front. For him too a memorial book was published by Sir
Oliver Lodge called *Christopher, a Study in Human Personality.*

[6]A younger sister who had died in infancy.

[7]Described by Sydney Smith as 'the safe and elegant imbecility of classical learning.' Lytton Strachey
referred to 'the bleak rigidities of the ancient tongues.'

[8]Less so when Madame Calviou arrived and introduced the French Play.

[9]Boys were required to wear white gloves for the occasion.

[10]Although the custom was established after a victory over Horris Hill (a somewhat rare occurrence)
of the whole school foregathering and joining in the singing of 'Ring the bell, watchman!'

Chapter 6

The continued success of West Downs meant that in 1913, sixteen years after the foundation, it was possible to proceed with the largest addition to the building yet – that of Chapel and Shakespeare. The latter was a splendid large recreation room – part library, games room, theatre and museum. At one end there was a gallery from which model aeroplanes were often to be launched, immediately below was an area where a stage could be erected for plays and at the other end was open space where model cars could be run. Shakespeare was partly below ground level and above it was built the new Chapel. There had long been a need for this. Until 1913 Chapel had been set up in a variety of places – first of all in Chapel Dormitory, then in a part of A, B and C classrooms, and then in a tin hut adjoining the gym where 'N' room was later to be. The new Chapel with its semi-Gothic windows and mediaeval style timber roof was an outstanding success. Kenneth Tindall used to claim with some justification that it was the finest Prep School chapel in the country. It was built entirely from benefactions,[1] and all the furnishings too were donated with the architect giving guidance so that each item blended in with the general design. Shakespeare and Chapel came only just in time. In the following year the First World War broke out, and the building of them would have had to be postponed.

War was declared during the summer holiday of 1914, and when the boys reassembled for the Autumn Term Helbert had a surprise for them. This has been described by Rolf Gardiner:

> It was L.H.'s custom to announce the names of the prefects in the gym parade on the first night of term. On this occasion he broke a well-kept secret dramatically: 'From now on,' he said, 'there are no prefects.' The School gasped. 'Instead there are Patrol Leaders and Seconds.'

The introduction of Scouting was a typically impulsive move on the part of Helbert. At the time it was probably intended as a patriotic gesture in aid of the war effort, but it had come to West Downs to stay and was to have a far-reaching effect on the character of the School. This was not actually its first appearance. A few months before Rolf Gardiner and two others had persuaded Helbert to allow them to set up a troop. But this was completely unofficial, operating only in breaks and free time. However, they had passed Tenderfoot tests and were sporting badges obtained from Scout Headquarters in the Buckingham Palace Road. They had also appointed Patrol Leaders who were a little miffed when they were superseded by official appointees, but on the whole they were delighted. Not everyone, however, was pleased. There were those who did not enjoy the parades and general regimentation that came with Scouting, and there were those who felt it impinged unduly on games. Rolf Gardiner recalls:

> Some boys may have disliked the idea; but they regarded it as a junior form of war service. Assistant masters may have felt likewise. But to Wilfred Brymer, for whom cricket was an holy game, sanctified by generations on the village green, the scheme was a bitter blow. However, he took it well. He went to L.H. and said 'Of course, I'll back you up, whatever you do; even if you proposed tiddle-de-winks, I should be there to help you through.' And so he did.

It was only to be expected that with the adoption of Scouting at West Downs, Helbert would throw himself into the movement wholeheartedly and would expect everyone else to do the same. For the time being ordinary school games were suspended. In their place came marches, parades and various scouting activities – signalling, tent pitching, shooting, fire making and cooking, and to make the parades more impressive a Scout Band was formed, and boys took lessons in bugle and drum. There were also a number of scouting games. West Downs was well placed for these, as on one side lay ideal open country:

> Beyond the School to the west there was nothing but open country. The Sarum Road was a rough lane, with only two small houses in it. The white, and often dusty, Romsey Road was also uninhabited from Sleepers Hill onwards, and Oliver's Battery was a stretch of open down, which made a good walk. Sometimes we had 'war-games' with wooden dummy rifles there or over the golf course.[2]

Perhaps the greatest benefit of scouting was that it brought boys into contact with this lovely country:

> Scouting brought colour and freedom to West Downs. It also linked the School with the Winchester countryside. This was a tremendous gain to a boy's education. We grew to know the lanes and by-roads, the woods and downs of a part of Hampshire, instead of being cloistered on a few acres of well-rolled lawn. We took part in scouting games and manoeuvres with other troops, joined in district parades, and went into camp. All this lit a candle of enthusiasm in our souls which time has never put out. One cannot be blasé at Scouting.[3]

For the time being there were no more cricket or football matches against other schools. In their place came flag-raiding matches or dispatch-carrying contests with Winton House.[4] In these every kind of subterfuge (or nearly) was allowed. The *Hesperid* for 1914 reports:

> Friday, October 23rd – We played Winton House at dispatch carrying. Four scouts carried dispatches: forty-four guarded the premises against enemies. Any disguise was allowed except female, and Scouts might not travel in vehicles. Two of the Winton House Scouts (dressed as a newspaper boy and a recruit) got into West Downs with their dispatch. None of our four were captured, but one was quite

rightly disqualified, the rule being that the dispatch-bearer should wear a red stripe upon the *top* of his arm – Beresford wore his as a good conduct stripe. He was dressed as a small child, with his hand in that of his mother, who was wheeling a perambulator. Another who was disguised was Napier, who went as a railway porter in the actual costume of a porter now at Winchester Station. The head porter kindly went with him up the main line until they reached a spot on the embankment close under the grounds of Winton House. Here Napier climbed the bank, and walked into Winton House without opposition. Mackeson and Hope went undisguised and deserve great credit for the way in which they delivered their dispatch after several hairbreadth escapes.

Sometimes scouting activities were of a useful nature:

> Wednesday, November 4th – Party of Scouts went to see the 8th Division pass through Chandlers Ford on its way to Southampton. The scouts made themselves useful by posting letters and telegrams, etc.

In the evenings scouting activities continued with such things as knotting, whipping (of ropes), first aid and uses of a Scout staff. And once a week round a camp fire there was a 'pow-wow' in which letters were read from soldiers serving on the Western Front – sometimes from General Sir Horace Smith-Dorrien (a West Downs parent), commanding an Army,[5] and sometimes from the son of Mr Stevens, the baker, serving in a humbler capacity.

With the extension of scouting there came the need for more space near the School. Crab Wood and Farley Mount were excellent but not near at hand. By a piece of great good fortune it became possible in 1914 to rent the land opposite West Downs on the Romsey Road belonging to Melbury Lodge. This comprised several acres of wooded uncultivated country, ideal not only for scouting games but also for numerous scouting-related activities. There were fences to be mended, firewood to be gathered, sheds to be restored, a telephone line to be laid and vegetable gardens to be cultivated.[6] As the U-boat menace began to threaten Britain's food supplies, these were taken seriously. They were operated on a patrol basis, and it would seem from a report in *Hesperid* that some were more successful than others:

> Lions: This patrol made a vegetable marrow bed from leaves collected in the autumn. There is some good fruit forming; another year the marrows should be planted out a fortnight earlier.
>
> Bears   have very promising beds of carrots and parsnips.
>
> Wolves   have quite a good onion bed and an excellent crop of beetroot. Both have been kept fairly clean.
>
> Hounds   have had a splendid crop of French beans. Their cabbages look quite promising.
>
> Buffaloes had two rows of peas. They were affected by the drought in May, but there was a fair crop.

Melbury

Early Scouting days

Swifts   grew turnips. The first crop failed owing to the ravages of fly; but a second sowing is coming on well.

Owls   had quite a success with two rows of broad beans.

Kangaroos have grown tomatoes; they are quite promising. Next year tomatoes should be planted earlier.

The value of Melbury quickly became evident and in 1916 the whole property was bought and became a vital part of West Downs life.

Apart from scouting other changes came to West Downs as a result of the War. Six masters (including Kirby, Ledgard and Rose) left to enlist, and these were not readily nor adequately replaced. Members of staff who remained found themselves with unfamiliar duties. C.S.B. Hayward took over Games and Miss Squilley, ever ready to put her hand to anything, took charge of junior scouting (in uniform?) along with Miss Playsted, the music mistress.

The War was brought home to West Downs all too vividly in the Christmas Holiday of 1914–15. Torrential rains had flooded out the military camps outside the City, and a desperate search was on for any kind of temporary accommodation. West Downs seemed very suitable and was filled to bursting as one unit after another sought refuge there. This is described in *Hesperid* of 1915:

On January 3rd two companies of the Welch Regiment and on January 4th the 3rd City of London Field Ambulance came from Hursley Camp, which was in a state of flood and had become uninhabitable. With the exception of one or two rooms belonging to the ladies of the School, and the servants' wing, every corner of the house was used by the soldiers. There were still 50 gunners in the house who had been billeted since December 22nd. The latter left West Downs on the day following the arrival of the Welch Regiment. The total number of soldiers billeted here in the holidays was something like 660. The state of the house baffles description. Of the top dormitories, the West was a subalterns' dormitory (with occasional pillow fights), the Top was filled with details who could not find room elsewhere, and the St Cross had 40 or 50 R.A.M.C. men quartered in it. The Long and Chapel dormitories had the same number of Welchmen. There were two sergeants in the front sick room, some R.A.M.C. officers in the music wing; the spare room was used once to rest an invalid, once for celebration of Mass by the Roman Catholic Padre. The gymnasium was filled to suffocation with soldiers; so was the changing room – almost all these being machine-gun section men. The machine-guns themselves were kept in the boot room, watched over by the inimitable Sergeant Hedley, now doing great work at the front. Of the classrooms, F was the Welch Regiment Orderly Room, E the office, D the sergeant's store, C, B, and A living quarters. Four men slept in Captain Rose's little lobby.

The greater part of the time the passages on the ground floor and the first floor were full of sleeping men most of the night. The Sanatorium was used as a hospital, and was generally full, as influenza was rife among the men. Russell's shed at the north-west corner of the field was reserved as an isolation hospital, and the old pavilion as a Scarlet Fever Ward (mercifully not required), and, funniest of all, the new pavilion as the butcher's headquarters.

Shakespeare was crammed with R.A.M.C. tackle and men; so, too, was the swimming bath. In the Lodge were 20 officers of the Welch Regiment, and in all parts of every building there was mud and plenty of it. No visitors could have been more charming or more considerate, but such was the state of the weather and the congestion in the dormitories where the men not only slept but fed all over the floors, that it took something rather less than 30 men working long hours for a fortnight, to make the house reasonably fit for the re-opening of the School. Mr. A.T. Bean, our Sanitary Engineer, told them what to do – and Mr Esmond Simpson, son of Mr J.W. Simpson, our Architect, saw that it was done.

In the event Easter Term was only two weeks late in starting.

To some headmasters this mass invasion of his school would have caused alarm and dismay, but not to Helbert. An officer who was there at the time later recalled how kind and self-effacing he had been:

> In December 1914, at an hour's notice, in consequence of bad weather, I had to find a billet for a unit which was mobilising under canvas near Winchester. Entering West Downs, I was informed that the place was already full of troops, that Mr Helbert had kept only a minimum of space for himself, and, moreover, that he was away. In examining the upper stories of the building I came upon one whom I supposed to be the Secretary, working at a desk covered with accounts. I informed him (with all the importance which an amateur officer, working against time, used to assume in those days) that I had taken over the billet, and that I wished to inform the proprietor of the fact. He then introduced himself as Mr Helbert, and in such a manner that I am convinced that he was not concealing, but actually did not feel any irritation – although West Downs was already housing more troops than the Law demanded. He at once showed me every available corner in the house, so that as few of the men as possible should be separated from the main body of the unit. Within a day he was everybody's friend, heaping kindnesses upon men and officers, entertaining wives and friends who came to see the last of us, complacently watching us as we spoilt the floor of his new School Library with our heavy packing cases of equipment. In that fortnight he earned and secured by his modest unselfishness and sympathy some four hundred real friends, who will not forget him. We shall remember our last sight of him, our blessed, cheery host, as he waved his farewells, standing at those dock gates at Southampton, through which our return seemed unlikely enough.

The outbreak of the First World War had been greeted in some quarters with enthusiasm. To youth especially it seemed a welcome relief from the hothouse atmosphere of Edwardian England. The young men who in 1914 rushed to join up had glorious visions of a victorious sweep across Europe culminating in the capture of Berlin before Christmas. How different was the reality! The opposing armies became bogged down in the trenches of France and Belgium, unable to advance even a few hundred yards without massive casualties. The War which had started as a joyous crusade had turned into a gruesome endurance test.

At West Downs, as in other places, the strains became ever more oppressive. Apart from the problem of replacing the six masters who had left for the War, domestic staff too was hard to find, and food became increasingly scarce. Most harrowing of all was the rising toll of dead and wounded, including relatives of boys at the School and a number of OWDs only just out of school. On no one did this strain fall more heavily than on Helbert. His immediate reaction to every problem was to take more on himself. Sleep for him became increasingly infrequent as he sat up through the night writing letters to parents and to OWDs at the front.[7] His burden had never been a light one; and by 1917 it had become intolerable; his nervous system broke down and it was necessary for him to go into a nursing home.

To some this may have come as a bolt from the blue, but there were others who had been expecting it for some time. As early as 1907 Sir Robert Morant (see p. 27.) had become worried about Helbert and had sounded a warning:

> But you must let me say one other thing. I am very gravely distressed at seeing, indubitably, that you are getting overdone, that it is seriously telling on you. I expect it is partly the 'flu attack at the commencement of this term, and your having to go at your work right on the top of it. But it may also have been your very inadequate holiday in December and January: or *that* which brought about the other.
>
> But apart from all this, I saw with my own eyes the ceaseless nerve-strain from 8.0 a.m. to 8.0 p.m. daily, including Sundays, to which you are submitted – *constant* touch with human beings, and in a relation which necessitates ceaseless control over your feelings, your temper, your very facial expression. *No* human frame can stand that year after year, as you have been, without one day breaking down badly. And on Sunday night you *looked* like it: and it *will* come. I know how difficult it is to lessen any of it: for every bit of it matters. *But*, you must not spoil it by spoiling too soon your own powers for doing it. You *must* get quite quit of it, and quite free from any invasion of boys *for an hour or so* in the middle of *every* day, and for *more* on *Sundays*. Forgive me for writing this. But I feel it deeply. Even Mr Beedle (or whatever his name is), who was staying at the Royal, told me at the station in the morning how your changed and tired look frightened him. But *I* saw it in the hourly strain on you. Won't you stedfastly (sic) arrange to set apart one hour *daily*, when you shan't be got at by *anyone*, and let nothing break this rule?[8]

Wise advice, but there was little likelihood of Helbert taking it. Already by then he had become a chronic workaholic and was incapable of slowing down. Not only did he fail to do any of the things urged on him by Sir Robert but he cut down further on sleep. After a long, arduous day – teaching in class, coping with problems of boys, masters, and domestic staff, and joining in all activities so that he never had a moment to himself, he would then sit through the night writing letters or talking to friends or old boys of the School who had dropped in and were always made welcome. When they urged him to turn in, he would reply that it was no use as he would not be able to sleep. When eventually he did, he was up again soon afterwards, never later than 6.30 a.m., often earlier.[9]

No constitution could stand up to this treatment indefinitely. By 1914 many people had become aware of the effect it was having on him. In that year his close friend, W.E. Cleaver, returning from abroad, had a long talk with him into the night, and afterwards wrote in his diary that he was 'very nervous about him'. Nor was the change in him lost on the boys. In the same year a perceptive newcomer to the School, Antony Knebworth,[10] in a poignant letter home wrote: 'Mr Helbert never looks nice now, but always looks cold and dull and stern.' And of the scout camp at Goodwood in 1916 Rolf Gardiner wrote:

But there was not the happy or carefree mood which had reigned at Middle Hall the year before. The battles of Jutland and the Somme, and a local epidemic of diphtheria, darkened its brightness. I succumbed to an illness, diagnosed as tonsillitis which affected my heart, and camp dispersed. While in bed with fever I shared a cottage with L.H. who used to come into my room to shave in the morning and discuss the situation or to read aloud to me. I felt that he was preoccupied by the increasing strain of things.

Following his breakdown Helbert was put in the care of Sir Thomas Horder.[11] A fortunate choice – the two men soon became close friends despite the fact that Helbert was not an easy patient. Sir Thomas later recalled:

> L.H. was a difficult patient to handle; not *difficile* – and of course far from unintelligent – but striving always to elude even the bare minimum of the limitations which it was my duty to impose upon him. I soon got to know that I must trust to one threat, and one only, in order to get his co-operation: that if he would not toe the line I should cease to take the responsibility of advising and of helping him. Again and again I caught him breaking through the barrier which I had put up, again and again he pleaded extenuating circumstances, and again and again I found myself smothering my provocation, resuming control of the health for which he seemed to care so little.

Sir Thomas emphasised that basically Helbert had a robust constitution and a sound nervous system, and there was no reason why he should not live to a ripe old age; but he perpetually overstrained himself, never relaxing and seldom sleeping and 'the stuff of his life oozed out of him'.

Meanwhile life at West Downs went on as best it could without him. Claude Hayward took over as headmaster with W.J. Brymer as second-in-command, and Lady Goodrich looked in from time to time to help with entertaining. The term passed smoothly, and Lady Goodrich expressed her appreciation in *Hesperid*: 'But the glorious staff, headed by Mr Hayward, has never faltered, and the good ship, West Downs, has been steered faithfully and well to Christmas harbour .... May I just say "thank you" from my heart for all the loyalty and grand spirit shown in my brother's absence.'

Helbert returned to the School in 1918, but after a time found the strain too much for him, and another period in a nursing home became necessary. Sir Thomas Horder was concerned at the deterioration in his condition:

> When I took charge of Helbert a second time in a nursing home in the summer of 1918 his condition was apparently not much worse than it had been on the former occasion. But his slower response to treatment, and certain new phases of illness that he showed, made me very anxious.

However, Helbert was back at West Downs in November when the War at last came to an end, and he announced the Armistice to the School. What happened next has been vividly described by Denzil Baring (1918–22):

> Whenever I remember West Downs there is one day which is photographed in my mind as clearly as if it all happened yesterday. It was a day which began in the most

ordinary way and seemed likely to continue as it began. Or so we thought until a summons came to go to the dining hall where we normally had our meals but didn't usually assemble for other purposes. What had happened?

Rather apprehensively we filed in, waiting for Mr Helbert. After a minute he came in. Then, standing at the end of the room, he raised both arms. 'I have just had a message,' he said, 'I am going to read it to you.

"At 11 a.m. this morning the Governmnts of England, France and Germany signed an armistice. The German army has surrendered. Fighting has stopped. The War is over."'

It took almost a minute for this to sink in. Then we broke into cheers which seemed as if they were never going to stop.

The war may not have been continuously in our thoughts nor did we study avidly the map in Shakespeare where coloured pins marked the positions of the various armies. But for as long as most of us could remember, there had been this heavy, dark cloud over our homes and families and, of course, over West Downs too. There were not many in that room who had not lost someone. Sometimes someone very close.

What happened next was quite unregimented (unnatural for West Downs?). There was a rush to put on our scout and wolf cub uniforms and to fall in outside. Then we all marched off down the hill into Winchester. By this time others were marching too and carrying flags.

At the bottom of the hill is the gate into the barracks, then as now the regimental depot of the Rifle Brigade. Through it went the throng of marchers, young and old, while somewhere a band struck up.

It was a marvellous, exciting moment. We felt somehow that a new life was about to begin. The future, of course, never quite lives up to one's enthusiastic hopes and there were to be disappointments in the years ahead, leading in little more than two decades to another war in which West Downs will have played its part. But here I conclude my own small footnote to history leaving others, better qualified, to continue the story.

The record of OWDs in the War was an honourable one. One hundred and seventy five (almost all who could) served in the armed forces, and of these thirty-seven were killed and forty wounded. Fifty were decorated. The names of the fallen along with those of the neighbouring district of West Hill and including the name of Lionel Helbert, who was felt to have been a casualty of the War, were commemorated on a monument sited outside the entrance to Melbury.[12] Later another memorial to West Downs boys killed in the War was erected in a special Memorial Garden. This beautiful tribute, the work of Lady Kennet, the widow of Captain Scott, is described later.

---

[1]The initials of each boy who contributed were carved on one of the bricks.

[2]Alan Rannie.

[3]Rolf Gardiner.

[4]A Winchester Prep School.

[5]Sadly not for long. After protesting against repeated orders for counter-attacks, which resulted in little but huge casualties, he was abruptly dismissed by Sir William Robertson, Chief of Staff to the Commander-in-Chief and an ex-ranker with the words: "Orace, you're for 'ome.'

[6]Another activity in war time was gathering chestnuts which were believed to be used in the manufacture of explosives.

[7]Letters from OWDs serving their country were published in special supplements of the *Hesperid* and

dispatched to all past members of the School. They were much appreciated by them, but were an extra burden on Helbert.

[8]It might be noted that Sir Robert did not practise what he preached. His biographer in the D.N.B. wrote: 'He knew no rest and enjoyed no leisure .... He died prematurely.'

[9]For a few weeks while his father was ill, he travelled up to London each evening, spent the night at his father's bedside, and then came back to Winchester on the milk train first thing in the morning.

[10]Son of the Earl of Lytton. High powered and adventurous, he was killed in a flying accident at the age of twenty-nine. His father subsequently published a memorial to him entitled simply 'Antony'.

[11]Later Lord Horder, son of a Wiltshire draper, he was to become physician to four sovereigns and two prime ministers.

[12]The names of the fallen were also underlined in red on the name boards in the Dining Hall.

Chapter 7

If the end of the war relieved Helbert of some strain, there was no improvement in his condition, and in the spring of 1919 it was necessary for him again to go on sick leave. The circular informing parents of this, although essentially sad in tone, yet contained flashes of his old humour:

> It had been my earnest wish and expectation to take up work before the end of term – certainly at the beginning of next. But my doctor, Sir Thomas Horder, is obdurate, and as I have unfortunately the most implicit confidence in his judgement, I suppose I must ask parents to excuse me till May. All being well I shall be at West Downs sometime before the middle of that month.
>
> If the parents of new boys would prefer to keep their boys at home till then and let them join up on my return it could easily be arranged.
>
> I don't know whom to thank the most – the parents, the staff or the boys of the School – for again carrying on so splendidly during some very trying times.

Through the good offices of two West Downs fathers, Rear-Admiral Sir Michael Culme-Seymour, second-in-command of the Mediterranean fleet, and Captain J.A.C. Henley, captain of the battleship *Emperor of India*, it was arranged for Helbert to go on a sea voyage on this ship in the Mediterranean and the Black Sea. Helbert was to be accompanied by Sir Thomas Horder, who was also in need of a holiday, and it was hoped that a complete change and enforced rest would bring a cure. But Helbert could never be inactive. Once on the battleship he wanted to know about everything that was going on and to keep a daily record of the ship's activities and to write innumerable letters home. Sir Thomas tried hard to make him relax, but this was something that Helbert had never found easy and he could not learn now. But at times he did seem to be better; there were bad patches, but for much of the time he was cheerful and lively. Everyone was very kind and he tried his hand, with varying success, at bridge and baccarat, and he had some interesting excursions ashore.[1] Moreover the voyage was not without excitement. The main war might have come to an end, but the civil war between Red Russians and White dragged on with the British helping the latter; and every so often the guns of the *Emperor of India* would be brought to bear on supposed Bolshevik troop positions. Helbert revelled in this, as he did in all that went on in the ship. But it is likely that he was at his happiest when taking classes of the ship's boys. Here he was in his element and being of use. Helbert could never really enjoy being just a passenger.

On his return to England in the early part of the Summer Term of 1919 it seemed that the voyage had had effect and he was rid of the torment that afflicted him. But then relapses occurred, and by the end of the term he was exhausted. At his doctor's suggestion he spent the summer holiday in Melbury, but the quiet and solitude of the place depressed him. At the beginning of the Autumn Term, however, he seemed better and a circular was sent to parents to dispel any ideas that he was thinking of retiring:

> Several friends have asked me lately whether I am going to give up the School in the near future, so I am taking this opportunity of saying that that is not my intention. At present time I am in robust health and hope to remain at West Downs so long as I am physically fit to carry on the School.

For a time there were grounds for optimism and as late as 5th October (a month before he died) he wrote a long, clear letter in a firm hand to a mother about her twin sons who had just arrived at West Downs. But then he broke down again. This was too much for him to bear. It seemed to him that he would never recover and that life had no more purpose for him. He made up his mind to leave West Downs. When he left Mrs Rannie had a strong feeling that she would not see him again.

Sir Thomas Horder wanted Helbert to go into a nursing home again, but this he refused to do and went instead to his great friends, the Wentworths, at Saxmundham in Suffolk. On his arrival there he might have re-echoed the famous words of Thomas Wolsey at Leicester Abbey: 'I am come to lay my bones among you.' In the weeks that followed his strength gradually ebbed away. According to Sir Thomas Horder he died peacefully in his sleep without a struggle. Lady Goodrich was with him at the end, and just before he died brought him news of a West Downs win at football against another school. On the back of a cheque nearby awaiting his endorsement he scribbled the words 'Well done, W.D. – as far as is known his last words. The cheque was later framed and hung in West Downs chapel.

Memorial services to Lionel Helbert were held at West Downs, Eton and Saint Martin-in-the-Fields. He was buried in Brookwood cemetery in the same grave as his father, and a special train was provided to take down the coffin along with those who wished to attend the last ceremony. Lady Goodrich arranged that the flowers from the graveside were pressed and these were presented to boys at the School for their Bibles. At West Downs the news of Helbert's death was received solemnly but undramatically. It was not perhaps altogether unexpected; and owing to his long illness and absences boys in the School at the time had not had the same opportunity to get to know him as had previous generations. To others who knew him well his death at the age of forty-nine came as a great shock, but there were some to whom it seemed in some ways fitting. His life had been so intensive that it could not be for long; his purpose had been fulfilled and death could not diminish it.

Tributes to Helbert poured in on every hand from boys, parents, masters and friends. The Headmaster of Harrow, the Revd Lionel Ford. wrote to his sons at West Downs: Lionel Helbert was 'the truest friend and noblest soul, and I simply can't tell you how I mourn that his lovely influence and sympathy should be lost to you.' In *The Times* Helbert's obituarist wrote: 'He will have the finest life after death that a great spirit can yearn for or attain to – the best that ever he would have wished for, since he cared only to live in and for his flock.' The most moving and impressive tribute was, perhaps, that from Sir Thomas Horder who knew most of the great men of that time, some of them intimately:

> L.H. was, I think, the most unselfish, and therefore the most saintly man it has been my lot so far to meet. To his doctor, bent upon saving this inestimable gift for the good of the world, and from self-destruction, the ceaseless exercise of such saintliness was sometimes very provoking. But L.H.'s nature was so simple and so beautiful, one could but love him, and stand in his presence barefooted, as being on holy ground. Two lines in Wordsworth's sonnet upon Milton come to me often when thinking of him:
> Thy soul was like a star and dwelt apart.
> Also:
> The lowliest duties on herself did lay.

[1] On one occasion in Istanbul he found himself in the middle of a mass panic when the sound of gunfire caused the inhabitants to rush for shelter. It was thought that the city was about to be bombarded, but the gunfire proved to be no more than a salute to a visiting admiral.

Chapter 8

The sudden death of the founder of West Downs, the man generally regarded as being the life-force of the School, might have precipitated a crisis. That it did not do so was due in the main to the stability and professionalism of the staff, recently reinforced by the return of the younger members from the War. As has been seen Helbert had chosen wisely in this matter and now, under the strong and stylish leadership of Wilfred Brymer they held firm and inspired confidence. Of great assistance to them was a surge of support from West Downs parents. At that time these were a close-knit body; many were related or were close friends and looked on West Downs as a family and were anxious to give any help they could. This might take the form of a sermon in Chapel, a talk to the School or even a comic turn in a concert. Certainly it was noticeable that in the period after Helbert's death there was an exceptional amount of parental participation in the School, and that this was welcomed by the staff, not, as is sometimes the case, resented.

After the death of Helbert West Downs lay in the hands of Lady Goodrich. Everything had been left to her, and she was never in any doubt as to what should happen: West Downs must continue as before, remaining as closely as possible the same school that her brother had created. In 1918 and 1919 there had been altogether four headmasters at different times: Helbert when he was there; Claude Hayward until he left to take up an appointment at Bradfield College; Walter Kirby, back from the War but almost at once struck down by mortal illness; and finally Wilfred Brymer. Lady Goodrich would have liked the new headmaster to have had West Downs' connections and would have been happy for Brymer to continue on a permanent basis. But, as has been seen, Brymer had great expectations from an uncle, and in the choice between becoming headmaster of West Downs and squire of Puddletown in Dorset he chose the latter. However, he was willing to stay on for the time being and 'play in' the new headmaster, something which he did with great tact and skill.

In looking for a new headmaster Lady Goodrich invoked the aid of Helbert's great friend, Nowell Smith, headmaster of Sherborne. Several people had shown interest in taking over West Downs, but to Nowell Smith the outstanding candidate was one of his housemasters at Sherborne, Kenneth Tindall. He recommended him strongly to Lady Goodrich who, after what was no doubt a careful inspection, offered him the post which he accepted.

Tindall had much in common with Helbert. Both were Wykehamists and Oxford men. Both were classicists and deeply convinced Christians; and both had the same ideals as schoolmasters, caring deeply for the boys in their charge and sparing no pains to get the best out of them. But in other ways notably in style, the two men were dissimilar: Helbert intuitive and visionary and very much an individualist, Tindall pragmatic and forceful and more of a professional school-master.

Kenneth Tindall, or K.T. as he came to be called, was the son of a businessman with scientific qualifications. After leaving Oxford he had thought of becoming a doctor, but had then opted for schoolmastering and obtained an appointment at Sherborne where, after only five years, he had become a housemaster. In time he might have gone on to a senior appointment in a Public School, but he had always felt drawn towards the Prep School scene – partly because of the badness of his own Prep School which made him feel how much scope there was for improvement in this field. And so he had no hesitation in taking up the offer of Nowell Smith and Lady Goodrich. His task at West Downs was not an easy one; Helbert was a hard act to follow. There were, no doubt, people all too ready to make unfavourable comparisons. With his appointment Lady Goodrich did not consider her role as guardian angel of West Downs to have come to an end. She maintained a financial interest in the School and kept in close contact until her death twenty-five years later. Each Advent she addressed the School alone in Chapel on the subject of Lionel Helbert's life and ideals and what he expected of boys at West Downs.[1] Each year too she presented a silver half-hunter watch to the head boy inscribed *Quod se optime gessit* (because of his excellent behaviour) and she never failed to send a congratulatory telegram to a boy winning a scholarship.[2] Also the custom was maintained of giving leavers the little gold cross, and John Stephenson (1919–22)[3] recalls that on his arrival at Winchester as a scholar he found waiting for him a letter from Lady Goodrich bidding him to 'hold tight to the little gold cross.'

In his first years Tindall acted with great discretion. As a stranger to the Prep School scene he relied heavily on Wilfred Brymer also on two senior boys, R.C. Allhusen and C.P. Dawnay whom he asked to stay on for an extra year. He accepted at once that the Helbert tradition was something special and should be maintained. At the same time some changes had to be made. His view was summed up with great clarity in a letter to the chairman of the OWD Society:

> Of all the remarkable features of West Downs, what has impressed us most is the spirit which pervades the whole place and everyone connected with it. I realise that it is in some subtle way an emanation from the wonderful personality of L.H. You and other OWDs will understand how difficult a task it will be to maintain the Helbert spirit and ideals without attempting anything in the nature of an artificial imitation of his character, which would be bound to result in failure.

In exchanging a housemastership at Sherborne for the headmastership of West Downs did Tindall, one wonders, know what he was letting himself in for? The life of a conscientious prep school headmaster is an exceptionally exacting one. During term time he has little time he can call his own. Routine duties of teaching and administration will take up what most people would consider a normal working day. But, of course, there are many other matters as well. People will be endlessly wanting to see him with problems, complaints and explanations. At the busiest moments parents will ring up and talk at length. Misdemeanours will have to be investigated and punished. Boys (and sometimes masters) will have to be reprimanded, exhorted or soothed. The nervous strain at times will be considerable. It has been seen how such a life broke Helbert down after twenty years and finally killed him at the age of forty-nine. That this did not happen to Tindall (he lived to a stalwart ninety-two) was due in part to an extremely robust constitution and in part to great inner strength derived from his religion. David Howell Griffith[4] wrote of him:

> Looking back over many years at West Downs one's mind goes automatically to the apparently inexhaustible and tireless energy of Kenneth Tindall. All day would be spent in taking an active part in all kinds of school activities, teaching two forms as well as dealing with his own administrative work; and often far into the night he would be discussing with would-be somnolent members of the staff ways and means of improving teaching or discipline, or new ideas for leisure activities.

In standing up to the strains of prep school life Tindall had one great advantage, denied to Helbert, in an exceptionally able and supportive wife. During the years of his headmastership Theodora Tindall (known from her initials of T.M.T. as 'Tumty') never spared herself. She took over completely all matters relating to boys' health, domestic staff and the organisation of big occasions. She took new boys under her wing and wrote soothing letters, sometimes erring on the optimistic side, to their parents. In addition she was always ready to undertake other miscellaneous duties, acting as sacristan in chapel, issuing books and stationery and even, when the need arose, wielding a broom and washing the dishes.[5]

Theodora Tindall was born and brought up in an English parsonage. She later went to Newnham College, Cambridge where she read History and distinguished herself at hockey, playing centre-half in the Cambridge Ladies team. She first met Kenneth soon after his family moved into her father's parish of Fordingbridge. The story of their courtship has been told with great charm by K.T. himself.

> During my last term at Winchester (June, 1903) my parents moved from Leighton Buzzard to Fordingbridge. Theodora and I first met at a mixed cricket match in the New Forest, where she was fielding point with her legs wide apart and wearing a hockey skirt at least six inches off the ground, which in those days was considered very daring and almost indecent ... We next met in the Christmas vacs at dances and I was interested to find that she and her sisters were keen on amateur acting, which was always one of my chief hobbies. This brought us together on several occasions in the next few years and with some of my Oxford friends we produced plays in the Town Hall at Fordingbridge ... It was in this period that I had the brilliant idea of writing a play in which I could make love to her ... the result was a

ridiculously mawkish drama; a happier outcome was that in August, 1906 we became engaged.

For a time after their engagement Theodora took a post at St Paul's Girls' School, teaching a junior form and coaching senior hockey while Kenneth started in at Sherborne. They were married a year later, and during their eleven years at Sherborne three children were born, one son and two daughters; another son was born soon after they came to West Downs.

[1] In 1938 she was unable to come for the first time because of ill health. So she sent a letter to the head boy (actually the present author) to be read aloud by him to the School in the absence of Tindall. It ran: 'I am not able to give you the message as usual. It is a very real grief to me. Will you tell the boys that L.H. says he wants to say to his boys that in all the turmoil they must stand fast, faster than ever, whatever happens in the world. It is loyalty to God and Courage and Truth that must be their undying watchword.'

[2] In 1929 Richard Norton (1935–39) who had just won a scholarship to Winchester, received such a telegram (delivered in those days in a special gold envelope) which ran: 'Three cheers. Tremendous, Congratulations. Vivat West Downs.'

[3] The Right Hon. Sir John F.E. Stephenson.

[4] Assistant master at West Downs (1923–60). See p. 82.

[5] The only thing she apparently never did, although she had a degree and teaching experience, was to take a class.

Chapter 9

Few people could take exception to the changes Tindall made during his first years. Challenges to boxing duels were discontinued, so also was the Court of Honour with its public confessionals. The ceremonies in connection with Trafalgar Day were modified and in time replaced by Armistice Day as the great patriotic occasion of the year. Also the School song was allowed to lapse into oblivion; written originally by two grandfathers of boys in the School it had surely become something of an anachronism.[1] More fundamental was the reorganisation of Scout patrols. In Helbert's time there had been nine of these with about six boys in each. Now they were reduced to five – one for each dormitory. Younger boys, before they were invested as full Scouts, were allotted to patrols as recruits, and a boy would normally expect to stay in the same patrol for the whole of his school career. So that in effect a kind of 'house' system was introduced.

Apart from these few changes and differences in style of the new headmaster West Downs remained at heart the same as it has been before. The teaching and practice of the Christian religion remained the cornerstone of the School. Like Helbert, Tindall had an exceptional gift for making Christianity come alive to the young. His readings in Chapel, particularly of his own version of the Gospel story made a great impression. The lantern slide services in Lent too were imaginative and vivid; and Carol Service, with Chapel decked in holly and lit by candles and with solos from boys and masters was always a great occasion. Advent continued to be regarded as the principal religious festival of the year; with a special service, and Advent Schemes on display. Tindall also continued Helbert's practice of giving the School a long talk basically on the theme of the School motto, but also touching obliquely on some of the dangers and problems that lay ahead of the growing boy.

In the course of time, as a result of gifts from parents and other well-wishers, Chapel had become fully and handsomely furnished. At first musical accompaniment had been by a harmonium (with a piano in reserve in case it gave out), but this had soon been replaced by an organ, at first hand-blown, not always totally dependably by a boy detailed for the job. But in the mid-twenties a fully electric organ was installed thanks to the beneficence of an assistant master, Arthur Broadhurst (see below p. 81). In most weekday services the organ was played by

Chapel

Shakespeare

boys which meant a somewhat limited repertoire of hymns but gave useful experience to the player. David McClintock (1922–26) remembers being co-opted into this:

> How I came to play the organ is a story. I am no musician and had persuaded my parents to let me give up the piano. On returning for my last year, there on the notice board was the usual roster of chapel officials, including McClintock as organist. I rushed off to KBT saying I was giving up music. His reply was that he thought it a pity and had arranged for Mr Broadhurst to teach me the organ. I was to go up at once and meet him there and practise a hymn for tonight's service. 'Thy kingdom come' (dead easy) was duly played after which Broadhurst told me to practise another for the next morning. After a while he said it wasn't good enough and I must repeat 'Thy kingdom come'. Afterwards as I left chapel G.M. Warr asked what I had against him that I had played twice a hymn containing the line: 'When comes the promised time that war shall be no more.' Thereafter it was a cushy job, for I chose to play only what I liked and could do.

I.M. Graham (1929–33) also has memories of being official organist:

> For about my last two years at West Downs I was school organist. My duties were to play the hymn at the weekday morning and evening services. On Sundays, when there was a full Matins and Evensong, the staff took over, and my duties were confined to finding the places and turning over the pages. I was too small to reach the pedals; but this did not matter, as I drew a 'double' stop on the manual sounding an octave lower which produced something like the same effect. The arrangement suited the staff (A.F. Broadhurst and Dorothy Lunn) who would otherwise have had to turn out morning and evening just to play one hymn..

There were other ways too in which boys played an individual part in chapel services. One of these was reading the lesson on Sundays. Boys were carefully coached by K.T. for this, but it was a task which usually caused them some alarm.[2] To some boys two chapel services a day were too much, but to some they were welcome. One described them as 'a haven of peace in an often troubled world.'

If the religious life of the School remained much the same under the new headmaster, so too, substantially, did the daily routine. At about 7.30 the Sisters began their rounds of the dormitories bearing trays on which were glasses full of thermometers in methylated spirits. These were put into boys' mouths, checked and then disinfected before going on to the next boy. Bells would then be rung and boys would get up and in silence go down to the nearest bathroom for a cold bath.[3] These were supervised, but not very closely and total submersion could sometimes be avoided. Back in his dormitory a boy, clad only in his pyjama bottoms, would go to his washstand to brush his teeth and at certain times to gargle with some pink liquid said to be permanganate of potash. After this he would get dressed, go downstairs and put on a pair of galoshes. In winter he would then go for a run along the front drive of the School,[4] but in summer he would go on to the playing fields where he might play some form of cricket, French or English, for which he might be able to borrow an old cricket ball and a cut down cricket bat known as a broomstick. Then came breakfast with announcements for the day and distribution of mail, always carefully scrutinised by K.T. to see that nothing unsuitable was coming into the School.[5]

Breakfast over, it was necessary to face the rigours of Sanitary Prep when at intervals between preparing a passage of Caesar, maybe, or learning French irregular verbs, boys would be despatched for the purpose of what was discreetly known as 'taking a number' (referring to the number on the lavatory door). For younger boys this was supervised by a Sister and his success or failure recorded on a chart. In the event of failure further efforts were required later in the day. It was at this time too that boys went off to Sister for various health foods – among others Radio Malt, Keplers, Virol, Glucose and, for the lucky ones, barley sugar – the nearest thing to a sweet allowed at West Downs.

Boys went straight from Sanitary Prep to Chapel after which came morning school, usually four periods with a break in the middle. During this boys were not left to their own devices but were required in summer to go for coaching in a cricket 'net' or fielding practice, and in winter to a 'punt-about' with boys standing in a circle and kicking any balls that might come to them as best they could.

At the end of the morning there was something of a rush to get ready for lunch. Hair had to be brushed and hands washed. If a boy had ink on his fingers – all too easy in those days of dip pens and overflowing fountain pens – he had to scrub away with pumice stone and Lifebuoy soap until his fingers were almost raw, because when he went on parade in the gym his hands would be closely inspected by a Patrol Leader or Second, and if not up to standard, he would be sent back to do better, and this might incur a Late Mark.

After lunch came a period of Quiet Time when some boys, if so required by their parents, had to go for a rest on their beds. Others, more fortunate, went to Shakespeare where they might read or play a sedentary game, perhaps borrowed from the Vickers Cupboard where there were sets (not always complete) of such games as chess, draughts, Halma and Dover Patrol.

On whole school days Quiet Time was followed by two periods of work after which came Games: cricket in summer, soccer in the Autumn Term and hockey and athletics in the Easter Term. If the grounds were unfit, there might be 'chivvy' down at Melbury. This was a simple, not over-exciting game which involved tempting members of the other side out of their safe base to chase and capture you so that someone on your side would then come out and capture him, and then someone on his side would come out . . . and so on.[7]

On rainy days there was always some anxiety about what would happen. The hope was that there would be Free Time, but this was not often fulfilled. All too often there would appear, chalked up on the little blackboard where orders of the day were posted, those dreaded words: 'Bottom half change burberry walk.[8] This meant changing into football clothes from the waist down, putting on caps and burberries, and go trudging through the rain up the Old Sarum Road. This was never popular.

After games came tea followed on some evenings by Free Time, always keenly looked forward to. At that time Shakespeare became a hive of activity, as Paul Morgan (1930–35) remembers:

> Shakespeare in Free Time allowed boys to do a wide variety of things – read books, play the piano, look at pictures and play chess or draughts. Alfa Romeos were model racing cars 10–12 inches in length propelled quite fast by clockwork with a steering wheel that steered. I think they cost about £3 (a lot of money then).[9] They were freely raced in Shakespeare. I would think there were about ten or fifteen. Gliders were launched from the gallery at one end of Shakespeare. They ranged from darts made of folded paper to quite elaborate constructions also of paper, with a paper clip or plasticine as weight, and even glued (seccotine or durofix). The best of these might almost go the whole length of the hall.

Shakespeare was, indeed, a splendid room of great character and containing a curious collection of miscellanea: Lord Kitchener's sword along with that of D.L. Rose regarded as of equal importance, a swordfish in a glass case, a framed letter from Lord Roberts to the School, an outsize python skin hanging on the wall, two captured German machine-guns, a cabinet full of prints of classical sculptuary and a glass case containing the School museum – a diverse assortment of objects ranging from rare birds' eggs to the gas mask worn by Walter Kirby on the Western Front in the Great War. There was also the library containing a not very wide variety of books of which the most in use, at least for casual reading, were, usually, the bound copies of *Punch*.

For those who wanted more violent activity during Free Time there was the gym where one might play indoor football or swing from one set of wall bars to another on ropes or, rather more dangerously, a game of 'forts'. This involved making use of boys' playboxes which were stacked in the gym and making them into forts at both ends of the room. The two teams, crouching behind them, then bombarded each other with old tennis balls. But this sometimes resulted in black eyes and was always being banned.

Each day ended with a service in Chapel, after which everyone filed out by the door at the East end, through the private quarters into the corridor outside the two lower dormitories. Here K.T. was waiting to say goodnight to each boy. As they passed, boys with guilty consciences looked anxiously for signs of trouble ahead; the hour of reckoning for any misdeeds was not far off. For the time being they moved further down the corridor where Sister was waiting with her thermometers in methylated spirits, and for the second time that day their temperatures were taken. Up in the dormitories the boys undressed and folded up their clothes as tidily as possible, placing them on a stool. Later the Patrol Leader came on a tour of inspection, and if one's stool was not up to standard, he was liable to 'take a flier' and kick it over, and one had to try again. Once in bed the only reading allowed at first was the Bible, but one was free to choose which part of the Bible, and the more lurid passages from the Old Testament were often sought out. Just before lights out K.T. came on his final round of the dormitories, and there could then be anxious moments for some boys. If in the course of the day one had lost a 'nuisance point' or, worse still, an 'all-rounder', an explanation was required, and this might result in a summons to the bathroom after which three or four whacks would be heard as K.T. wielded his slipper. It was a ritual as K.T. left the dormitory for him to call out, 'Goodnight all', and everyone would reply, 'Goodnight, sir. Goodnight, all.' After this boys were supposed to go to sleep, but they were not always in the mood in which case much depended on the strictness and vigilance of the Patrol Leader. Some boys might read by torchlight under the blankets; some, if it was light enough, might converse by deaf and dumb signs with their neighbours; some, more adventurous, might go 'bed crawling' under the beds to a friend the other end of the dormitory. But he would have to be careful to avoid the chamber pots, and he would also have to be careful to be back in bed by the time the night sister came on her rounds, flashing a torch onto each bed to see that it was occupied. If one was sleepless and felt like a little light refreshment one might tell the night sister a sad story in the hope that she would bring one a cup of ovaltine or, even more popular, a beverage known as Instant Postum. But the night sister had not been born yesterday, and usually all one got was a pill or a bracing talk.

Such then was the weekday routine. On Sundays it was more leisurely. In those days West Downs was rather strictly Sabbatarian. The only work consisted of learning by heart Scripture Verses during Sanitary Prep. Otherwise there were two quite long chapel services, and one was required to write a letter home; this had to be taken to K.T. for inspection to see if it was adequate; but as part of it was always read by him, it was also a form of censorship. Generally time passed slowly on Sundays; there was often not much to do. In summer the afternoons were spent on the playing fields, where boys were required to wear a rather terrible felt hat, but in deference to the Sabbath games were severely restricted: no cricket balls or cricket bats (or broomsticks) were allowed, only soft balls and pieces of wood borrowed from the carpentry shop; but games with these soon palled. Monotony might be relieved for some by a rehearsal of the Shakespeare play in Melbury, and some scouting activities were allowed. Some boys might try to pass tests in Fire and Cooking down at Melbury. For this it was necessary to find one's own firewood and with no paper and only two matches to get a fire going. Then one was provided with the wherewithal for cooking potatoes and a lump of meat, and if the master in charge could get his teeth into these, one passed the test. Boys who scored heavily on Sunday afternoons were those senior boys with bicycles. With parental permission they might be allowed to go on rides outside the School or take part in scouting-related activities such as 'Messenger's Badge'. In the winter terms the usual activity on a Sunday afternoon was a burberry walk (not necessarily bottom-half change). These were not popular unless the master in charge had a gift for story telling in which case there was great competition for a 'side' next to him or as near as possible so that one could hear what he was saying. These walks were usually up the Old Sarum Road, then hardly more than a lane, where traffic was infrequent. But it was not non-existent, and when it came, could catch a long, straggling line of boys unawares, as shown by an incident recalled by I. M. Graham (1929–33):

> School walks were a feature of life at West Downs – in all weathers, at all times of day, even in darkness on winter mornings. Known often as 'Burberry Walks', they were also known by their locations, e.g., 'Long Triangle', 'Short Triangle'.
>
> One walk, the 'Long Triangle', in July 1933 could have been disastrous for two boys. We had just emerged from a by-road onto the main Winchester-Romsey Road for the return to the School – as usual walking on the wrong side of the road – in file, with Anthony Gibbs (the late Lord Aldenham) and myself in the rear. Without warning we were run into from behind and knocked down flat like ninepins. Luckily the wheels did not go over either of us, and we crawled out one each side from under the car.
>
> I had a badly cut ear, Anthony a back injury. The driver said he had been looking at the view over towards St Cross on the right, and luckily was only going about 20 m.p.h. He was naturally most concerned and offered to drive us back to the School. But the duty master (Mildmay) said we should walk the mile back, and so we did, supported by other boys. We were then put into darkened rooms in the Sanatorium ('Sanny') suffering from shock. Mildmay, I believe, got into serious trouble afterwards for this.
>
> The sequel for me was that I missed Confirmation, and had to be confirmed a week later by the Bishop of Winchester at a private ceremony in his chapel.
>
> The Epilogue for both of us was a few weeks later attending the case in Winchester Guildhall. As prospective witnesses we were not allowed in court and had to sit outside in a draughty corridor where a kindly policeman looked after us. In the event we were not called. At the conclusion of the case K.B.T. came out and said the driver had been fined £1, 'which shows that you boys are only worth ten bob each.'
>
> We did not think this very funny.

There were other ways, besides being run over, in which burberry walks could be livened up. At one time, after the procession had gone a certain distance, it was the custom to release the boys into the adjacent countryside for a time while they 'did their own thing'. For one boy this presented the solution to a problem which had been vexing him. He had just been visited by his mother who had given him a tin of Fortnum and Mason biscuits. By rights this should have been handed in and shared with the other boys at his table. But this seemed to him rather a waste, so he smuggled it out on a burberry walk and then, when on his own with another boy, buried the tin by a certain landmark known as Gar Moses. Afterwards during each succeeding burberry walk he disinterred it and replenished his stock of biscuits. History does not relate how well the biscuits survived underground even in a Fortnum and Mason tin.

If most Sundays at West Downs tended to be tedious and long drawn out, there were some that were total happiness – when one was taken out for the day by one's parents. It was not that life at West Downs was actively disagreeable and one was longing to get away from it, but conditions there were, indubitably,

Chess in Shakespeare

The burberry walk. Even on hottest days burberries were always carried.

somewhat plain and economical, and the joy of being reunited with one's family and going to places where there were such things as curtains, carpets, sofas, silver and large lavish meals was indescribable. There were boys at West Downs to whom the Norman Mead Hotel, an establishment of no great pretensions, was a veritable paradise.

Those OWDs who look back on their time at West Downs as being unduly hard and rigorous should, perhaps, make comparisons with some other prep schools. The opportunity for this did sometimes occur, while they were still at West Downs and went to another school for an Away Match; they might have noticed then how primitive were some of the facilities compared with their own. And there were other schools where the comparison would have been even more pronounced. West Downs in the thirties was not still being illuminated by gaslight, as at Temple Grove; nor were there several classes being taken in one large room; and there was nothing like the horrific Vinery at Summer Fields with its doorless lavatories and open drain.[10] And before the Second World War not every Prep School had its own swimming bath, and very few could rival the West Downs playing fields or had an open air theatre comparable with Melbury. And then there was Shakespeare and Chapel – spacious, graceful and with a unique ambience of their own. Surely OWDs have much to be thankful for.

---

[1] The first verse ran:

> Come join the merry chorus,
> We've a jolly time before us.
> So away with melancholy and with frowns
> At play, boys, as at work
> None of us will shirk
> Three cheers for past
> And present at West Downs.

[2] So much so that one boy once concluded by announcing: 'Here endeth the first eleven.'

[3] In the summer boys who had 'passed their length' would go for a very quick swim in the swimming bath known as 'Plunge'. This was eagerly looked forward to.

[4] Originally it had been round the triangle formed by the Romsey Road, the Old Sarum Road and Chilbolton Avenue, but with increased traffic this was considered dangerous.

[5] On one occasion a somewhat dubious magazine was discovered which was promptly torn to shreds, and the unfortunate boy for whom it was intended made to stand on his chair.

[6] Including in some years a match against the ladies of Winchester.

[7] One such game occurred soon after a class had been reading the story of David and Goliath. One boy recalled the words of David, taunting the Philistines: 'Come on out, ye sons of the uncircumcised', and started bawling them at the opposition. But Mr Stanton (see p. 81) who was taking the game, was not amused. 'I don't think that sort of language should be used in a game,' he said somewhat stiffly.

[8] Another version from earlier times was: 'Caps, burberries, footer stockings and up the road.'

[9] Not a bad investment. The author saw one of these in an antique shop recently priced at £300.

[10] Described by one of the governors of Summer Fields as 'one of the classic horrors of British education.'

Chapter 10

It is, almost always, a traumatic experience for a boy of eight or nine to leave home and to find himself in totally alien surroundings. In some Prep Schools little was done to make it easier for them and they would be left to fend for themselves as best they could; but at West Downs some steps were taken to make this sudden transition less painful. A new boy was encouraged to catch the 'mush' train from Waterloo where he would be gathered into Tindall's compartment with other new boys. Here Tindall would be kind and genial, and it may or may not have been a comfort to the newcomer to see other boys as tearful and apprehensive as himself. On arrival at West Downs he would be put into the care of a 'pater', a boy about a year older than himself, who would show him round, tell him what to do next and generally 'clue him up'. In due course he would have his first experience of school food, which he was probably not in the mood for, and soon afterwards he would go up to his dormitory. Here he would be shown his bed and his 'box', a small space between his bed and that of the boy beside him; this contained a chest of drawers and a stool on which to place his carefully folded clothes,[1] He would also be allotted a washstand with a basin and jug of cold water, and under his bed there would be a chamber pot, known as a '*foricas*'.[2] For the first night immediate necessities were unpacked from a Gladstone bag he had brought with him. Next day his trunk would arrive with all those smart new clothes obtained from Billings and Edmonds and marked with name tapes from Messrs Cash. That night in a strange bed in a large, bare dormitory – no carpets or curtains – shared with about fifteen other boys, he might feel very forlorn and before going to sleep there might be tears. Next morning he would have to cope with the problem of dressing. West Downs uniform in the pre-war years was not simple, involving, as it did, shirts with separate collars; these needed front studs and back studs as well as a tie pin to go through the collar and a clip to keep the tie in place lower down. Then there were braces (suspenders in America) which kept up not only one's trousers but also one's underpants by means of two loops – elastic tops in those days not being common. It was necessary, therefore, to unbutton the braces each night to get the pants out and button them up again each morning to put them back in again. Some boys were tempted to cut down on time by leaving them in, but this was regarded as unhygienic in the extreme and distinctly bad form. Having finally completed this ensemble, your new boy had to face up to the fact that later in the day it would have to be dismantled for games and then put together again, and then again taken apart at bedtime. It took time to get used to this

During the first week or two Mrs Tindall kept a motherly eye on new boys, often gathering them into the private dining-room and reading to them. Miss Squilley too was adept at putting boys at ease and keeping them busy so that they forgot their troubles. But, inevitably, there were many boys in their first days who felt sharp pangs of homesickness. C.J.B. Wood (1932–37) recalls:

> One's first few days and weeks were utterly miserable. Never been away from home before, probably over-indulged by grandparents, nannies, etc., no previous school as such. Dreadful shock to the system. The School made little effort in those days to soften the blow. One was just thrown in at the deep end, and that was that. One sank without trace in a corner of a vast dormitory and longed for oblivion. My saviour was a boy called Cleminson, who I think must have been the Patrol Leader, who came and sat on my bed and offered encouragement. Eventually one found one's feet and formed friendships, so that life became bearable and eventually enjoyable.

Some boys wrote impassioned letters home, begging to be taken away. One of these was Robin Ferrers (then Tamworth):[3]

> I remember being asked, on my second day there, whether I had had 'a new boy's squishing' yet. It did not take a vivid imagination to conjure up what that was – and it was not a very agreeable prospect. I was so miserable that I asked KBT for some writing paper and an envelope to write home. I was offered a postcard, but I declined this, as the postman would read it. In my letter I begged my parents to fetch me back by the first train on Monday, and I offered to refund them my tip. I 'knew' that they would come. They did not, but it reduced my mother to tears. She kept the letter, which I still have somewhere.

Some new boys took more desperate measures like Tom Pocock (1934–38):

> The day that remains clearest in memory from my four years at West Downs is the first. I can see that bland, sunny September day in 1934. Dressed in my new suit of tweed knickerbockers, I am standing by the clump of trees at the edge of the playing-fields near the green-painted wooden building known as 'N-Room'. Other small boys are running about and playing games on the grass where the late afternoon sun picks out the white puff-balls and glints on cobwebs.
>
> Upstairs in the school, my trunk, tuck-box and Gladstone bag are doubtless being unpacked as May and her maids emerge from their warm lairs in the airing-rooms to make up our beds with the obligatory tartan rugs we have brought with us. Everybody is friendly and I have as my 'pater' a charming boy, David Ackers, the son of friends. I have been looking forward to this day for many months and all is as happy as could be expected, so I am surprised by my own reaction to it.
>
> As I look at the animated scene, I make up my mind and think to myself: 'I do not want to stay here, so I will go home.' On reflection, this was prompted not so much by simple homesickness but by the realisation – acute in an only child, accustomed to the familiar streets of London – that he was in exile and that his life would be arranged and dominated by those he did not know.
>
> I did not burst into tears – unlike the little boys already blubbing in matron's room – but remained cool and determined; indeed Mrs Tindall was to tell my

parents that she had never known a child of nine show such control. I did not make an immediate plan of escape but simply a decision to do so. Once that was taken, I could consider the options and so remained calm and outwardly content, even sending the compulsory postcard home with the news, 'I got here all write. (*sic*) Write soon.'

I have forgotten the later events of that day, except that presumably we all had our temperatures taken then and again next morning. But while the other boys were engaged in exploring the school, I was quietly assessing the more practical means of escape. There would, I realised at once, be no point in asking my parents for help; they would only urge me to 'settle down' and, in any case, I did not know how to make a telephone call, and an exchange of letters would take too long. So it had to be a lone action by myself. It had to be a *fait accompli* achieved by my arrival at the house in Chelsea to announce in a perfectly friendly way that I had decided that I did not want to stay at West Downs after all. Instead, I would prefer to resume my education at Mr Gibb's day-school in Sloane Street, where I had already spent a year and at which boys could stay until the age of thirteen.

But how was I going to reach London? The railway was the obvious answer. We had walked up to the school from Winchester station that day and I could probably find my way back. When I reached Waterloo, I could take a taxi to Chelsea. It seemed simple.

There was one problem. The single, third-class ticket to London would have to be bought and would almost certainly cost more than the sixpence or half a crown in my trouser pocket. So how could I find enough money? The answer came quickly for I remembered that in the days when I was taken about London by a nanny, she had sometimes gone into the Post Office near our home for this purpose and, after a brief consultation at the counter, had come away with a pound note or two in her hand. If she could do that, so could I.

Just how I discovered the whereabouts of the Post Office, I cannot remember. Probably it was an apparently casual question to a master, matron or maid but I do remember the sudden leap of excitement when I learned that it was just across the road from the entrance to the drive. I decided to go there next morning.

That first night at West Downs was happy. It would not only be my first night there but, I assumed, my last. The following night would be spent in my own bed from which I could see the frieze of sailing ships my father had painted on the wall. I was, I remember, deeply content in this knowledge and sorry for the other boys who would have to remain in these alien surroundings.

Exactly what time of day I made my escape, I do not recall. But I do remember dodging through the laurel bushes beside the drive until I could not be seen from the sash windows of Mr Tindall's study and finding myself beside the road that runs down the hill into Winchester. Opposite stood a row of little houses and a shop that did not look like the Post Office in the King's Road. However, I ran across and entered. Behind a wire lattice on the counter was a pleasant, middle-aged woman, who smiled at me and asked what I wanted. I enquired whether this was the Post Office and was told that it was. In that case, I replied with all the nonchalance I could muster, I would like some money, please.

How much did I want? she asked. This was wonderfully easy, I thought, and told her that I only wanted enough to buy a railway ticket to London. She gave me a odd little look, then asked me to wait and disappeared into a back room, there doubtless to count out the money she was going to give me. While waiting, I idly wondered when the London train would leave and whether I would be home in time for tea. Gazing through the glass panel of the Post Office door, I could see the entrance to the drive leading to West Downs and it was odd to think that I would never walk up it again. Just then, very suddenly, Mr Tindall appeared at the bottom of the drive, running.

The headmaster will be remembered as a large man but light on his small feet, like a salmon balancing on its tail (as Kenneth Tynan once wrote of Charles Laughton). These little feet now propelled his bulk swiftly across the road and into the shop. He was not so much angry as stern as he led me back to school; I showing the stoicism I was later to recognise when actors such as John Mills and Jack Hawkins played brave prisoners of war whose escape tunnel had been discovered by the Gestapo.

My frustration was exceeded by an outraged sense of betrayal. The postmistress had been acting upon the instructions of a customer but, while pretending to carry them out, had telephoned the school. I am not sure that I ever forgave this treachery.

Once back at West Downs, Mrs Tindall's relief and rehabilitation service went into action. There were telephone calls to my worried parents, who were summoned to visit me. Meanwhile I was accorded individual attention by the headmaster's wife, usually in the private dining-room where she would read aloud my letters from home – as I could not read my parents' handwriting – and give me the enclosed slip of paper on which my mother would have written a private message in capital letters. I was allowed – on condition that I did not try to run away again – extra visits at weekends provided my parents waited for me in their car parked outside the entrance to the drive; opposite the house of the treacherous postmistress, as it happened.

Some boys at West Downs were regarded as 'delicate' and allowed extra cream with their puddings and dosed with that glutinous and rather delicious 'tonic' called Virol. Others were thought to be 'highly-strung' and their special privileges might include a standing reprieve from beating – both those delivered vigorously with a cane and those administered with a slipper in a bathroom after the offending child had been plucked from his bed under the soft-focus gaze of his parents' obligatory photographs in their leather frames on his little chest of drawers – or a recommendation that the boy be taken to be seen by an expensive psychiatrist in Harley Street.

I suppose I was regarded as highly-strung for I was never beaten by Mr Tindall. During that first term, I came to realise that escape was impossible and decided to settle down and serve my time. Although I never really enjoyed West Downs – in retrospect, the place seemed to lack heart – some vaguely happy memories remain. Several are connected with friendships but most relate to an approaching end of term when we could chant,

This time next week, where will I be?
Out of the clutches of K.B.T.![4]

Was the pure ecstasy of the ending of term ever to be experienced again? It was, of course, but one has to think for a moment and then try to equate it with the major moments of happiness in adult life. As one looks back after half a century, West Downs seems as insubstantial as an uneasy, recurrent dream. We can never forget it and, for better or for worse, it made us the men we became. Now that it has gone, there is only sadness to be felt for a part of us has gone with it. West Downs deserved a better fate.

On the whole young boys are adaptable creatures and there were not many in whom homesickness persisted for very long. Often life was transformed by, perhaps, a great friendship, or some success at work or games or the discovery of a new interest. And as the term progressed and the holidays drew nearer,[5] excitement mounted and most things, even burberry walks, became bearable.

[1] A boy's box was sacrosanct; no other boy might go into it without dire consequences.
[2] Known colloquially as a 'fokeye'.
[3] The Right Hon. the Earl Ferrers.
[4] Other doggerels sung at the end of term included:

> No more spiders in my tea
> Making googly eyes at me.
> No more beetles in my bath
> Trying hard to make me laugh.

[5] One sign of this, always joyously acclaimed, was the arrival in the dormitories of 'calico bags' in which to put end of term laundry.

Chapter 11

Soon after Tindall's arrival at West Downs it became clear that he had exceptional talent in the field of drama – in all its aspects: acting, directing and writing. This was something he had in common with Helbert; but whereas with Helbert the talent and interest seemed to dwindle with age, and at West Downs were only occasionally in evidence, with Tindall they increased and burgeoned. His output was remarkable. In his first year he instituted a School Shakespeare Play. The first, *The Merchant of Venice*, was performed in Shakespeare, but thereafter they were performed in Melbury where a splendid outdoor theatre was created. Many OWDs remember the skill and patience with which K.T. directed these.[1] And they remember in particular the memorable performance he himself always gave in *The Tempest* as Caliban. R.P. Norton (1935–39) recalls:

> K.T. really went to town when making himself up for the part of Caliban in *The Tempest*. I was quite taken aback at the dress rehearsal when this fearsome apparition, blacked-out teeth to boot, suddenly emerged from the bushes at Melbury. It was the talk of the School for days – I don't think any of us had previously appreciated that K.T., normally a rather austere and Olympian person, was capable of letting his hair down to that extent.

Another OWD remembers K.T., made up for the part and waiting off-stage for his cue, setting fire to his long artificial fingernails while lighting his pipe. Other OWDs have vivid memories of other plays. Peter Howell (1928–32), later a professional actor, recalls:

> Kenneth Tindall, a great genial bear of a man, loved Shakespeare and had the priceless gift of communicating his love to us. In this he was greatly assisted by the existence of Melbury, one of the most perfect settings for open-air Shakespeare imaginable. I remember the sound of the flute stealing gradually upon the ear, as *Twelfth Night*'s Feste wound his way down through the wooded hills onto the stage.

C.A.G. Campbell (1926–29) also has memories:

> Melbury then was quite untouched and unspoilt, and was a dream world of its own. Since you could not see the outside world from inside its valley, it might have been Prospero's island itself. For me, with all the echoes of Stratford-on-Avon and the old English countryside ringing idyllically in my ears it soon came to represent the Elizabethan countryside, a place of sheer joy. In those happy summers every

The Tempest in Melbury. K.T. as Caliban.

Thursday and Sunday there would be rehearsals lasting the whole afternoon. That, of course, is the way to learn to love and enjoy the greatest poet of Britain and of the world – not being made to write 'criticisms' of his plays for exams which turns joy into what is regarded as school 'work'. I need hardly say that K.T., as a producer, was excellent, combining artistic sense and the power of showing us how things should be acted with his great practical sense of getting results. The only thing he never taught me was how to manage my real life goats when I was Audrey in *As You Like It*. They, like me, wanted to be on stage as much as possible and, having uprooted the stake they were tied to, made a formal but untimely entrance in one of the scenes where Shakespeare had not included them. This upset me a lot at the time.

The other performance which occurred regularly and which K.T. directed in conjunction with 'Madame', was the French play, usually by Molière – *Le Malade Imaginaire, Les Fourberies de Scapin, Le Bourgeois Gentilhomme* among others. These did much to make the French language come alive. In one of them D.N.F. Wilson (1933–37) was required to smoke on stage; he wonders today if this was the reason for him later becoming a chain smoker.

In addition to these School performances there were also do-it-yourself plays put on by the boys. The custom was carried on from Helbert's time that every year each patrol performed the plot of a Shakespeare play, but using their own words not Shakespeare's. Rough and ready these certainly were, but almost always gave great pleasure to both audience and performers, not least when things went wrong, as when Desdemona suddenly rose from the dead and Iachimo emerged from his trunk too soon and had to go back. Edward Ford[2] has a vivid memory of a performance of *Macbeth*. The curtains parted and two boys emerged from opposite sides of the stage and ran into each other. One of them, Charles Romer Lee, acting Lady Macbeth, said to the other: 'Let's murder Duncan.' 'Yes, let's,' said the other, at which the curtains were once again drawn.

Sometimes too a boy would write and produce his own play in an attempt to gain the Scouts' Entertainer's Badge. But he had to be careful here. There were bounds which could not be transcended. One boy was failed flat for introducing a drunk into his play.

But perhaps the event which boys looked forward to most in the course of the year was the Masters' Play at the end of the Autumn Term. These were usually written by a character called Bassett Kendall whom nobody had any difficulty in identifying as Kenneth Bassett Tindall. In addition K.T. directed the plays and acted in them – no mean feat on top of all his other duties. Each year there was the same charade before the play was put on. K.T., if asked, would reply that there was not going to be a Masters' Play this year, and other masters would disclaim all knowledge of any such thing. Then, as the term proceeded, tell-tale signs were observed. Boys in West and Chapel dormitories heard strange sounds after lights out coming from Shakespeare – raised voices perhaps or even a pistol shot. And the next morning there would be further evidence – a circle of chairs, ash trays and other odds and ends not normally found in Shakespeare. But still the myth was maintained that Masters' Plays were things of the past. But then in the last week of term there appeared a large, mysterious painting with a flaming title: 'The Destroying Angel', 'The Yellow Peril', 'Wild Geese' by one Bassett Kendall. The excitement caused by this was intense. Over the years the fantasy had developed that the pictures contained clues about the nature of the play and boys scrutinised them minutely. In fact they never contained anything of significance, but this did not stop some boys from looking very knowing and secretive and in deepest secrecy swapping their discoveries with those of others. When performed the play never failed to hold the audience spellbound. Several OWDs have recorded that they have seldom since enjoyed plays so much. One of them, *The Destroying Angel*, is remembered with fascination by C.A.G. Campbell:

> *The Destroying Angel* I remember well for varying reasons, though not for the fact that it anticipated in 1930 or so our present situation of 'Mutually Assured Destruction', rightly abbreviated to MAD. The story was that a mad professor had invented a bomb which could destroy a whole city, and in his bitter hatred of the futility of mankind, had appointed himself 'a destroying angel' and planted one of his bombs in each of the capital cities of Europe. Each of these bombs was fused to a radio receiver, which would cause it to explode whenever a certain chord was played on the grand piano in the professor's home. All he had to do was to play all these chords, which in fact were the chords of Chopin's Prelude in C Minor (which I have been playing ever since), one after the other and all the capitals would blow up in turn. 'Beany' Broadhurst, as music master, was, of course, the professor in question, and duly carried out his dastardly aim, playing the Prelude in great style. I remember how he pronounced in triumph the name of each city as he banged down its chord: 'Berlin! Vienna! Bucharest!' while we wondered whether the explosion of London would be heard in Winchester. But unfortunately for him some mean person had cut the wires so that Europe survived to undergo instead the ministrations of Hitler and the R.A.F.

As if the Masters' Play was not enough to be getting on with, in some years in the following Christmas holiday K.T. would produce and take the lead in an amateur production of a Shakespeare play down in the Winchester Guildhall.

Of the out-of-school activities besides drama most were related to Scouting. As has been seen Scouting had come to the West Downs to stay – it was no mere patriotic gesture in wartime. It is not too much to say that in the twenties and thirties it permeated the life of the School – for some people's taste too much so. It did, indeed, involve rather a lot of saluting, parading and other quasi-military activities, but few would disagree with the basic ethos of the movement – self-reliance, consideration for others and the ability to render them practical assistance, as well as a sense of brotherhood which transcends class and race. The only time in the year when West Downs boys came into contact with boys from a different background was on Scouting occasions, notably the Baker-Wilbraham Competition when all Winchester troops competed at West Downs in Scouting activities. One of the most solemn occasions of the term was Investiture when recruits, who had come of age, (after taking oaths of great solemnity), became fully fledged Scouts. This was sometimes followed by the election of patrol leaders for next term in which all Scouts took part, preceded by a prayer for divine guidance. In their free time West Downs boys were kept busy passing Tenderfoot and Second Class tests in such things as knots (bowline, sheepshank, round turn and two half-hitches), signalling and triangular bandage, and then later trying for one of the Scout badges in such things as basket work, book binding, ambulance or friends to animals.

Another out-of-school activity which was well provided for at West Downs was music. Compared to the present day when most Prep Schools have their own orchestras or groups and choirs which perform all over the country and indeed outside it, West Downs' efforts during the twenties and thirties were somewhat modest.[3] But there were two first class piano teachers in Miss Lunn and Miss Playsted, and times for practising were carefully organised. It was also possible to learn other instruments, although this option was not often taken up.[4] Otherwise singing classes were part of the school curriculum as also was choir practice for the whole school.[5] Lionel Helbert used to take the latter with great verve (so too later did K.T. with the help of a large ebony ruler). But between the wars they were taken first by Arthur Broadhurst, an enthusiastic choir trainer who took choirs to participate in local festivals, and then for a time by a Colonel Cowland who was in command of the Winchester College Officers' Training Corps and whose musical style was often reminiscent of the parade ground. Singing classes were also taken by Arthur Broadhurst and then by Dorothy Lunn, a gifted pianist who believed quite rightly that with a class of mixed musicians enjoyment was more important than expertise. Songs, therefore, tended to be uncomplicated and to have a country flavour. Classes blew away the morning dew, bade dull care begone, told of the exploits of Sir Eglamore that gallant knight (fa-la, fa-la, fa-la lanky down dilly) and recounted the various noises made by the animals on Old Macdonald's Farm. And then at the end, if the class had behaved reasonably, it was allowed to let itself go on favourites like 'The British Grenadiers', 'Men of Harlech' and 'John Brown's Body'.

Musical life at West Downs received a great lift with the arrival in 1936 of G.S. ('Gussy') Leach, (see p. 69) who took over choir practice from Colonel Cowland, conducting this with a rather more delicate touch and with more ambition, introducing new descants, anthems and part-singing. In singing classes too G.S. Leach was innovative, bringing in Gilbert and Sullivan as well as songs from the American deep South, which today would almost certainly get the School into trouble with the Race Relations Board, about 'darkies living a happy life playing on the old banjo.'

Each year a musical competition was held for the Peacock Cup; this was open to pairs of boys playing or singing together. Sometimes this might be an instrumentalist accompanied on the piano, but more usually it was a singer and a pianist. The offerings on these occasions varied considerably – from 'The Swing' ('How would you like to go up in a swing, up in the sky so high.') to 'Silent Worship' by Handel ('Did you not see my lady, go down the garden singing.')

The judge on these occasions was usually a distinguished musician – Sir George Dyson, Plunket Greene, Steuart Wilson and Dr E.H. Fellowes among others – who would give a brief performance of his own when the competition was over.

As well as music and drama the social graces were not overlooked at West Downs, and in the Autumn Term dancing lessons were provided. By the 1930s Miss Tuite had withdrawn from the fray and had been replaced by Miss Dunlop, a commanding lady of uncertain age, who came with a pianist and violinist and a rather glamorous assistant. In taking one's partner there was always, of course, strong competition to be the gentleman rather than the lady. But there was also competition of a different sort. For if there was an odd boy out at the end, he would be paired off with the glamorous assistant. To some boys this was something to be dreaded, but to others, rather more mature, it was a consummation devoutly to be wished; and some boys went to great lengths not to have a partner. One boy achieved great success at this for a time until it was spotted by the ever-vigilant K.T. and the culprit (a future major-general) was warned off. It should be recorded that Miss Dunlop's repertoire was a wide one, including not only such standard fare as the Waltz and the Fox-trot (with great emphasis on the chassé) but also 'golden oldies' like Paul Jones and Sir Roger de Coverley as well as up-to-the-moment items like the Lambeth Walk and the Chestnut Tree.

In the twenties and thirties entertainment at West Downs was, for the most part, 'homemade'. It was not possible then, as it is now, to get instant entertainment at the push of a button on a television set. Nor was advantage taken of modern inventions that were then available. There were no cinema shows at West Downs and the radio was heard only very occasionally – at times of national crisis like the General Strike or the Abdication and sometimes briefly for a test match. There were, however, some entertainments brought in from outside and to get an idea of these one might look at an entry from *Hesperid* of 1928 under the heading of 'Entertainments':

> October 27th – Mr Charles Dodds gave a delightful recital of songs and recitations which everyone enjoyed.
> November 9th – A concert party of four people from the Small Towns and Villages Concert League gave a very pleasant performance. A reciter was included.
> November 12th – Mr Porterfield of the C.P.A.S., gave a lecture on the steel industry at Sheffield, and incidentally gave the School an idea of the slum quarter there.
> November 26th – Colonel Haddick kindly lectured on 'The Romance of Turkey'. He gave a most interesting account.
> December 10th – Captain Greenstreet enthralled the School by his lecture on 'Two Years in the Antarctic with Sir Ernest Shackleton.' The fact that he himself had been present in all the dangers made it all the more exciting.
> December 14th – the carol party from Connaught House visited the School and sang in Shakespeare. The School subscribed £7 towards their Christmas treat.
> December 17th – The top table chose as the last lecture of the Term 'Charles Dickens'. It was as usual read by Mr Ledgard.

Lectures, usually with lantern slides, became a regular feature of life at West Downs. Some were more popular than others. It seems that by 1926 the School had had enough lectures on the Great War:

> Mr Phelps was the first lecturer this term. He told us some interesting information and anecdotes of Zeebrugge. Some of the audience knew too much about that great naval exploit already to make it as enthralling as it might have been; but it was very well delivered.

And some performances were received with polite restraint:

> On May 26th Miss Elizabeth Ann recited some poetry in Shakespeare.

But there were some which must have been very exciting, notably the visit of the famous cricketer A.C. MacLaren:

> Mr A.C. MacLaren, the great cricketer and ex-captain of England, came down and lectured with films on the great game. His lecture was perhaps the most important of the term and far the most eagerly expected. He showed some very excellent moving pictures of the first class cricket of England, Australia and South Africa. The slow motion pictures were very amusing but they also showed very clearly how some of the great bowlers bowl and how some of the great batsman bat. In the intervals he gave some excellent hints for the different departments of the play in cricket, which, we hope, will prove very useful in the next Term.

And it must have been very exciting too when a real, live Mohawk chieftain appeared on the scene:

> Saturday, February 22nd – Oske-Non-Ton, a Mohawk chieftain, gave a display. He started by singing some Indian folk-songs and hunting songs. He showed us how to make a tom-tom, and he played upon one of his own, and also sang a war song. He showed us also some masks and rattles, used at Indian concerts. Finally, much to the School's enjoyment he made a fire by friction with a bow and some tinder which ignited a mouse's nest found in the Study. The School greatly enjoyed this entertainment which it owes to the kindness of Mr and Mrs Blow.[6]

Sometimes lecturers ran into unexpected hazards. Lt.-Cdr. G.G. Marten (1927–31) recalls an 'organised laugh' when an unfortunate lecturer essayed a none too funny joke and the ensuing false laughs not even a glowering K.T. could subdue. And Michael Howard (1929–33) recalls another untoward incident:

> In my day at West Downs (and for all I know until the end) the custom was for the whole School to register its thanks to a visiting lecturer with a cry in unison of 'Thank you very much, sir' at the conclusion of the talk. This was triggered by the head boy.
>
> Usually there was no difficulty in picking the appropriate moment but I recall one memorable evening when the little ceremony went astray.
>
> We had been treated to a seemingly endless lecture on slum clearance by a minister of the Crown. His dissertation went on and on and he showed no inclination to bring the proceedings to an end. Eventually I, as head boy, decided

that enough was enough. I whispered to my second-in-command, who was sitting next to me, that we should initiate the customary vote of thanks when the next suitable pause occurred in our lecturer's flow.

A moment or two later, when I have to say I had not registered a significant pause, a solitary shrill treble voice beside me called out 'Thank you very much, sir!' No one joined in.

Our distinguished and, no doubt, surprised lecturer, pausing only to say courteously 'Well, thank *you* very much,' continued steadily on his way.

Relations between me and my deputy were somewhat strained for a time thereafter, each of us, no doubt, holding the other responsible for what was a highly embarrassing episode.

As well as lecturers and musicians, conjurers sometimes gave performances. One of these overstepped the mark. He asked for a volunteer from the audience who was wearing a waistcoat, and K.T. came forward. The conjurer then said that he would remove his waistcoat without taking off his jacket, which he proceeded to do but only by submitting K.T. to some indignity including picking his pockets and revealing the contents. K.T. went through with it bravely but clearly had some difficulty in being amused. So too, perhaps surprisingly, did many of the boys who felt that undue liberties had been taken.

---

[1] Usually the same in rotation: *Midsummer Night's Dream, As You Like It, The Tempest* and *Twelfth Night.*

[2] Sir Edward Ford, K.C.B., K.C.V.O.

[3] But not compared with other Prep Schools at that time. At Horris Hill, for example, learning a musical instrument had to take place during games and, as can be imagined, this was not encouraged.

[4] When the present author started taking lessons in the oboe, which had to be given, for want of a better place, in the swimming bath, it was considered mildly eccentric, but it has to be admitted that the noises emanating from the swimming bath were rather bizarre.

[5] Not quite. Sir Jack Boles (1934–38) recalls his chagrin when it was suggested to him that his time might be better spent at some non-musical activity.

[6] This is taken from *Hesperid* of 1930, sadly the last to be issued. From then on there was no West Downs magazine until it was revived in 1954.

Chapter 12

There was a rule at West Downs, observed by most parents, that boys should not be visited during the first two weeks of term and thereafter on occasions but not too often – too many visits being regarded as 'unsettling'. But there was one occasion when all parents were encouraged to come. This was for Paters' Day which, as in Helbert's time, was a great family occasion, and parents who did not visit the School at any other time, usually made a point of coming for that weekend.

Festivities began on Friday with the performance of the Shakespeare play in Melbury. On Saturday more parents would arrive, awaited by their sons with eagerness but at the same time with a little apprehension – apprehension that their female relations would not be dressed in too bizarre a fashion and would not do anything which might attract ribaldry.[1] In the afternoon, as before, two teams of paters took on the boys at cricket. An innovation in the Tindall era was a Maters and Sorors match with a junior team. For this some maters, perhaps co-opted at the last moment, were not always dressed for the part, and smartly dressed ladies in high heels and large, decorative hats could be seen doing their best with a cricket bat or gently hustling after a ball in the field. During the afternoon too a band would be playing and later on there would be a strawberry feast; it is remembered that while this was in progress there was almost complete silence. There were more important things at that moment than mere conversation.

Another event always welcomed by the School because it provided a break in routine and a whole holiday was OWD Day, held on the Saturday nearest to 13th June, Lionel Helbert's birthday. This usually attracted a number of OWDs, particularly from Winchester College. In the morning they attended a chapel service where was read the passage from Isaiah containing the words 'Here am I. Send me.', the words inscribed on The West Downs War Memorial.[2] Also 'Jerusalem' would be sung fortissimo. Then there would be a meeting of the OWD Society followed by lunch and cricket and shooting matches against the School.

Something else which always caused excitement was a School expedition. Compared to the present day when there seems to be an endless succession of 'field trips', 'project work on site' and outings to places of historic interest there

73

Junior Game versus the Maters and Sorors. The boy plays an impeccable forward stroke. Mater behind the stumps not an altogether convincing wicket keeper.

The fire lit, some serious cooking takes place.

were very few of these – not more than one or two a year, if that. For several years Tindall kept going the picnic on Helbert's birthday, sometimes to Crab Wood, sometimes to the New Forest and the stone marking the place where William Rufus was killed. Here is a description from *Hesperid* of the expedition of 1921:

> On the Monday morning the School, garbed in cricket clothes, were conveyed in char-à-bancs[3] to the Rufus Stone in the New Forest, the spot selected for the picnic.
>
> Everyone was in very high spirits and the journey took a good hour, as it was past 12 when this large party arrived at this spot. A slight misfortune occurred in the fact that one of the char-à-bancs, being a little defective in the engine line, did not arrive till some time later.
>
> Everyone seemed ravenously hungry, and the appearance of lunch was hailed with great delight, but a rather unwelcome order was soon after issued to the effect that no one should begin the feast until a given signal.
>
> After lunch the School was briefly divided into five parties, besides the private walks in threes and fours. Mr Brymer and Mr Wilkinson each organised a bird's nesting party; a third party was formed under the leadership of Mr Ranger for the purpose of catching butterflies; fourthly Mr Rose supervised the games, and Mr Perry-Gore led a small gang armed with cameras; and so with these various occupations the afternoon was whiled away very pleasantly.
>
> After tea came the sweet scrambles which were one of the most amusing features of the afternoon. Mr Tindall mounted an old tree stump; first the Lower School gathered in an expectant crowd round his feet, and he proceeded to throw the contents of two large boxes of 'mixed boiled' into the air in handfuls. At the descent of each handful there was a general rush to the place where most of the sweets seemed to fall, a number of sweets being squashed and trampled in the ground. Next came the turn of the Upper School, which was no less amusing, after which the time arrived to re-embark in the char-à-bancs, in which the whole school returned to West Downs where a much enjoyed plunge was indulged in.
>
> Many thanks are due to Mr and Mrs Tindall who so kindly and thoughtfully organised the day.

Later the birthday picnic was replaced by other outings such as a trip by steamer on the Solent or a visit to a Naval Review at Portsmouth where there were usually ships commanded by OWDs ready to welcome the School on board. Brigadier B.A. Pearson remembers the Naval Review of 1924:

> One very special occasion I remember vividly was the whole School (about 90 boys) going off to see the Naval Review at Spithead in 1924. We went in vehicles known as char-à-bancs (pronounced sharrabangs). Three of the boys – Burmester, Forbes and Sinclair – all had fathers who were Senior Captains R.N., commanding H.M.S. *Barham*, *Queen Elizabeth* and *Warspite* respectively; they had kindly invited the School to witness the Review from aboard their battleships. The Review was terribly impressive with its mass of naval craft at anchor in straight lines, but as a small boy with little or no knowledge of the sea, I have only the dimmest memories of the day apart from two excitements which I recall in detail – P.H. Nowell-Smith's accident and our return trip to Winchester in the evening.
>
> I was in the *Warspite* party, so was Nowell-Smith. As we went out from the dockside in an open 'barge', we were repeatedly warned by the coxswain not to put our hands over the outside edge of the barge. Of course one boy in his excitement

forgot and, as we drew alongside the *Warspite*, held on to the outside edge of the 'barge' and all his fingers were crushed to pulp. From having been a promising pianist Nowell-Smith never played another note.

The other excitement that day was on the way home after the Review was all over, when the char-à-banc in front of ours (we were travelling in convoy) capsized, depositing its contents into the ditch! Something had caused it to swerve suddenly to its near-side where there was a large heap of gravel on the road's verge. Luckily the vehicle fell over onto its nearside; had it been the other way, all the boys would have been thrown out onto the road in the path of the oncoming traffic. I remember seeing one lone figure sliding down the vehicle's side and onto the ground. Apparently he had had the presence of mind, when everyone else was being tipped out into the ditch, to hang on to the hood struts and in his own time to let himself down to the ground slowly and gently – that was Richard D'Oyly Carte, son of the opera company magnate. It might have been a nasty accident, but remarkably no one was hurt; the char-à-banc was righted and we continued on our way back. It had been quite a day!

In the late 1930s there was an annual expedition to the Military Tattoo at Aldershot which was keenly enjoyed. And occasionally a group might be taken to Southampton to watch a First Division soccer match or, even more exciting, to watch Hampshire play the Australians at cricket. The author will never forget the thrill of seeing the great Don Bradman in action.

---

[1]On one occasion a particularly large mother in voluminous, flowing clothes made her way into the dining hall where she clasped her son to her bosom. He was to suffer for this later.
[2]See (p. 85).
[3]A primitive motorbus.

Chapter 13

It soon became clear after their arrival that the Tindalls shared Lionel Helbert's preoccupation with health. For the time being boys continued to be put through Puffing Billy,[1] their heads were regularly examined for nits, and their bowel movements ever more closely monitored. For constipated boys this almost amounted to a persecution, as John Aldridge (1929–33) recalls:

> When I was at West Downs, constipation was considered to be a terminal ailment. There was a rumour among the boys that if you failed to open your bowels for three days, your rectum would seal itself up – and then where would you be? Anyway, I was suspected of being constipated, and was given frequent doses of Prunol, Syrup of Figs and other nostrums, none of which, luckily, had the slightest effect upon my good-natured and imperturbable digestive system.
>
> So that the throughput, so to speak, could be monitored, I was not permitted at Sanitary Prep to 'take a number' in the ordinary way, but had to retire upstairs to some far-distant bathroom, where a commode awaited me. As there was no way of flushing it, the results or non-results of my labours were clear for Sister to see. Overshadowing this situation, as the atom bomb was later to overshadow civilisation, was the ultimate horror-weapon of the time – the enema. I am happy to record that a combination of innate good health plus an occasional economy with the truth saved me from this fate worse than death. Eventually Sister called off the hunt; I was permitted to excrete unsupervised, and my bowels and I lived happily ever after.

An innovation of Mrs Tindall's was the taking of boys' temperatures twice a day – in sickness and in health. Some adults objected to this as being psychologically damaging, but there was little evidence of this. Most boys took it light-heartedly, and it did, indubitably, often catch illnesses at an early stage. Sister Guy (see below p. 80) said later that the actual taking of temperatures was not so important, but it gave her an opportunity to look into boys' eyes, and this was usually enough to spot trouble.

Besides the daily taking of temperatures there was other evidence that Mrs Tindall was somewhat susceptible to way-out ideas about health. Perhaps the most notable of these, certainly the most rigorous, was the introduction of 'The Ice Age'. This perhaps originated with the School's connection with Captain Scott. The School had raised quite a large sum of money towards fitting out his fateful expedition – enough, so the boys were told, to buy one of the ponies which proved so impractical. No doubt, like many others, the boys of West Downs had followed the progress of the expedition eagerly and had been thrilled by Scott's words when everything was going wrong for him: 'How much better it has been than lounging in too great comfort at home!' Perhaps because of these words Scott's widow (see below p. 85) became convinced of the benefits of cold. Certainly her son, Peter, who came to West Downs, was brought up with the greatest rigour[2]. This may have made an impression on Mrs Tindall, but it was not until several years later that she took rather drastic action in the matter. This followed a lecture given to the School by a Dr Levick. The report on this lecture in *Hesperid* of 1930 runs:

> February 26th – Dr Levick lectured us in Shakespeare on 'How to keep fit'. He said that it was necessary to live in the open air as much as possible, and always to have lots of air indoors. He said that it was good for the health to be cold and a very good exercise to shiver. He also told us some of his experiences in the Antarctic. Since then the School has had all its windows wide open, and food which contains vitamins.

The results of this lecture were indeed Draconian: not only were all classroom windows thrown wide open (including the French windows in Melbury) but the newly installed central heating system was allowed to fall into disuse.[3] John Aldridge (1929–33) describes the scene:

> About 1930 the School was given a lecture on health by a Dr Murray Levick. He had at one time been attached to an expedition to the Arctic, Antarctic, or some other frigid waste, in the course of which he had noticed that no one was suffering from measles, mumps, whooping cough or 'flu. Unfortunately he concluded that this was solely due to the extreme cold; and from that moment on most of the inhabitants of West Downs were doomed. I write 'most' because the Tindalls, throughout the Ice Age which descended upon us following the lecture, maintained roaring fires in their private apartments, whence Mrs Tindall ventured forth in fur coat and fur gloves, the general effect being not unlike the well known picture of Captain Oates setting out on his last walk.[4]
>
> Indeed such was the severity of the weather in the lower passage that on one occasion a lady's hat was torn from its anchorage upon her head, and sailed a considerable distance to leeward.
>
> Mr Rose and Mr Ledgard, veterans of World War One, may have compared their classrooms unfavourably with the trenches of the Somme, where they were at least allowed to light braziers to offset hypothermia, whereas no such luxury was allowed at West Downs. However, as no one at the School was trying to shoot them, they probably concluded that, by and large, West Downs was just preferable to winter on the Western Front.
>
> Madame conducted her classes wearing an overcoat, gloves and, as I remember, some sort of head cover. Her aspect suggested that her comments on the temperature, in whatever language they had been expressed, would have been unsuitable for the ears of her pupils.
>
> The junior masters wore their varsity scarves and turned various shades of purple and blue.
>
> In spite of mittens I got chilblains on my hands, which broke and went septic, and I arrived home for Christmas with my fingers swathed in bandages and hot fomentations. The Georgian vicarage in which we lived was far from cosy by

modern standards, but compared to West Downs was as Aden is to Murmansk. My hands healed rapidly, only to revert to square one when exposed to the rigours of the Spring Term. I can honestly say that I suffered far more from the cold at West Downs than I ever did watchkeeping on the open bridge of a destroyer in the Barents Sea. And, alas for Dr Levick's theory, little boys, blue and miserable with cold, fell prey to any passing germ far more rapidly than if they had been luxuriating in a thoroughly unhealthy fugg.

Other eccentric ideas too Mrs Tindall had on the subject of health, although not as extreme as 'The Ice Age'. For a time, but only a brief time, if a boy fell ill, Sister Guy was required to take a spot of his blood which was then put on a card and despatched to a doctor of sorts in London who then used it to diagnose the disease and prescribe treatment.

Another idea concerned onion bags. A parent had convinced her that raw onions put into net bags would act as a germicide and greatly reduce chances of infection. Accordingly a number of these evil-smelling bags were placed at strategic points throughout the School – lavatories, bathrooms, passages, changing rooms. But whatever was the effect of onion bags as an aid to health, they were not, regrettably, always used for that purpose. At times they became detached from their hangings and were used as missiles. The author can vouch with great fervour for the horrendous impact of an onion bag received full in the face. Many years later an OWD admitted shamefacedly, as well he might, some responsibility for the advent of onion bags:

> The reference in your note to 'bags of raw onions hung around the School as an aid to health' suggests to me that it is time to confess to an appalling secret which I have successfully concealed for some sixty years.
>
> The conviction that such bags prevented the spread of colds was strongly held by my grandmother, Lady Mary Meynell, who convinced my mother, who convinced the powers that be at West Downs – presumably K.T. or perhaps more likely Mrs Tindall – of their efficacy.
>
> Even now the thought that my connection with such bags might have been revealed at the time induces feelings of severe panic.
>
> Yours sincerely
>
> Richard Meynell (1932–35)
>
> P.S. Actually I have a suspicion that my grandmother may have been on to something!

There was one further occasion when dire consequences were threatened as a result of a visit by a health 'expert'. A Swedish P.T. instructor had been called in to advise on gym, games and life in general at West Downs. It seems he found fault with almost everything including the school desks which, he said, were having an entirely deleterious effect on boys' physiques. How seriously Mrs Tindall thought of replacing all the desks is not known, for the 'expert' then went on to denounce hockey and the harmful effects of all the stooping which it entailed. But this was too much for the ex-Cambridge centre-half, and the man was discredited.

It must not be thought that Mrs Tindall was a health 'crank'. Basically her views were entirely sound; it was only occasionally that an element of the unorthodox came to the surface. Among OWDs there are a number who speak highly of her care and efficiency including C.A.G. Campbell (1926–29):

> I would like to say that as regards efficient admin., my life after West Downs became a steady descent downhill. Mrs Tindall was undoubtedly one of the finest administrators ever and one of the most thorough ... Mrs Tindall was responsible for the health of nearly 100 children of varying strengths and physical idiosyncrasies, and apart from this very onerous responsibility, the goodwill of parents, and especially mothers, depended greatly on their confidence in her management of our health. Likewise the very great disadvantages to a school of this size of having epidemics spreading widely among the inmates justified any reasonable precautions to spot anyone who was catching any of the common childhood diseases at the earliest possible moment.

In connection with the health of the School mention must certainly be made of Vera Guy. Other Sisters came and went at fairly brief intervals, but Sister Guy was at West Downs from 1930 for thirty-four years – and even after that came back for a spell in response to an urgent appeal for help. In the years between the Wars Sister Guy always had two Sisters under her and in times of epidemics three or four. It was she who sorted out boys' ailments – some real, some imaginary and some plainly contrived. At times too parents came under her care, as when one had a bout of malaria while at the School and when another cut his head open while doing a back dive in the swimming bath.[5] Many OWDs remember her skill and care, not to mention her adeptness at reading over eighty thermometers at great speed twice a day.

---

[1] See p. 25.

[2] He was excused School uniform; throughout the year he wore only an aertex shirt and shorts, and there were no blankets on his bed.

[3] Among other stories rife at this time was that of ink freezing in the inkwells in certain classrooms.

[4] This picture was hung in Shakespeare and is vividly remembered by several OWDs although more than one remembered it as Titus Oates setting out on his last walk!

[5] He subsequently presented a trophy for high diving to the School.

Chapter 14

Of the qualities that Helbert and Tindall had in common one was the ability to attract and to keep good staff. During the War, with all young and able-bodied men away in the armed forces, the position had been extremely difficult. Inevitably among their replacements there had been one or two oddballs. Fortunately there had also been stalwarts like Claude Hayward and Wilfred Brymer who had kept the School going. Also deserving of mention, perhaps, is Norman MacMunn, a gentle, mildly eccentric idealist with progressive views about education in which discipline played little part. 'I want you all to feel free,' he used to tell the boys in his class. They were quick to take him at his word.[1] At the end of the War he left to start a school for handicapped children, and West Downs raised a sum of money to help him in this.

With the coming of peace the situation became easier, and in Tindall's first years there was an exceptionally strong team. Messrs. Rose and Ledgard, with an M.C. to his name, arrived back from the War, looking little changed, and were to remain much the same for the thirty or so years in which they were still to serve the School. In 1920, during the interregnum between Helbert and Tindall, there was a notable addition to the staff in J.L. Stanton (soon to be known as 'Starkie'), a neighbour of Lady Goodrich in the West Country and a considerable cricketer, having played a number of games for Gloucestershire. Tall, carefully dressed and with a slight tendency to pomposity and, as some boys thought, rather too gallant towards the ladies, he was to be in charge of cricket and a senior member of the staff for the next twenty years. There were those who looked on him as being something of a 'figure behind the throne.' Certainly he became a close friend of the Tindall family (he was godfather to their fourth child), and although not officially second master, it was assumed by some that he would take charge in the event of Tindall being out of action – but this was something which never happened. On the outbreak of the Second World War Stanton joined the army and in time became military assistant to the Chief of the Imperial General Staff, Lord Alanbrooke – no mean feat for a middle-aged schoolmaster. After the War his career continued to flourish and he became a personnel director at Unilever. He also got married.

An affable and highly popular member of the staff who arrived soon after the Tindalls was Arthur Broadhurst known by the boys as 'Beany'[2] Broadhurst.

Arthur had been a pupil at West Downs in early days (1900–04), and then after Winchester and Christ Church had joined the family firm of Tootal, Broadhurst and Lee. During the War he had served in the Royal Flying Corps and on demobilisation had decided that he did not want to spend his life in the textile industry, so he sold his shares in the Company (fortunately at the top of the market) and devoted himself from then on to Education. He had been very happy at West Downs, where Helbert had made a great impression on him, and was glad of the opportunity to take up an appointment there. During his eight years at the School he taught mainly Geography and Music and acted as organist and choirmaster. With his considerable wealth he was able to indulge his taste for high-powered cars, the latest cameras and the best Parker pens which were the envy of the School. He was also something of a gourmet[3] and his figure was rotund. His show of wealth might have been resented but for his great generosity. He presented the School with a new electric organ, took parties of boys to Switzerland at his own expense and passed on his discarded cars to his colleagues on the staff at knock-down prices. West Downs was a brighter place because of him.

After he left he wandered the world for a time, looking for an ideal place to found his own school, and finally decided on the North Island of New Zealand. St Peter's, lavishly equipped (including two farms) and run on West Downs lines, was to prove highly successful. One of its features was that every boy had to learn a musical instrument. Broadhurst was subsequently awarded the O.B.E. for his services to Education.

In 1924 there arrived at the School perhaps the best loved of all West Downs masters, David Howell Griffith, 'D.H.G.' or 'Griffin', as he was sometimes called, had been born in Australia where his father was Archdeacon of the Goldfields in Western Australia.[4] But David's origins were in Wales and it was there that he was educated at the Ruthin School where he had a distinguished career, becoming head boy, captain of the Rugby XV and Victor Ludorum in athletics. David, who became of military age just after the First World War, thought first of making the Army his career, but then decided on schoolmastering. So, after a spell at a school in Felixstowe, he joined West Downs in the early Tindall era and stayed there for thirty-seven years. During that time he was for a long time in charge of Scouting, became Second Master at the outbreak of the Second World War, was the mainstay of the School while in Scotland, and finally was to be chief prop and support of J.F. Cornes when he took over from Tindall.

Stocky, of great physical strength and with a brisk but kindly manner, D.H.G. was a master in whom boys could have complete confidence. Robust, down to earth, with little time for airy-fairy notions and tortuous modern theories, he believed in hard work, a well ordered routine and a firm but not oppressive discipline. His main interest in schoolmastering was building up the self-confidence of the less talented. He had a gift of wonderfully clear exposition and knew instinctively how fast a boy could learn. It was very rare that a boy did not respond to him; he felt instinctively that D.H.G. cared for him and in return he was always anxious to prove his worth in his eyes. With his athletic distinctions he was qualified to take top games, but here too he preferred to work with the 'also rans'. Certainly he never spared himself; nothing was too much trouble; during the school term he was always at hand, hardly ever taking time off. And yet he was no drudge; he never lost his zip nor his humour.

With new members of staff, as well as boys, D.H.G. was unstinting in his help, and many new and nervous teachers were helped to find their feet. Maisie Richardson, who taught at West Downs from 1944–81, recalls a typical incident when at one of the busiest times of the term he rewrote all her exam papers which she had done incorrectly for the duplicating machine.

It is notable how many OWDs kept up a correspondence with D.H.G. after they had left the School. Tributes to him are numerous. I.M. Graham writes:

> The most popular master without a doubt was D.H.G., but I also feel in his case that the epithet a 'great' prep schoolmaster would not be out of place. I am sure that only his extreme modesty and shyness kept him from going on to higher things.

And Christopher Wood:

> Among those I remember particularly was D.H.G., a kind of mobile Rock of Gibraltar. The kindest and fairest of men and a most gifted teacher. I always looked forward to the days when he was duty master. Somehow the School took on a different appearance.

And Colin Campbell:

> It was in his class that I first began to learn how to learn and to get real confidence in my own ability. He was very thorough and very clear in his explanations. Above all he taught the gospel of 'Determination' – that with enough Will you could always do more than you expected.

J.F. Cornes, his last headmaster, recalls a sixth sense he had for trouble brewing in any part of the building even when he himself was far away. Simon Macdonald-Lockhart (1925–29) remembers his unfailing touch in instantly subduing incipient trouble when he visited the School once as an old boy:

> We talked for a while watching the boys amuse themselves and then he suddenly said: 'Excuse me.' Raising his voice he called: 'Smith minor', or whatever the boy's name was. He did no more than call the name, but that was sufficient. He did not tell me what he had done, but merely turned to me with a smile saying 'W.D. does it again.' The story shows not only his complete command but also his attitude to his job. It was not 'I've done it again.' or 'We've done it again.' but 'W.D. does it again.'

The high quality of the masters in the early Tindall years is shown by how many of them later became headmasters of other schools. Among them were C.A. Ranger who went off to Pinewood and C.A.G. Browning (known from his initials as 'Cabbage') who went to Fernden. There was also R.E. Wheeler[5] who took over his father's school in Norwich and K.A. Gaskell who became headmaster of

Ravensbrook, at the same time marrying the Tindalls' eldest daughter, Rachel. Later on came G.M. (Mike) Singleton who became headmaster of The Elms near Malvern, also chairman of the I.A.P.S.[6], a magistrate and a member of the Solicitors' Disciplinary Tribunal. Mike, a county cricketer, was at West Downs for only two years (1936–38), but he has vivid memories of it. He recalls that his salary was £180 a year and that on this he ran a car costing £10; he remembers the Masters' Lodge as being a happy place where the residents were well looked after by a man known as Herbert and his wife. There was also a lively interest in racing. John Stanton would collect the bets (including an occasional flutter from Tumty) and phone them through to his bookie. One year they had a notable success:

> I remember strongly advising Mahmoud for the Derby. We all had a good bet, and John told me to run the senior cricket game on the afternoon of the race so that he could listen to the wireless. I can still see him coming out in front of the pavilion, raising his arms and shouting to me, 'The grey won.' We kept a drinks cupboard in the Lodge, and it was punished that night.

A contemporary of Mike Singleton's was Robert Schuster who became joint headmaster of Ravenswood School in Devon after the Second World War. During the War he had served in the army and was captured in Italy. Later he had an exciting escape disguised as a Roman Catholic priest. It could well be that Robert, not a very military figure, would have been more convincing as a priest than as a soldier.

Another master who was at West Downs for a few years before the War was G.S. Leach, a classicist and a notable musician with a tenor voice of near professional standard. He had taught at West Downs before under Helbert, but had then gone to be headmaster of the Wick School at Hove. His contribution to West Downs music has already been noted. What was not generally known, as he was the most modest of men, was that in his younger days he had been a considerable mountaineer, making several climbs, although not the most famous, with Mallory and Irving.

There were two outstanding women teachers at that time who should be mentioned: Margaret Tempest who taught Art and was a well known illustrator of children's books, and Dorothy Lunn who taught Music. Reference has already been made to her skill as a class teacher, but she was also an exceptional teacher of the piano. Here too she realised how important it was that her pupils should enjoy what they were doing. She did not, therefore, overburden them with scales and exercises nor did she impose on them pieces to learn for which they had little enthusiasm; within certain limits she let them learn what they wanted to and made them enjoy it. The author would like to express a great debt of gratitude to her.

One other woman teacher who should certainly be mentioned is Madame de Coutouly, sometimes genial, occasionally explosive, who struggled to impart a French accent into West Downs boys – no mean task. With much flair and success she carried on the tradition, started by Madame Calviou, of an annual French play. For this she not only taught the players their lines but also contended with the costumes and scenery, her none too svelte figure being seen at times perilously high on a ladder.

Inevitably not every teacher was a success. Some came and went fairly quickly. *Hesperid* of 1923 reported: 'Mr Russell came this term, but, as he hopes to be a professional singer, he left, for schoolmastering tired his voice.' There was also a supposed naval commander who was in and out of the school in a couple of days. But generally during the inter-War years West Downs was fortunate. Masters were gifted and sometimes inspired and their idiosyncrasies innocuous. There were very few to whom OWDs felt a strong aversion.

As well as inheriting a strong staff from Helbert, Tindall also inherited some illustrious parents. Prominent among these was Nancy Lady Astor, the first woman to take her seat in the House of Commons. It was while her eldest son was at West Downs that she fought and won the by-election at Plymouth – an event followed with great excitement at the School. Lady Astor is said to have had rather a strong aversion to schools and schoolmasters and, with her famed outspokenness, it would have been interesting to have been a fly on the wall during her interviews with K.T. On her visits to the School, one with the Queen of Romania in tow, it was improbable that she would have kept a low profile, nor did she. When the school was parading in the gym she took over from the master on duty and started barking orders. If the boys happened to be standing they would be told: 'On the floor, SIT.' And if sitting: 'Stand UP.' And at occasions when parents were expected to sit quietly and applaud politely she did neither. Also during her visits she would conduct a small Christian Science seminar in the private garden, a privilege unlikely to have been accorded to many parents.

Another eminent parent was The Right Hon. Leo Amery who was Secretary of State for the Colonies while his ill-fated son John was at West Downs. John, happy in the knowledge that his father had forbidden him to be beaten, was apt to play fast and loose. He is remembered arriving for the 'mush' train at Waterloo, where other boys were in school uniform and attended by sorrowing mothers, flamboyantly dressed with a female companion and smoking a cigarette. While at the School he is said to have attempted to run away with Richard D'Oyly Carte, son of the Savoy Operas producer. This event has passed into mythology and there are several versions of it. One says that they succeeded in reaching the D'Oyly Carte yacht at Southampton; another that they were recaptured in a neighbouring vegetable patch; another that they were found asleep in the Scout wagon in the back yard; and yet another that it was not John Amery at all but another boy. The truth, it seems, will never be known.[7]

A parent of a different ilk was Lady Scott, widow of the Antarctic explorer (later Mrs Hilton-Young and Lady Kennet). A very gifted sculptress, she created the West Downs War Memorial – a striking and beautiful statue of a naked boy with raised arm, and underneath the words from Isaiah: 'Here am I. Send me.'[8]

'Here am I. Send me.' The West Downs War Memorial.

The Memorial is described in *Hesperid* of 1922:

> He stands with right hand raised, ready for any service to which he may be called. There is nothing depressing or sentimental about this boy; he is just the ideal human boy – fit, sound and active in body and mind; in his face can be seen hope, eagerness and joy in the thought of noble service, but there is also a suggestion of seriousness, as if the young boy had some realisation that his work would be difficult and that its very difficulty made it more worth the doing. And on the stone pedestal beneath his feet are carved the words, 'Here am I. Send me.'[9]

---

[1]On one occasion, when his class was in total disarray, the headmaster of Harrow passed by the window and was shocked to see his son in the forefront of the fray. He was a strong admirer of Helbert and West Downs and had altogether four sons there, but this particular one was removed and sent to a rather stricter regime at Summer Fields.

[2]Prep school slang at that time indicating something good. Since then 'super', 'smashing', 'wizard' and, more recently, 'cool' and 'groovy' have at times taken its place.

[3]When on duty during boys' teas he eyed avidly the choicest cakes from home and usually managed to obtain a slice – giving rise to a variation of a well known hymn:

> Kinkering Kongs their slices take
> From my great big birthday cake.

[4]He seems to have had a *penchant* towards mining communities. He was later to become Priest-in-Charge of the Diamond Mines in South Africa.

[5]Rather a diminutive figure remembered by some OWDs for his singing in concerts in a high tremulo voice. One song particularly remembered began with the words 'I am small, sang the wren.'

[6]Incorporated Association of Preparatory Schools.

[7]John Amery's life ended in tragedy. He joined the Fascist Party and in occupied Europe during the Second World War campaigned actively against Britain fighting with Russia against Germany. For this he was subsequently convicted of treason and paid the ultimate penalty. But, like the Thane of Cawdor, 'nothing in his life became him like the leaving of it', and he met his death with unflinching courage, joking lightly with the hangman.

[8]It is believed by some that Peter Scott was the model for the statue, but he is very definite in his autobiography that he was not.

[9]On the closing down of West Downs the statue was re-established in Peter Scott's bird sanctuary at Slimbridge.

Chapter 15

When Tindall succeeded Helbert he inherited a school deeply imbued with Victorian values: the Christian faith, hard work and clean living – these were the hallmarks of West Downs and Tindall, himself a strong Victorian, had no inclination to change them. In this he certainly had the support of most people connected with the School, but there were some who thought that without impinging on its basic character he might have done more to bring West Downs into line with modern times. The twenties and thirties were a period of great social and technological change. They saw the emergence of the radio, the cinema, the Labour Party and the Modern Woman. But these and other upheavals were kept remote from West Downs.

Was West Downs then too protected? Did Tindall in his dread of the vulgar and the trivial keep the School over-sanitised? Was he, like Dame Partington, trying to keep at bay forces which were ultimately irresistible? Certainly he put up a strong rearguard action. Film shows were almost unknown at West Downs; the wireless, even Children's Hour with dear, innocuous Uncle Mack, was ignored; and reading matter was closely censored. At the beginning of each term all books brought back from the holiday were inspected, and anything savouring of the cheap and sensational was confiscated. Conan Doyle, Rider Haggard and John Buchan were quite safe. Not so Edgar Wallace and The Saint and certainly not *The Well of Loneliness* which one brave soul tried to get through. Magazines too were rigidly restricted. Respectable Establishment periodicals like *Punch* and *The Illustrated London News* were allowed, but no comics, not even such harmless publications as *Rainbow* or *Tiger Tim*. The popular press too was excluded. Each day carefully selected strips from *The Times* were posted in Shakespeare, but apart from the cricket scores and other sporting results these were not widely read.[1] What did manage to get through were pictorial strips cut out of a daily paper. In the late 1930s the *Daily Mirror* ran an exciting series called Buck Ryan, and a weekly consignment of these used to be sent to the author by an obliging nursery maid, and no objection was made to these. Whether it would have been the same if the strips had been *Jane's Journal*, also a *Daily Mirror* feature at that time, must be doubtful.

Life at a boarding Prep School must, necessarily, be restricted. Too much freedom cannot be given to boys between the ages of eight and fourteen.

88

Responsibility for the safety and welfare of up to a hundred of these is a heavy one. Without supervision and regulation things can all too easily go wrong. Bullying can take place, so can accidents. Boys can put their heads, hands or other parts of their bodies through a glass window, they can decide to investigate the electricity supply and get a shock, they can swallow a coin or some other extraneous object.[2] And in each case the School is held responsible and parents will want to know why it was allowed to happen. In striking a balance between freedom and constraint it is possible that West Downs under Tindall erred on the side of caution. There were, indubitably, rather a lot of rules, the point of some of which was not immediately obvious. Was it necessary to ban all sweets[3] and comics? To have to get permission at all times to go to *foricas* and to maintain total silence while there? And was it not a little excessive, if one boy wanted to take out another on a parental visit, for both to have to obtain written permission from their parents?

It may be argued that these were minor points of no great significance. Maybe they were. Certainly they should not be allowed to obscure the fact that the Tindalls took good care of the boys in their charge and ran a well organised school. This was, perhaps, too readily taken for granted; it was not realised how wretched school life can be where the organisation is chaotic. It was also not realised how hard the Tindalls worked to achieve this good order.

A well run school requires a well disciplined school – not too lax and not too severe. If the former, organisation will be under strain and may break down and some boys will be confused and distressed. If the latter, the harsh measures taken to enforce it will not only cause fear and misery, but will also be counter-productive, and when indiscipline breaks out it will be disagreeable rather than merely mischievous.

There are those OWDs who would say that K.T. in holding the balance between punishment and mercy was more inclined to the former than the latter. And it may be that there were occasions when he over-reacted and 'blew his top' too readily. But most would agree that at heart he was a just man. No one accused him of having favourites; one knew where one was with him; and one thought twice about trying anything on with him.

In maintaining discipline he did certainly use the cane and the slipper, sometimes perhaps to excess, but it was not in his nature to bludgeon boys into virtue. He tried too to win their hearts and minds.

Like Helbert, Tindall delegated certain disciplinary powers to Patrol Leaders, although not, as before, corporal punishment. But he did retain Patrol Leaders' Meeting, a sort of kangaroo court which met in the private dining room and summoned before it those boys who were considered to be a nuisance and generally doing badly. This was liable to abuse as Colin Campbell recalls:

> When the culprit came in he was made to stand in front of us on a stool (like the old Kirk's 'stool of repentance') where he would be harangued by the head of the School with extra remarks thrown in by the other Patrol Leaders. I well remember when I

was first summoned before it at the age of about ten. It was a pretty frightening experience, and though prepared to admit to myself that I was rather obstreperous, I did not feel that all the rude things they said to me were justified. When I became a Patrol Leader and saw the thing working from the other side, I was at times disgusted with it. I learned then of Parkinson's Law of Bureaucracy that if you set up a body to do something, it will do it to justify its existence even when what it is doing is unnecessary or even wrong. Often we could not think of anyone who really deserved to feel the heat, and yet we cast about until we found someone to jeer at.

It is common practice to find fault with Prep Schools; often they are easy targets. This is perhaps especially the case with a school which has a strong and distinctive character of its own; it is liable to arouse strong feelings for and against. Thus at West Downs there were those who valued greatly the strong Christian ethos of the School, while there were others who found it rigid and oppressive. Tindall was a forceful character whose strengths and weaknesses were manifest and to whom one reacted strongly one way or the other. But it must be certain that, consciously or unconsciously, nearly all boys in his charge were influenced by him to some degree. At that impressionable age it was inevitable. And few would deny that he went to great pains on behalf of the boys in his care. This was especially the case in all religious matters. His inspired efforts to bring chapel services to life have already been noted, and he was also at his best in preparing candidates for Confirmation. Some OWDs remember this with great gratitude. I.M. Graham (1929–33) writes:

> He prepared candidates himself and took immense trouble over this. I still have his notes which my mother bound up for me in ecclesiastical purple. Surely this was exceptional for a layman, and I don't think one could have been better prepared by the Archbishop of Canterbury himself.

Another matter over which Tindall took considerable trouble was the leaving talk he gave to each boy. These were partly physiological and partly exhortative with warnings of what might lie ahead at Public Schools.[4] Today the imparting of the facts of life is often delegated to doctors or some semi-scientific 'expert', or considered unnecessary because boys already know them. But fifty years ago it was very different. Then the subject was treated with a certain amount of awe, and headmasters like Helbert and Tindall regarded it as a sacred duty. Boys were seen individually and first sworn to secrecy. Explanations were frank and factual but not always adequate. It must be astonishing to boys today how innocent were their counterparts fifty years ago. Most of them knew nothing and were not particularly curious. Consequently when all was revealed to them 'out of the blue', they tended to be somewhat bemused. It was not until they reached their Public Schools, where further information was freely vouchsafed, that their understanding became more complete.[5] Like Helbert, Tindall kept a record of what he had told each boy and a summary of this was sent to his parents.[6]

Like Helbert too, Tindall considered that his responsibility for boys at West Downs did not end when they left the School. Boys arriving at their Public

Schools would find waiting for them a kindly and affectionate letter full of good wishes and urging them to get in touch with him if they were in any kind of doubt or trouble. Lord Horder (1919–23) remembers the words he used: 'It is your right and my privilege.'

If West Downs under Tindall scored highly for organisation and care, what of academic standards? At first the School did well and there were a number of scholarships including some at Winchester and Eton. But then the record languished and in the late twenties and early thirties the Honours Board was not overladen. Compared to a school like Summer Fields, where it was expected to win six or seven scholarships a year, the toll was meagre. Of course this does not tell the whole story. Scholarships at this rate are usually only gained by intense cramming, and West Downs did not go in for this. Also concentration on scholarships often means that middle-of-the-roaders and doubtful Common Entrance candidates are neglected and this was certainly not the case at West Downs where Common Entrance failures were almost unknown.[7] Certainly to David Howell Griffiths and maybe to Tindall too a weak candidate gaining a place at a Public School was just as much an achievement as a strong one gaining a scholarship. Academic standards at West Downs then should not be under-rated. Edward Ford, who won a scholarship to Eton, has given it as his opinion that his years at West Downs were 'enjoyable, productive and educative'.

West Downs is more open to criticism, perhaps, on the matter of the School curriculum. This remained narrow and severely classical. In class boys were still mainly occupied with such matters as the ablative absolute, isosceles triangles and irregular French verbs, and hardly at all with the great works of literature and the great figures of history. Nor had any significant concessions been made as yet to Science. It is likely that to Tindall as to Helbert Science was a closed book. The only member of staff who showed something of a scientific bent was D.L. Rose who occasionally gave lectures on such subjects as Water and Electricity. Otherwise the only field of Science where there was some activity was Natural History. This had been given a great boost by Peter Scott during his time at the School; his great enthusiasm had been infectious. Both on the playing fields and down at Melbury there was considerable scope for activity, as Jack Boles recalls:

> I remember the Natural History interest in the grounds at West Downs and at Melbury and the encouragement some members of the staff gave. The steep fringe of woodland around the two sides of the sports field were rich in birds including crossbills. I found a lark's nest with eggs on the steep bank between the main playing fields, and many slowworms. Lime and privet hawkmoth caterpillars seemed to cope with captivity, and somewhere there were newts.

In taking West Downs to task for the narrowness of the curriculum one must remember how restricted it was by the requirements of Common Entrance and the scholarships exams. So long as these were unchanged there was little room for new subjects.

During the 1930s West Downs, like other Prep Schools, went through lean times financially. Worldwide depression meant that money was in short supply and everyone, including the Government, was looking for ways of cutting costs. At Prep Schools the situation was exacerbated by the incidence of a fall in the birth rate ten years previously, and there were places unfilled. At West Downs numbers fell from over a hundred at the beginning of the decade to just over eighty in the middle, and this made a great difference to profitability and the availability of funds for less essential items. It meant too that no improvements or additions could be made to the school buildings. Probably few realised at the time on what a tight budget West Downs was being run.

The criticism most frequently levelled at Prep Schools and, indeed, at all independent schools is that they are snobbish and exclusive – bastions of privilege, remote from the ordinary life of the country. But it is easier to say this than to know what to do about it – apart from abolishing independent schools altogether; and this is not the place to get drawn into an argument on that subject. At boarding Prep Schools particularly, owing to the restraints that have to be put on young boys, it is all too easy for them to become narrow and enclosed societies. Before the Second World War it was usual for no home visits to be allowed during term time and parental visits to the School were few and far between, sometimes non-existent. It could happen, therefore, that boys went for weeks on end without ever emerging from the School except, maybe, for burberry walks or a visit to the dentist. During this time their only social contact would be with a small circle of other boys and fragments of conversation with masters or matrons. It is claimed for boarding schools that they make boys independent and self-sufficient, and this may be so, but they can pay a heavy price for this in terms of a narrow and uninspiring social life.

At West Downs under Tindall it was recognised that there was a need to keep in touch with the outside world and to be aware that there were boys from a different social background from one's own; but not a great deal was done about it. As a gesture the School 'adopted' an inmate of the Waifs and Strays and helped him with money and other gifts. At one time he used to make annual visits to the School, but these were discontinued – they must have been a great ordeal for him. Association with local boys was rare except on Scouting occasions, notably the annual Baker-Wilbraham competition between Scout troops. Other contacts were less friendly, as when there were ugly confrontations with lean and hungry looking youths[8] across the fence surrounding the playing fields. A somewhat grimmer indication of a different world came from the Winchester Prison a few hundred yards down the road. At times the black flag would be seen flying and sounds of rattling tin cans could be heard as prisoners made their protests. On one occasion a prisoner escaped, and all the staff joined in the search, but unsuccessfully, and on arrival back at the Masters' Lodge it was found that it had been entered and a master's suit removed.

---

[1]An exception was shipping movements. Some boys took a great interest in these.
[2]One unfortunate boy who swallowed a marble was made to sit on a commode until the marble had

made its way through his gastric system and emerged the other end.

[3]With wartime rationing this rule was relaxed.

[4]Possibly this was overdone. One OWD recalls that when he arrived at Harrow and a much senior cousin came and said a few kind words to him, he became alarmed.

[5]Later when boys knew much more and these matters became less sacrosanct, these talks were sometimes taken rather lightly. It was the custom with some boys to lay bets on how many times K.T. would relight his pipe in the course of the talk.

[6]In those reticent days some parents found this instructive. At least one mother was able to fill in gaps in her knowledge.

[7]On one occasion when a boy did fail the entrance exam to Winchester, a prayer was offered for him in Chapel.

[8]Known in the School, regrettably, as 'guttergrubs'.

Chapter 16

Any history of a Prep School would be incomplete if some reference was not made to some of the indigenous customs, language and taboos prevalent at certain times. Some of these originate from the headmaster and some from the boys. Of the former several have already been mentioned, especially those connected with health. But there were quite a few more, notably in the matters of dressing and eating.

Dressing and undressing at West Downs always had to be done with great care. It was thought very important that what St Paul called one's less seemly parts should not be exposed to view. Boys might have just been to a bath or a swim where they had plunged naked into the water, but subsequently they had to be punctilious about the order in which they put on or took off their clothes so that they did not 'show sights.' To do so would cause comment.

School food is a subject on which Old Boys tend to hyperbolise. Horrendous stories are told of the gruesome things which they were expected to eat. Some of the food at West Downs was certainly unappetising, but generally, it must be said, it was wholesome and reasonably nutritious.[1] But it did take some getting used to. Inevitably certain things were placed in front of a boy to which he felt a strong aversion – spinach, perhaps, liver, tapioca or prunes – but he was always expected to eat them. Sometimes he did his best, but sometimes he resorted to other methods of disposing of them. The author has to confess with shame that he has in his day deposited quite large quantities of liver under the table, usually, truth must be told, under someone else's chair.

Elegant table manners are not something which come easily to most boys; their natural tendency is to gobble, speak with their mouths full and reach impulsively across the table for anything they happen to want. In theory they have been taught not to do these things at their mother's (or nanny's)[2] knee, but this has not always happened, some mothers feeling that it is the function of the school to which they are paying large fees to do that sort of thing. West Downs, it must be said, did not shirk its duty in this respect and strenuous efforts were made to instil in boys a reasonable standard. Boys who transgressed were sometimes made to stand on their chairs or in extreme cases were sent to the 'Pigs Table', a table normally used only for piling up dirty dishes. In table manners, as in other matters, K.T. was not free from personal fads, as Paul Morgan (1930–35) recalls:

94

> In the early 1930s K.B.T. held that it was improper to eat puddings with a spoon only. It had to be a spoon *and* fork. If he saw any boy eating with just a spoon, he would roar in the dining hall 'Cannibal!' and everyone would look to find the offender who seldom repeated the offence. A fork only was, of course, permitted. In the 1980s a spoon only is common, but personally I still hesitate!

One of the rigidities of life at West Downs was the custom of always addressing others boys by their surnames. Christian names were never used even among brothers who solemnly addressed each other as Smith major, minor or even mus. (minimus). Indeed Christian names were often closely guarded secrets. In the case of first names this was difficult to maintain – name tapes and letters from home often giving them away – but middle names were never revealed except under extreme duress or in exchange for some equally prized piece of information. Also kept closely secret were the Christian names of one's closest relatives. Edward Ford's uncle was a master at West Downs for a time and he remembers the dismay he felt when his mother, down on a visit, came into the Dining Hall where the whole school was standing in respectful silence, and greeted her brother-in-law with the words: 'Hullo, Gus. How nice to see you!' This was heard with glee by the boys and from then on Edward and his twin brother, Christopher, were known as Gus. Another custom was always to refer to one's near relations by their Latin designation – pater, mater, frater and soror. For some reason the English form was considered unworthy of them.[3]

In the early days of West Downs it seems that not many sedentary games were played. Apart from the immortals like chess and draughts few have been mentioned. Diabolo was in fashion for a time, but then disappeared. In the 1930s, however, 'table' games became more widespread: Dover Patrol, Attaque!, Aviation and Tri-Tactics were very popular; and it was at this time that Monopoly made its first appearance. One very simple homemade game, which had the advantage that it could be played by oneself, perhaps surreptitiously in a dormitory on a summer's evening when one was supposed to be going to sleep, was Code Cricket. Here each letter of the alphabet was assigned a result of a ball bowled – a certain number of runs or dismissed in some way. Then two teams were made up and a passage taken from a book and each letter read off and then taken into account. But perhaps the most popular of all games, certainly the cheapest and simplest, was conker fights. Other games might fade from the scene, but this one never failed to reappear each autumn.

Toys, like games, were subject to the whims of fashion, but in the 1930s there were certain hardy favourites – models of all kinds of ships and vehicles, high speed racing cars, aeroplanes propelled with elastic bands and, of course, yo-yos. Of personal possessions in those days perhaps the most highly prized was a watch. Watches then were not the tough, reliable things they are today. Unless expensive, which was discouraged, their time keeping was erratic and they frequently went wrong, usually finished off altogether if dropped. Great store was also set by a good fountain pen (perhaps a Conway Stewart) and for these ordinary school ink was considered unworthy and deleterious and a private supply of superior quality was always kept. Propelling pencils were also popular, particularly a 'four-in-hand' which wrote in four different colours. One possession allowed at that time which is usually strictly banned today, was a penknife. This may have been because of its use in many Scouting activities, and the most popular were those with numerous gadgets – corkscrews, bottle openers (little use for these at West Downs) and one said to be useful for getting stones out of horses' feet (surely very rarely used!).

At most schools weird customs, rites and initiation ceremonies are liable to evolve. At ancient establishments these are handed down from generation to generation and attain almost mystic significance. At West Downs such customs tended to be short-lived but they did exist and H.J. Simpson (1922–26) recalls one of them:

> There was a 'Rite de Passage' which entailed going down a hole and a tunnel in the chalk and coming out the other end. This was somewhere beyond the beech woods up the Old Sarum Road. On getting back one had to try to clean the chalk stains off one's burberries and hope to get away with it.

Colin Campbell remembers one with religious undertones:

> This took place in Chapel Dormitory and shows our devotion to Old Testament studies. In those days everyone used to plaster his hair with some concoction – Brilliantine or Honey and Flowers were the favourites. Now in the middle of the wooden floor planking there was a knot hole with the knot missing – a real hole about one inch across. This some bright spark, mindful of his Scripture researches, designated 'The Holy of Holies', and persuaded the rest of us to render due worship to it in ceremonial fashion after Lights Out, at the same time propitiating it with sacrificial libations from our Brilliantine bottles. It certainly produced a 'sweet savour', but in due course it also produced a crop of earwigs which was less desirable. So that particular cult came to a premature end.

Modern historians, who like to scrape up every detail, would probably consider it necessary in a Prep School history to devote space to schoolboy humour, especially the scatological. But the present author does not propose to follow this trend; the subject is not an edifying one. Faint memories come floating back of mildly smutty jokes, rhymes and 'revised versions', but these had surely better remain in semi-oblivion. There is no need, for example to resurrect the Old Lady of Spain and certainly not the Old Man of Madras. Let them rest in peace.

Brief reference should be made though to schoolboy slang if only to show how dated it soon becomes. From the 1920s and 30s the following is a random selection:

Bate	temper – at signs of which the taunt 'batey, batey' was apt to be rendered.
Bish:	a foolish and avoidable mistake.
Blub:	to cry, hence blubberation.
Bunkum (bunk):	nonsense.

Bunk:	be off! Later replaced by *scram*.
Cad:	mean, despicable fellow.
Cave (pronounced K.V.):	watch out; danger is approaching.
M.Y.O.B.:	mind you own business.
Poop:	idiot, fool. Sometimes poopstick. New boys were sometimes sent on an errand to Sister 'to fetch their poopstick'.
Mingy:	(sometimes squingy) mean, niggardly.
Rotter:	variation of cad; alternatively stinker, louse, swine.
Quis:	used to indicate that something is going free; first to answer 'ego' obtains.
Sense of common decency:	absence of which in a boy often sadly bewailed after some dastardly act.
Sneak:	teller of tales, lowest of the low.
Snubs:	so there! Used when scoring off someone. Variations: snibs or 'take a boosy one!'
Spread:	to tell everyone, usually a dark secret.
Squish:	to apply physical violence to someone.
Swear on one's Bible honour:	the most solemn of oaths.
Swizz:	swindle; used to indicate unfair treatment. Sometimes 'chiz'.
Tight smack:	blow with the flat of the hand. Bets with money being impossible, tight smacks (usually ten) were often substituted.
Trademark:	imprint of hand left on bare back after a tight smack.
Warpath, on the:	indicates approach of headmaster or others in authority in ominous mood.

---

[1]The Tindalls were careful to see that this was so. On one occasion, when a titled parent made a complaint about the food, K.T. made a special journey to London, armed with statistics to convince her of the fact.

[2]Sister Guy noticed a marked difference in the table manners of new boys who had had nannies and those brought up by mothers.

[3]Rather curiously this was a privilege they shared with the lavatory which was always known as the Latin *foricas*.

Chapter 17

When war broke out in September 1939 it was expected that the Germans would immediately launch mass air raids on the British Isles, and long prepared plans were put into effect for dealing with this contingency. At West Downs, as elsewhere, gas masks were fitted, sandbags filled, and windows crisscrossed with sticky paper to prevent splintering. Also, for the first time ever, West Downs dormitories and classrooms were fitted with curtains – yards and yards of black-out material so fitted that no chink of light would be visible from the outside. Already at the time of Munich amateur attempts had been made by masters and others to dig air raid trenches, but these had caved in and had had to be replaced by more substantial affairs. But in the event heavy air raids did not come, not at least during the first winter of the War. Occasionally warnings were sounded, and boys were roused from their beds, assembled in Shakespeare and marched off to the shelters. But there was no sign of activity overhead and no bombs were dropped anywhere in the neighbourhood. And so for six months, during the so-called 'Phoney War', life went on much as before. Some inconvenience was caused by food and petrol rationing, but the expectation was that this would not last long and that soon Allied troops would be breaking through the Siegfried Line and advancing into Germany.

From this mood of false optimism the country was rudely awakened by the events of the spring of 1940. Despite British sea power Norway was invaded; with only brief resistance Holland and Belgium were overrun; and in France the much vaunted Maginot Line proved useless as the German armoured divisions poured through where it ended and even in places over it. By a miracle the trapped British Expeditionary Force escaped by Dunkirk, but the French had little stomach for the fight and capitulated soon afterwards. It seemed that the Germans were unstoppable, and most people expected that their next move would be across the Channel into southern England.

At first at West Downs the Tindalls did not take this threat too seriously, but then it was impressed on them by some senior officers among the parents that in the event of invasion Winchester would be in the forefront of the battle and might even be caught in a German pincer movement. A decision was then taken with great promptness: the Summer Term would end forthwith, waiting only for the performance of the Shakespeare play, and West Downs would then move to a building in a safer area. But the search for this was to prove extremely difficult as Ann Bass (then Ann Tindall) recalls:

> Immediately after the weekend of Paters' Match and the Shakespeare play my parents set off to the West Country and Welsh borders to look for a new site. They came back realising that all the desirable places had already been taken by the schools which had evacuated from the south coast at the start of the War. They even considered very seriously going to Canada and began negotiations for a place in Ontario. But this was advised against by Government contacts. How many parents would have applied to send their boys abroad cannot be known, but it is difficult now to put oneself back into the rather panicky feeling of that summer.

The Tindalls then embarked on a search in the British Isles for a large, empty, more or less habitable building which could be turned into a school. West Downs had for many years had strong connections in Scotland and Northumberland and it was there that the Tindalls concentrated their efforts. Once again there were a number of false trails, but eventually they came across Glenapp Castle in Ayrshire which, although not ideal, might suit their purposes. By this time they were beginning to become rather desperate, fearing that if a building was not found soon the School would have to close down, as many Prep Schools had already done. And so, with some misgivings, they took a lease.

The task of moving West Downs from Winchester to Ayrshire during the tensest period of the War was herculean. Ann Bass recalls it vividly:

> Then came the planning of the move. Everything on the school side had to go: beds, bedding, chests of drawers, dining hall tables and chairs, desks, books, kitchen equipment – including even the Aga cookers which had been installed at West Downs not long before! The task seemed impossible, but each department had to sort out its priorities. On the private side of the house not so much was needed as the Castle was let furnished. So N-room[1] was packed with sofas and chairs, antique furniture, pictures, magic lantern and all else not required, and kept locked up till the end of the War.
>
> To find furniture vans at that time of the War to travel so far was difficult, and Pickfords advised using the railways; Stranraer Station was only fifteen miles from Glenapp, and there were main line trains from Euston to catch the ferry to Larne. Containers were a fairly new idea – not large ones as one would use now but just the size to fit on a standard flat railway truck, and as many of these as possible were chartered; but much of the school furniture had to go in open trucks – desks, beds, chests of drawers. This was worrying, but we were assured that all would be quite safe under tarpaulins. It could not, of course, be guaranteed to arrive in less than a week or so, goods trains being rather slow.
>
> We arrived at Glenapp before the containers and lorries which brought the furniture from Stranraer. My first impression was the beauty of the place and the almost incredible luxury of the parts of the house which we were to inhabit.
>
> In those days fitted walk-in wardrobes with lights which went on when the door was opened and bathrooms with fitted carpets and bidets were a new experience! Our sitting room with French windows onto a balcony or terrace had a Reynolds (insured for £7,000!) over the mantlepiece and Chippendale chairs with antique gros point tapestry and other furniture which would now fetch a fabulous price. But all the rooms which were to be used by the boys had been stripped of furniture.

In the advance party to Glenapp were David Howell Griffiths, Harry Ricardo, Robert Schuster, Mike Simson (who had recently married my cousin Betty Wilkinson who acted as an extra under-matron), May (who for years had been in charge of clothes and linen and the upstairs domestic staff), the Housekeeper and resident kitchen staff – three young 'lady' cooks ('cooklets' my father called them!).

At last the furniture arrived. What had come in the containers was intact, but the dormitory chests of drawers had been badly knocked about and all had to have a quick coat of paint by Mr St Germier, the very deaf handyman who had been resident in the Masters' Lodge at West Downs where his wife had cooked the masters' breakfast and supper. But far the worst problem was the dormitory iron beds. They had been taken apart in Winchester and bundled all together into the trucks. Some were relatively simple to reconstruct, being more modern – two ends and a spring mattress on a frame which slotted in so one only had to find a matching top and bottom and a frame which fitted the slots. But many more were the older kind which had a top and bottom, two side irons and a spring mattress which had to be secured by two bolts and nuts at each end – at least nine pieces altogether for each bed and of all different patterns. Over a hundred beds left Winchester, but after two days solid work by all available not more than eighty or so were put together. A terrible pile of unmatchable pieces were left over. However, the situation was not as immediately serious as that sounds as some boys did not follow us to Glenapp, and even though about half a dozen Ayrshire boys joined the School, the total number had gone down from just under a hundred to eight-four. That actually was the maximum number which could be squeezed into the dormitories even though they were not spaced as generously as in Winchester.

When the furniture had come the rest of the staff arrived – Messrs Ledgard and Rose, Miss Lunn and Miss Playsted and Miss Coombs, the P.E. instructress who had taken the place of Sergeant in the gym. Except for the latter, all of these had gallantly left comfortable homes in Winchester to become living-in members of staff. The male members of the staff lived at Auchairne Lodge nearly a mile away and came and went in a minibus which cannot have been very convenient for them. The Estate Factor, Mr Hewitson, was most helpful in putting us in touch with local services and tradesmen. For him it was probably more exciting than looking after a castle empty for much of the year. One thing which had to be done was to check the inventory of all that was in the Castle and which would have to be accounted for at the end of the let. When this had been done a lot of things which were not needed like burnished fire irons in rooms used as dormitories were collected up and stored, which made it considerably more difficult to sort out when we left Glenapp!

Glenapp, of course, was not a genuine castle. It had been built in the 1860s in what was known as Scottish baronial style, complete with numerous turrets, castellations and other mock fortifications. In the 1920s it was acquired by Lord Inchcape, the Scottish shipping magnate who might have been king of Albania.[2] He had enlarged it and embellished it and lived there until his death in 1932. In some ways Glenapp suited West Downs well. The building was in first class order, the rooms were large and suitable for classrooms and dormitories, and there was a splendid if rather small hall where assemblies and chapel services could take place and plays performed. Outside there was a large, attractive garden full of rhododendrons[3] and lovely open countryside with a magnificent view down to the sea with the rock of Ailsa Craig, and beyond, visible on fine days, the Isle of Arran. Also Ayrshire was a safe area far away from the firing line: there were no air raids and few signs of troop movements; the only indications of the War were the coastal defences and the convoys sailing up and down the Clyde. Nevertheless Glenapp was not ideal. Basically it was too small: there were not enough classrooms and temporary huts had to be erected outside – subsequently blown down in a storm. But the main disadvantage at Glenapp was the lack of any flat land suitable for playing fields. During the year that West Downs was there football, cricket and hockey had to be very makeshift.

Certainly it was an act of considerable courage on the part of the Tindalls to take on Glenapp. At the time they could not be sure how many West Downs parents would be prepared to send their sons to school in Scotland. In addition there were all the problems of running a school in war time, notably that of finding suitable staff when all able-bodied young men were away in the armed forces. The Tindalls themselves were not young at that time and, according to Ann Bass, were feeling the strain:

> My parents must have been under great strain, working in improvised and cramped conditions, not knowing if the School would be financially viable, and how many of the staff would be called up. John Stanton had gone in the first month of the war. Luckily David Howell Griffith was just over the call-up age. Mike Simson left for the navy before Christmas, and Robert Schuster for the army before the move from Glenapp – but not before he and Harry Ricardo had aroused considerable suspicion in the local Home Guard with their foreign names. Harry, of course, being a diabetic, remained as a mainstay throughout the war. The replacements to the staff were of uncertain quality. There was one major who was said to spend much time scanning the shipping lanes into the Firth of Clyde and was suspected by all of being a spy, especially as he collected all his mail from Stranraer Post Office.

In spite of all difficulties the move from Winchester to Glenapp was achieved with complete success. The Autumn Term of 1940 started only two weeks late and by then everything was, as one boy put it, in apple pie order. The 'mush' train had been laid on as usual, this time from London via Rugby to Stranraer, and until the last moment some boys had little idea where they were going to – one, indeed, not until he had joined the train at Rugby. On arrival at Stranraer there was a drive of a few miles through the lovely Ayrshire countryside past a somewhat macabre memorial to a postman who had died in a snowdrift on that road only the year before; then through the rhododendrons of Glenapp, and finally there was the Castle itself. Once inside the boys could not believe their eyes at the luxury and splendour – finely carved mantelpieces, moulded ceilings, panelled rooms and chandeliers in the dormitories[4] – a far fling from Top and St Cross. Altogether Glenapp could hardly have been more different from the outskirts of Winchester and the Romsey Road – open country with woods, lochs, panoramic views and hardly another house in sight. The excitement of this contrast is recalled by Robin Bendall (1936–41):

> After the rather institutional feel of the Romsey Road building and its restrictive boundaries, Glenapp imparted a sense of romance and freedom. The wonderful grounds with their woods and ponds and a waterfall – complete with suspension

bridge – gave us in liberal doses the feeling of adventure that we had only glimpsed at Melbury. Furthermore, bicycles were encouraged, and with several long drives leading to the Castle there was plenty of scope for their use. Unfortunately, the drive leading to Ballantrae[5] was rather steep, and after one boy had fractured his skull racing down it, I think that it was put out of bounds. This was an incident of considerable drama with the patient's mother summoned to his bedside. When he was declared out of danger a few of the more honoured friends were permitted a brief visit to the sick-room.

Certainly Glenapp had much to offer a school taking refuge from the war zone, but there were certain things which it lacked. Of these much the most important was a playing field, but the surrounding countryside was ideally suitable for scouting. And so, as at the beginning of the First World War, although for different reasons, scouting games and other activities replaced football and cricket. In this the School was fortunate in having on the staff at the time a scoutmaster of great enthusiasm and expertise. Harry Ricardo came to West Downs at the end of 1938 where he was at once found to be a skilled artist and an excellent teacher of English; and he also took over as scoutmaster from David Howell Griffith. Prep School masters are not normally notable for sartorial elegance, but Harry Ricardo was an exception, always a dapper figure in well cut suits, carefully tied ties and what used to be known at that time as 'co-respondent' shoes.[6] His scouting uniform was no less impressive. It is remembered that the brim of his scout hat (long before the days of berets) was always in place, unlike others which tended to sag, and that his toggle was always skilfully made up. Certainly he made excellent use of the opportunities for scouting in the Scottish countryside, inventing new games (notably 'Smugglers and Warehousemen') and reintroduced Scout camps which had not taken place since the First World War. At Glenapp one of his main projects was the construction of a log cabin thatched with heather. Michael Priestley (1940–44) recalls:

> After a violent storm once, the Scoutmaster decided to build a log cabin with fallen young pine trees which we were told to collect while he did the building. After a while fallen trees ran out, so we began cutting down live ones with the result that when the hut was finished the Scoutmaster saw that the surrounding woods were filled with stumps of trees cut off three foot from the ground – it was something like a Bateman cartoon! We were set to sawing off the stumps at ground level and covering them with pine needles.

West Downs was to spend a quiet and happy year at Glenapp. There were some misfortunes, as when the temporary huts blew down, and in the Summer Term a projected production of *Twelfth Night* had to be cancelled at the last moment because of an outbreak of mumps which laid low most of the cast. This was a particularly virulent epidemic and several sickrooms were needed to cope with it. Sister Herbert, one of the matrons at that time, had not had the disease and to protect herself used to put on her gas mask while tending her patients – apparently an effective precaution. There was also an unfortunate incident inside the Castle when a boy of a curious disposition decided to investigate the plumbing arrangements. Robin Bendall recalls:

> K.T.'s study was in the rather gloomy basement, and it was here, late one winter's night, that he saw a trickle of water approaching his desk. On opening the door to investigate, he discovered the whole Castle basement awash with hot water. Staff was called out and issued with buckets, the boilers were damped down, and many hours were spent baling out. It later transpired that a boy in the School, renowned for his interest in experimentation, had dislodged a pipe in one of the turret-rooms. K.T. was, understandably, not amused and the usual punishment was meted out – enabling, I believe, the very delightful perpetrator of this incident to claim a new record for strokes received!

On a happier note the year at Glenapp also saw the wedding of Ann Tindall to Richard Bass. The School was given a whole holiday for the occasion and attended both the wedding service and the reception. Ann recalled later that this made up for the paucity of the congregation which otherwise consisted of only a few close relatives and local residents.

After West Downs had settled into Glenapp so well the hope was that it would remain there in relative peace for the rest of the War. But this was not to be. In a West Downs News Bulletin of January 1944 Kenneth Tindall described what happened next:

> Early in September, 1941, we had a visit from officials of the Scottish Health Department who informed us that they were instructed to find a house suitable for a hospital. On hearing that the Castle was occupied by a school, they told us that we should not be disturbed. But the relief was short-lived. On the following day they reappeared, saying that they had orders from the Department to inspect the place and make a report.
>
> On September 8th, just a fortnight before our Autumn Term was due to begin, Glenapp Castle was requisitioned and we had no idea where we were going to move to.
>
> It is not an exaggeration to say that during the next three weeks we made enquiries about more than sixty large houses in Scotland and North England. In almost every case these were either being used or were already earmarked for war purposes; the others were quite unsuitable for school premises.[7] It was during these weeks that we first heard that Blair Castle might possibly be available. We came up to Blair Atholl to see it. From the outset it seemed clear that the Castle would answer our purpose well, though the basement of one wing was occupied by forty children evacuated from Glasgow.
>
> Blair Castle was formerly the property of the Dukes of Atholl, but it is now owned by a Company. As soon as we had seen the place, I entered into negotiations with the Chairman of Atholl Properties Ltd. and arranged the terms of a lease.[8]
>
> It was at this point that the Glasgow Corporation stepped in and said that they proposed to press for the whole Castle to be requisitioned for the accommodation of more evacuees, although it had been empty since the beginning of the War. After some weeks of uncertainty it was decided by the Perthshire County Council that it would be unsuitable for this purpose, a fact which was self-evident from the start.

---

[1] An extension to the main building of West Downs used for carpentry, bookbinding, basket making and other miscellaneous activities.

[2] A tentative approach was made by certain Albanian interests with an offer and beseeching Lord

Inchcape not to regard it as something out of musical comedy. Lord Inchcape's reply was terse: 'Not my line.'

[3] In which one boy discovered a cannon ball which has been used as a door prop ever since.

[4] Inevitably, perhaps, boys were not able to keep their hands off these. For a bet, it is remembered, one was dismantled and put together again – without detection.

[5] The nearest town, remembered with affection by some boys especially for the potato scones on sale there.

[6] Shoes of more than one colour, usually brown and white.

[7] Including, according to Ann Bass, a very dilapidated castle in Northumberland with many legends of ghosts, but nothing else to recommend it.

[8] The rent agreed was £500 per annum, the equivalent of the rates in Winchester in 1939.

Chapter 18

Fourteen pantechnicons were needed to transfer West Downs from Glenapp to Blair Atholl. Moves are always traumatic, but this went more easily than the one from Winchester. Everything had to go, so no decisions were needed as to what should be taken and what left behind. Also much had been learned from previous mistakes; this time each bed was tied together separately, not put into a common pool. Six weeks after Glenapp had been requisitioned, West Downs was installed in Blair Castle and ready for the Autumn Term.

In retrospect it is surely the case that the expropriation of West Downs from Glenapp was a blessing in disguise. Blair was in every way more suitable. There was much more space, so that the whole school could be accommodated under one roof; outside there was flat ground which could be used for playing fields, and the surrounding country was even more beautiful and dramatic. It was, moreover, further removed from the war zone.[1] Also Blair, unlike Glenapp, was a genuine castle, dating back to the thirteenth century and rich in history.

The Castle had its origins in 1269 when an intruder into the Atholl domains, one John Comyn (grandfather of Bruce's antagonist) built a tower there when the Earl of Atholl of that time was away in England. Later it was appropriated by the Atholl family and expanded into a full-scale castle. During its history Blair Castle has been besieged on many occasions and partially destroyed, and on four occasions occupied by enemy forces, including Cromwell during the Civil War. It has had associations too with most of the great figures of Scottish history. Mary Queen of Scots was entertained there to a massive hunt, involving the killing of 350 red deer and five wolves; the Earl of Montrose was based there for a time during his rising; Bonnie Dundee slept there before riding to victory and death at Killiecrankie; and Bonnie Prince Charlie stayed there soon after landing in Scotland in 1745. The Castle has the distinction of being the last castle in the British Isles to be put under siege – in 1745 when it had been occupied by the forces of George II and Lord George Murray attempted to recapture it. Soon after the Forty Five rebellion the Castle was 'de-fortified' and converted into a manor house. However, in Victorian times, to suit the baronial tastes of the Duke of Atholl of the time, turrets and castellations were added on.

It was here that West Downs arrived in October of 1941. It cannot have been often that a Prep School has been accommodated in such state. Many of the

Blair Castle. Home to West Downs 1941–45.

Front Hall. Weapons and banners were left in situ *during West Downs occupation.*

splendid rooms had been emptied of furniture to create the necessary space. The Dining Room, once a sixteenth century banqueting hall, was turned into a dormitory as also was the splendid Drawing Room with its finely moulded ceiling[2] and the Blue Bedroom Suite and the Red Bedroom where not long before the Crown Prince of Japan, now the Emperor and about to order the attack on Pearl Harbour, had slept. Nearly all the rooms occupied had historical associations. The Tindalls' sitting-room (The Tea Room) was where Queen Victoria had once written her Highland Journal. The Stewart Room, a vaulted chamber under the Great Hall, built by the third earl, became K.T.'s study. And Mr Ledgard found himself in Earl John's Room, devoted to the memory of Lord George Murray, one of the Jacobite leaders at the time of the Forty-Five Rebellion. And a bedroom cut into the ancient eleven foot thick wall of the Old Keep, where Bonnie Prince Charlie is said to have slept, was occupied by Harry Ricardo. It would be fascinating to know what connections there were with other rooms. Perhaps Madame de Coutouly taught French in a room where Bonnie Dundee had once caroused with his men? Or Miss Playsted was giving her piano lessons where once the Earl of Montrose had taken refuge? And in a chamber which centuries ago had been ringing to the 'lascivious playing of the lute', West Downs boys were now bawling out 'The Rio Grande' and 'The British Grenadiers'. The possibilities are endless.

Before the arrival of West Downs all the furniture and pictures of the Castle had been stored away in locked rooms, but there was still abundant evidence of the Castle's history: the walls of the Entrance Hall and the passages were lined with armour and every kind of weapon of war – crossbows, pikes, halberds, claymores, arquebuses, muskets among others. It was, of course, expecting too much that these would be left entirely untouched by boys of Prep School age. Nor were they. One OWD remembers discovering a pistol in the handle of a claymore, presumably for use when confronted with a mightier wielder of the claymore. Another remembers finding a walking stick with a cavity for a dram or two of whisky, unfortunately empty. There are also stories of boys getting into suits of armour and causing terror by uttering ghostly noises when anyone passed. Something else which provided not altogether innocent amusement to the boys was a large circular staircase, as John Pratt (1942–47) recalls:

> Blair Castle was a paradise for small boys; it was a real life adventure playground in today's idiom. There are dozens of memories and among them the best marble helter-skelter I have ever seen. This consisted of a large circular staircase starting on the second floor and terminating outside the headmaster's study. A marble placed in a groove inside the banister rail would whizz down two flights of stairs and exit on the ground floor – the hazard being K.T.'s eagle eye and hearing.

A particularly magnificent room was the Ballroom, added in the nineteenth century for the twenty-first celebrations of one of the Dukes of Atholl. This was lined not only with weaponry and battle trophies from distant lands but also with numerous prizes from the hunting field, mainly stags' heads.[3] These could present

Red Room. For 4½ years a West Downs dormitory.

Ball Room. Used as a chapel, dining room, lecture hall, recreation room and for general purposes.

hazards which were nearly lethal to Sam Cameron (1943–47):

> There were high windows and these had to be opened and closed with cords. There was a piano at one side of the Hall near a radiator. At the end of one term, while we were waiting to be taken to the station, I was sitting on the radiator swinging one of the window cords while the piano was being played. Quite unknown to me, the cord hooked over one of the antlers, and as I swung the cord, down came the whole trophy. One horn went through my ear and into my shoulder. By the start of the next term all the stags' heads had been removed!

The Ballroom, which West Downs called Shakespeare, was of enormous size, large enough to act as dining hall, chapel, reading room and occasional gym and badminton court. Along the top ran a minstrel's gallery where musicians had once performed, but this was now given over to Scouting with displays of knots, lashings, splices and triangular bandage.

If there was scope for adventure inside the Castle there was, of course, much more outside. OWDs of this period regard themselves as having been marvellously fortunate in living amidst country of such unique beauty. There was so much to attract and absorb a young boy: woods to explore, large expanses of unspoiled country with Highland cattle and ponies and abundant wild life, a river and a loch on which to fish, a salmonleap, as well as a splendid formal garden with well kept flower beds and rhododendrons, peacocks, statues, follies and a tomb from which a ghost was said to emerge at midnight.[4] There must be few boys on whom such surroundings did not make a deep impression. Caird Biggar (1941–46) remembers them vividly:

> The most memorable thing about Blair was the 'ducal estate' and the wonderful grounds around the Castle. Near the Castle these were laid out according to the Victorian concept of the 'romantic Highlands'. There was the 'Hercules Walk', a formal grass-covered ride, leading between banks of rhododendrons up to a great statue of Hercules. There was a garden with mock battlements and cannon, around which peacocks and squawking peahens paraded. There was the statue of the goddess Diana[5] in the woods and the Marble Grotto overlooking the river Tilt. There was the back drive, the grand front drive, the West drive, and the Nine Mile Drive. Looking down from a hill above the West drive there seemed to be another castle until one realised that they were mock towers – a 'whim'. I thought it was all splendid.

Jonathan Pinhey (1945–48) remembers with great intensity the long lime avenue leading up to the Castle and his terror at walking along this alone at night after being taken out to dinner at the Atholl Arms. Nick Hodson remembers the woods fragrant with garlic in spring also his mystification (still unresolved) at discovering an old, overgrown railway track in the Castle gardens. Michael Cripps (1939–43) remembers the Banvie burn which flowed through the garden and which was supposed to have been out of bounds. In practice, however, this appears not always to have been the case, and a number of explorations were made upstream. Many OWDs remember the large variety of wildlife to be seen, and sometimes stumbled across, in the surrounding country – pine marten, grouse, snipe, woodcock, wild cat and capercaillies ('as large as turkeys'). Sam Cameron remembers disturbing one of these and thinking the end of the world had come. There were also, of course, herds of red deer. In wartime, when there was no stalking, ghillies carried out occasional culls, and a carcass would be seen across the back of a pony on its way to the Castle – a sure sign of what was coming up for lunch for the next few days.

---

[1] The only outward and visible signs of a country at war at Blair were units of the Canadian Army at work as lumberjacks in the neighbouring forests and an outpost of the Royal Observer Corps manned by a band of particularly dour and uncommunicative local inhabitants.

[2] It has been told that the heavenly bodies on the ceiling were sometimes used by West Downs boys as targets with flannel and sponge – highest points being scored for a direct hit on the naked backside of a cherub.

[3] It fell to the lot of Mr St Germier, the very deaf handyman from Winchester, to keep the Ballroom clean. His only comment on surveying it was: 'Cor! All them 'orns.'

[4] As a result of a 'dare' a number of boys broke out of bounds to put this theory to the test, but with negative results.

[5] This caused some confusion to one new boy who knew of only one Diana – Diana Bass, the Tindall's newly born granddaughter, and he could not equate the two.

Chapter 19

One of the many advantages of Blair over Glenapp was that, although it was further from London, the railway journey was easier. There were special reasons for this, as Ann Bass found out:

> The station was at the end of the main drive and all trains stopped there on the way from Perth to Inverness. When the railway was built the Duke had said: 'Yes, it may go through my land provided that all trains stop at Blair Atholl Station and I can stop any train on my land if I wave a red flag at it.' So the railway company installed special equipment for filling up with fuel and water and sheds to house extra engines to pull the trains up the pass of Drumochter and over to Kingussie and Inverness. And so all the trains still stopped to hitch on the extra engines. You could leave Euston at 7.00 in the evening and arrive at Blair at 6.50 next morning, having only stopped at Crewe and Perth. Or there was a day train each way. Early on third class sleepers were still bookable for the 'mush' train, but in later years some pretty uncomfortable journeys were suffered by David Howell Griffith who always went down to accompany the boys back. Sleepers were generally reserved for government officials, but sometimes there were vacancies.

For an eight-year-old, leaving home for the first time, the journey from London to Blair in wartime Britain with an interruption, maybe, for an air raid could be daunting – not least at the end when he woke up and found himself in the middle of the Highlands. Tony Mullens (1945–49)[1] remembers this clearly:

> Blair Castle and Scotland were to a small boy of eight and a half a different planet. Mountains were a new phenomenon, and that first morning, having travelled overnight from Euston, seeing them for the first time was a traumatic event. Those train journeys became, of course, routine after a while, and one feature I well remember was the rug. The rug was needed, I recall, to keep warm during the night, but it had to be carried in a special way. It was rolled into a sausage and secured with a rug strap – in fact two straps with a handle. A new one was an early present, as I remember.

Nicholas Hodson has a vivid and detailed memory of his first journey to Blair:

> The train chugged slowly through England. We all learned the Litany: Leamington Spa, Rugby, Crewe, Lancaster, Carlisle, Coatbridge, Airdrie, Lanark, Stirling, Perth. At Lancaster there was a great deal of hissing and bumping as a second locomotive was attached for the steep climb to Shap Summit.
> On this first time up Sister Guy came into our carriage, selected a boy, and then to

111

my amazement down came his trousers and a big needle was firmly stuck into his buttocks. I had been prepared for a new way of life at West Downs, but this was not the sort of thing I had expected. However, I was soon reassured that he alone had to have this treatment as he was a diabetic. One of a pair of twins, his name was Fuller, and his father had been the School doctor when West Downs was at Winchester. Sadly his diabetes later took a turn for the worse and he was taken away from the School, dying soon after.

Rugby was rather a surprise because, in contrast to the total black-out of London, we always stopped for a while in a brightly lit marshalling yard. Scrutiny revealed that each of the overhead lights had a large cone-shaped cover which would have screened any direct glare from enemy bombers. In actual fact there once was a raid while we were waiting there and all the lights went out until the all-clear was sounded. So our fears were unfounded.

There was always the same guard on the train. We used to look out for him as he had a fabulous party trick which always kept us amused. If you listen to a train passing through the scenery the various diddy-bumps, sushes, whooshes and other sounds are characteristic of the viaducts, bridges, level-crossings and so forth which the train passes. Points, of course, made a different sound to ordinary track. The number of diddy bumps in 41 seconds gave you a speed of the train in m.p.h. What that guard could do was to predict from inside the carriage, with all the curtains drawn tight because of the black-out, with complete confidence and accuracy exactly when each change of rhythm for bridges in particular would be heard. He would say: 'Bridge number 241 coming now, 5 – 4 – 3 – 2 – 1. There she goes.' Eventually Sister would come and shoo him away, but we loved this trick.

When the train arrived at Perth we would all emerge on to the platform and be conducted into an otherwise empty upstairs restaurant. An ancient waitress creaked around slopping out porridge for each boy. This porridge was quite unlike the delicious variety we had at home, as it was highly watered down and had a gritty texture. We then got into a different train which grated its way up the Tay valley as far as Ballinluig where it followed the River Tummel. Then came in quick succession Pitlochry, Killiecrankie and finally Blair Atholl.

We all got out and our luggage, which consisted of a playbox and a handcase each, was piled up onto a farm cart. This was drawn slowly through the village and across the main road, then through large wrought iron gates and up the long drive to Blair Castle itself, all the boys of the London 'Mush' following in a long crocodile. At this point we met the Tindalls for the first time. T.M.T. had driven K.T. down to the station. He walked back with the boys while she put in her car those of the new boys whom she judged to be most overcome by the moment. The roof-rack and opened boot were piled high with hand cases. Inadequately roped, invariably some of the cases fell off and were picked up by hastily volunteered members of the crocodile.

On arrival at the Castle the new boys were taken at once to Mrs Tindall's sitting-room on the first floor. Here, usually with a pair of binoculars round her neck, as she was a keen bird watcher, she broke us into the disciplines of Castle life.

Soon afterwards the new boy would be handed over to his 'pater' who would keep a watchful eye on him and see that he did not get lost. The relationship between a 'pater' and his protégé was usually a warm one, but sometimes it was put under strain as when a nervous new boy, unaccustomed to strange objects under his bed, mistook his 'pater's slipper for his chamber-pot with disastrous results. Fortunately the 'pater' (a future lieutenant-general) was forgiving about it. Sometimes a 'pater' might require services in return for help given, as when a new boy, H.D.Y. Faulkner (1942–44) found himself reading aloud from Southey's *Life of Nelson* while his 'pater' practised knots and splices – William Staveley on his way to becoming Admiral of the Fleet Sir William Staveley, G.C.B. and First Sea Lord.

After reassembling at Blair in November of 1941 it was not long before West Downs settled down to its time-honoured routine. Breakfast was followed by Sanitary Prep, but this had now a touch of class about it – the luxury WCs of the Castle being rather different from the severely functional 'numbers' at Winchester.[2] At the same time Sister Guy, who had established her surgery in an old kitchen, dispensed Virol and Radio Malt to boys considered to be in need of 'building up'. Sanitary Prep over, the school returned to the Ballroom where breakfast had been cleared away and morning chapel was held. Then to morning classes.

In the afternoon came games, and at Blair there was much more scope for these than at Glenapp. There was quite a large area of short grass by the Banvie burn, into which many a cricket ball was to disappear, and there were other more or less flat bits of land on which makeshift football and cricket pitches could be improvised. Something that was difficult to arrange owing to petrol rationing and the distance involved was matches with other schools, although an occasional fixture was possible with the junior department of Leys School which had been evacuated from Cambridge to the Atholl Palace Hotel at Pitlochry. Henry Beresford–Peirse (1943–46)[3] remembers some of the efforts that were made to keep games going at that time:

> As regards games we were at a disadvantage at Blair because of the weather and the lack of matches. Nevertheless, we were taught well and there were nets on the lawn on the far side of the burn from the Castle. A rather eccentric master, Captain House, taught me the off-drive by spending long summer evenings in the nets pitching the balls on precisely the same spot until I had perfected the stroke; I never learnt any other stroke so well.
>
> We did better at football and never tired of watching Mr Howell Griffith in plus-fours and stout shoes demonstrating deadly accurate place kicks from somewhere near the half-way line and always putting them right over the bar. Some of the football pitches were distinctly uneven, and as for the cricket pitches, I remember one where the wicket was in a small valley and the fielders stood on the slopes of the surrounding hills.

There was less difficulty about organising athletics, and finals day was, as always, a notable event. Caird Biggar recalls having some success here but with modest rewards:

> I can remember Sports Day on the lawn by Banvie and my winning the 100 yards, hurdles and long jump on the same day. I was very proud of my prizes which added up, I think, to four shillings and sixpence (22½p) in National Savings stamps!

If conditions for regular games at Blair were limited, conditions for Scouting were perfect, and West Downs with its long tradition of Scouting and two excellent scoutmasters in David Howell-Griffith and Harry Ricardo was well-placed to take full advantage of them. Michael Cripps (1939–43) remembers how skilfully and imaginatively this was done:

> Scouting became a very important feature of school life. A Scout circle was built, a mile or so from the Castle, with a flag mast. However, the halyards were invariably pinched during the holidays, so the mast had to be stepped between two railway sleepers so that it could be lowered and the halyards removed at the end of the term. Weekend camps were held on a site near the circle in the summer, two patrols at a time and one for the 'Pioneers'. I managed to get into this select band and we considered ourselves great experts with such things as felling axes, and we were in charge of splitting and carting logs to K.T.'s study and the masters' common room. The Duke's factor generously gave us a free run of the Atholl estates.

Harry Ricardo had a great talent for making up scouting games or 'wide games', as they were known. Nicholas Hodson remembers these with great pleasure:

> On two days a week we played wide games in which every aspect of the forests and moors were utilised. The most usual game was 'Smugglers and Excisemen' in which the goods being smuggled were a couple of playboxes. We learnt to use all sorts of ruses, such as decoys, to get the goods through. Lives were represented by a piece of wool tied round the arm. We all became experts at semaphore and could get messages across large tracts of country while the enemy's attention was distracted or when natural features could be used to ensure that they could not see the signaller.

In the depths of winter Blair Atholl is liable to be under several feet of snow. During one winter, while West Downs was there, Sister Guy remembers taking a walk and finding herself on a level with the tops of the adjacent hedges. When this happened and normal games were impossible, there were other exciting attractions, as Henry Beresford-Peirse recalls:

> I remember one fantastic winter at Blair when we were in the grip of ice and snow for the whole Easter term. Being wartime there was no skiing equipment and we had very few sledges. Everyone wrote home immediately, pleading for anything on which to slide down the slope. Meanwhile we prepared a long toboggan run with banked turns and as icy as we could make it. Finally my father, home on leave, managed to knock together a sledge, and the excitement of going down to pick it up from the station at Blair Atholl I can well remember.

And Nicholas Hodson remembers the considerable preparatory work that was needed in order to establish a 'Cresta Run' at Blair:

> The field had a good slope on it. In winter, particularly Common Time, we used to make a fabulous toboggan run on it, and boys who had toboggans were assiduously courted by those who did not. In order to build the track as much snow as possible was brought to it, usually by rolling up snowballs until they became boy-sized. On arrival at the track these would be cut into bricks with a spade. The whole school would then shuffle down the track and tread it into a shape as near resembling the

Cresta Run as we dared make it. Last thing at night containers of water were brought to the track and poured on to where they would instantly freeze.

One West Downs tradition, which seems somehow out of place in the Highlands but was nevertheless carried on, was the burberry walk. To some like Caird Biggar these were interesting and enjoyable:

> Even when Sister Guy put us off-games because of a cold or something, we had fun on the walks we had to go on. There were always things to see – plenty of ornamental lakes to fling stones into, or better still to whizz things across if they were frozen over in winter. Sometimes the attractive gym mistress, Miss Coombs, would be in charge of such walks and then we were apt to visit a wartime sawmill near the Castle which was operated by a band of real live Canadian lumberjacks from the Canadian army. We were fascinated to see how the huge tree trunks were handled and sawn up. Miss Coombs, we thought, was more fascinated by the Canadians and vice-versa. A few miles from Blair Atholl up the river Garry there was a wonderful salmon leap where one could watch salmon all the time trying to get up a tremendous waterfall. Very few ever seemed to manage it. The Canadians from the sawmill were also aware of them and thought they would do a little experimental fishing – with hand-grenades. The water bailiffs were not amused!

Nicholas Hodson too has idyllic memories of these walks:

> Off-games walks were hikes in the nearer lanes, while bad weather walks were through the forests and even on to the moors beyond. We soon learned to recognise and to eat herbs like sorrel, to look for the droppings of the capercaillie, and to appreciate the secret inner life of the ponds and lochans.

But to some like A.J. Wodehouse (1945–48) burberry walks in the Highlands were less pleasurable:

> I recall those long walks in the heather when the whole school, or so it seemed to a shy and somewhat disorientated nine-year-old boy, took off into the hills two-by-two like animals entering Noah's Ark. These walks were pleasant and joyful expeditions when the summer sun shone, the sky was blue and the going dry and springy; but they were tedious and miserable in the winter when the cold wind blew, dark rain clouds scudded overhead, and conditions underfoot were wet and squelchy. It is of my deliverance from one of these latter that I would like to tell.
>
> It is unlikely that it was actually raining when we set off, otherwise we would not have gone, but everything else was just as I have described it, and the rain itself duly arrived when we had gone too far to turn back. So there I was, a picture of misery, plodding along in my burberry and gumboots through the wet boggy heather, the rain running down my neck, my hands cold and blue, tears not far from my eyes. On and on we marched, I had no desire for conversation and there was nothing in my mind except a faint hope that sometime in the distant future I would be warm again.
>
> We had reached the mid-point of this hellish journey when a car drew up alongside the master in charge (David Howell Griffith as I recall). This in itself was a rare occurrence in that part of the world in those early months after the war, so we all stopped and stared. A man got out, immaculately dressed in a dark green uniform, and approached D.H.G. in a smart and confident manner. I was standing close enough to hear the conversation. He said, and from that day to this the various

accents of America have been music in my ears, 'I am a friend of Brigadier Wodehouse.' (My father was then Military Attaché in Dublin where this officer also worked.) D.H.G. turned to me and said: 'This is Wodehouse', or similar words. I shook hands with my saviour, whose name, sadly, I cannot remember, got into the car and we drove away. I will never forget the expressions of envy on the faces of my fellow pedestrians.

The rest of the story will not take long: I was whisked away into Blair Atholl, filled up to the brim with delicious cakes and buns and subsequently taken back to the Castle armed with sweets and, most forbidden fruit of all, chewing gum. These were immediately confiscated by Sister, though how she discovered that I had them I will never know, for I am convinced that I did not declare them, but it was a small price to pay for my rescue from durance vile.

As I have said, it is my great regret that I have forgotten the officer's name, but if this tale is deemed worthy of inclusion in the annals, and if by chance it reaches the ears of my Deliverer as he enjoys the evening of his life in the United States, he can be sure of the best dinner money can buy if he should get in touch with me.

Once the school was established at Blair, it was not long before the main West Downs institutions were revived. Patrol plays started again in the first term, and in the following summer a particularly successful performance of *The Tempest* was given by the school. The grounds of the Castle abounded in natural theatres and an ideal setting was found – a bare stony hillock on which grew two lonely fir trees. As usual K.T. took the part of Caliban, on this occasion eating, or seeming to eat, raw fish he had caught in the loch a short time before. The following year *A Midsummer Night's Dream* was given for which a different setting was found – a tree-covered knoll. This too went well but with snags typical of such occasions – one performer catching his foot in a tree root and falling flat on his face, and one of the fairies feeling exceedingly self-conscious because he had lost his gym shoes and it was necessary for him to appear in fairy costume and a stout pair of walking shoes.

Outside lectures and other entertainments were also arranged. Many OWDs remember recitals given by Megan Foster (Lady Spooner), the mother of a boy in the school and a professional singer. There was also a Chinese conjurer, remembered by Michael Cripps:

> . . . a Chinese conjurer called Col Ling Soo (actually an Englishman called Collings) who ended his act by spinning plates and saucers on the tips of bamboo canes. Boys tried to copy this, and much china was broken resulting in threats from K.T. of putting canes to other purposes if the practice did not cease.

Vividly remembered is a Captain Knight who arrived on foot in a kilt and soaked to the skin. He was accompanied by a golden eagle which he used to give a lecture on that species. At one stage this was let loose and allowed to fly around and caused considerable alarm among the audience, particularly to red-headed boys for whom it was said to have a fancy.

A regular visitor to the Castle at that time was the Bishop of St Andrews, Dunkeld and Dunblane, a kindly and jovial figure who, with a long grey beard and a fund of salty stories, fully lived up to his splendid title.[5] As well as keeping the company entertained, he also prepared boys for Confirmation and took Communion in the multi-purpose Ballroom. At Blair, as at Winchester, religion was the bedrock of West Downs life. It was at this time that Kenneth Tindall completed a remarkable work, his own version of the life of Christ (or 'The Unholy Gospel' as dubbed by his family). This made a deep impression on many boys including Wilfred Grenville-Grey (1939–43):

> Mr Tindall's felicitous rendering of the New Testament in Chapel created a 'fascination with Jesus'. Through all the vicissitudes of reading Theology at Oxford, deciding *not* to be ordained, working seventeen years in Africa, lobbying for Human Rights at the United Nations in New York, I find that those readings by K.B.T. left a deposit of commitment which remains with me to this day.

[1] Lieutenant-General Sir Anthony Mullens, K.C.B., O.B.E.

[2] Some of the baths too were super de luxe, notably the Duke's which required steps to get into it – this was always much sought after.

[3] Sir Henry Beresford-Peirse, Bt.

[4] These were square wooden boxes and part of boys' luggage – used mainly for footwear.

[5] Remembered by Sir James Spooner is his definition of the principal races of the British Isles. A Scotsman: keeps the Sabbath and anything else he can lay his hands on. A Welshman: prays on his knees on Sundays and on everyone else during the rest of the week. An Irishman: has no principles but is prepared to die for them. An Englishman: a self-made man who worships his maker.

Chapter 20

West Downs had settled quickly and smoothly into its new home in the Highlands, but there were some adjustments which had to be made notably, as Caird Biggar recalls, to the hours of darkness:

> The first thing I recall about Blair Atholl was the very strong contrast between the seasons. How dark it was in the winter evenings and how spooky it was scurrying in pyjamas and dressing-gown from the dormitories in the main part of the Castle down to remote bathrooms in the South Wing, miles away down long corridors hung with innumerable antlers, each pair sticking out of a ghostly white skull! Also in winter I remember how the lights used to go dim when frost affected the stream of water which was channelled down from the hills to work the Castle's own hydro-electric power station.
>
> By contrast in summer I remember how impossible it was to go to sleep at 'lights out', when *double* British summertime combined with the northerliness of Perthshire meant that it was broad daylight until nearly midnight. We surreptitiously read our books, hoping the patrol leader was asleep or, more likely, reading his own book.

The Castle's hydro-electric system did, indeed, have its idiosyncrasies, as Anne Bass remembers:

> All the electricity was generated from the stream, the Banvie, which ran past the Castle. It was 100v. D.C. which made it useless for most of the electrical equipment we had, but some replacements were available. The only thing that worried Mr Boland, the estate engineer, was that not too many lights should be turned off at once; it was much better for the system if lights, once they had been switched on for the evening, should be left on. Thus when the rest of the country was being urged to save electricity, we were being urged to squander it. It cost nothing at the time, but it was very bad training for future electricity bills.

Something else to which acclimatisation was necessary was the extreme cold of the Castle in winter. There was no central heating and classrooms and sometimes dormitories had to be heated by stoves which required a lot of attention and fuel which had to be carried long distances. The hot water system of the Castle depended on four or five separate boilers tended, not always reliably, by a musty old Highlander called Mungo. There would be little hot water available on days when Mungo had had a dram or two the night before! Of unkempt appearance and none too clean in his habits, Mungo came in for certain amount of ribaldry from the boys which usually he took in good part. But one thing shocked him profoundly as Nicholas Hodson recalls:

He firmly disapproved of our Sunday activities and used to line up all the other old retainers outside the changing rooms as we made our way back from our Sunday afternoon wide game or other sport. 'Ye should na day-secrate the Sabbath,' they would mutter to each boy as he wended his way in.

As well as stoking the boilers Mungo also undertook other odd jobs such as shoe cleaning and carrying coals. On occasions he also gave boys lessons in salmon poaching – with the help of a sledge hammer!

Apart from Mungo and a few estate workers it appears that West Downs had little contact with its neighbours at Blair. It seemed to some as if they were disapproving of the occupation of the Castle by a school, and were courteous but remote. It was said that the Duke of Atholl at that time, who was an invalid, had been strongly opposed to the letting of the Castle, but his wife, the so-called 'Red Duchess'[1] had insisted. This may have fuelled the resentment of some of the locals for when, a year or so later, the Duke died, the head gardener, who had always been particularly stand-offish, was heard to murmur: 'They killed our Duke.' The funeral of the Duke, which took place at Blair, was a splendid and moving occasion. The coffin was carried to the family burial ground on a farm cart suitably decorated and accompanied by a contingent of the Atholl Highlanders in full dress – the last remaining private army in Britain.[2] Norman Arthur (1940–44)[3] remembers being surprised at seeing these elderly men, kilted and grizzled, with tears in their eyes.

That was all West Downs ever saw of the Duke, but it did have occasional visits from the Duchess. She took boys on tours of the Castle and took a kindly interest in the welfare of the School. She also took a calm and reasonable view when there was an 'incident'. This occurred when curiosity overcame a group of boys and they decided to break into one of the locked rooms in the Castle where the Atholl treasures were stored. It proved all too easy – a screwdriver to unscrew the lock was all that was needed – and once inside, a veritable Aladdin's Cave confronted them. Inevitably they could not keep silent about their escapade and word of it finally came to K.T. who felt obliged to report the matter to the Duchess. He did, of course, take other steps as well.

Neighbours of whom the School saw virtually nothing were the Glasgow evacuees in the South Wing of the Castle. On one of her visits the 'Red Duchess' had remarked how nice it was for West Downs to have the evacuees so close at hand and, no doubt, there was frequent contact between them. But in fact there was none; it was strictly prohibited. It seems that there was no open warfare, but an Iron Curtain there certainly was. Forty years later some OWDs could not even remember that the evacuees had been there.

Contact with some local inhabitants was, of course, essential – with tradesmen, hoteliers and the local doctor. With the latter, contact was not easy as he lived fifteen miles away and only came over in emergencies – very different from Winchester where a red flag in the window brought Doctor Fuller in promptly from his rounds.

Another matter in which local assistance would have been welcome was that of haircutting but, as Nicholas Hodson recalls, this could be erratic:

> In order to get boys' hair cut K.T. invited over a couple of men from a Canadian lumberjack camp up the road towards Rannoch Moor. They took one and a half minutes to process each boy, providing him with a crisp crew cut. At first no one could recognise anyone, but we learned quickly enough and rather enjoyed the temporary anonymity. The shearing had been in honour of the approaching parents' weekend at the end of June, so there were a few complaints from parents. One of them, Mrs Savege, volunteered to come up and cut our hair professionally. She would stay a week and tidy each of us up, as though we had been done at Trumper's. The parents might have been less pleased if they had known that boys lost about half a period in order to get their hair cut.

[1] The Duchess had been a member of the House of Commons and one of the first women junior ministers, but had always been to the left of contemporary Conservative thinking. At the time of Munich she resigned from the party and from her seat in Parliament, and stood as an Independent in the ensuing by-election. This was fought very hard and with some bitterness by the Tories who were determined to hold the seat at all costs; they succeeded but with only a narrow majority.
[2] It included Mungo who had cleaned up considerably for the occasion.
[3] Lieutenant-General Sir Norman Arthur, K.C.B.

Chapter 21

Perhaps the greatest problem confronting schools in wartime is that of staff. The young and the fit go off to the war and can only be replaced by the elderly, the unfit or the unsuitable. West Downs was to have its share of all of these – inexperienced idealists full of impractical notions, ex-army officers who, despite a certain ferocity of appearance, cannot keep a class in order, and various others who for one reason or another had to leave hurriedly. But on the whole West Downs was fortunate. It continued to be served by three older teachers of exceptional ability. D.L. Rose, now nearer eighty than seventy and racked with rheumatism, went on gallantly until the end of the war. W.H. Ledgard, a somewhat incongruous figure in the Highlands, impeccably dressed in neat sub-fusc suits, stiff collars and well polished shoes; he too was in his seventies[1], but as mentally alert as ever and still capable of a good turn of speed, as when he gave chase to a boy who was trying to escape from the school train in Buchanan Street Station in Glasgow. Apparently ageless, he was to be at West Downs for another ten years yet. Miss Squilley came up to Glenapp and on to Blair, but soon afterwards, owing to increasing deafness, had to call it a day. She had taught at West Downs for forty-two years. Kenneth Tindall wrote of her at the time: 'She is one of those rare people who radiate peace and good will. I have heard her described as a powerhouse for good; and this description could not be bettered.'

It was surely West Downs' greatest good fortune during these difficult years that it retained the services of David Howell Griffith who was too old for the armed services but still in full possession of his formidable powers. Now officially designated second master, he bore the brunt of keeping the daily routine of the School running smoothly – organising, improvising, ironing out difficulties and soothing ruffled feelings. There was no task he himself was not prepared to undertake when no one else could be found to do it, even the most menial as Anne Bass recalls:

> Each classroom had a Coustier stove for which fuel had to be carried. D.H.G. made this one of his tasks, often involving relighting several stoves before breakfast. He was a tower of strength, and so many of the jobs he took on were quite unknown to others. In the latter years when fewer of the staff were experienced, he was around almost all the time, unofficially 'on duty'. When one remembers that he was also in the Home Guard – out for one or two nights a week – it is amazing how he kept going.

Temporary staff were, predictably, rather a mixed bag. OWDs remember with affection Arthur Pyper who was at Blair for a year before going on to Merchiston College in Edinburgh.[2] But others were less successful. One ex-military gentleman laid it down that he would undertake no duties other than classroom teaching; and it was found that even here he was not particularly adept. He did, however, have some aptitude with a scythe, and he was kept contentedly and more or less profitably occupied for some hours cutting nettles. Another ex-army man also failed to find his niche in schoolmastering. Nicholas Hodson writes of him:

> He usually wore an ugly scowl. He was a keen fisherman and helped the anglers among the boys with their fly-tying. If he had any other talents he kept them well hidden. K.T. tried to use him to teach various subjects that he claimed he knew, but with each he was a more dismal failure than the last. Finally he came to French where his ignorance was so amazing that even the most junior classes would laugh at him. Prone to violent rages he ended his career at West Downs by hurling himself in one of his tantrums against the safety guard surrounding the stove in the changing rooms. The structure broke and his trajectory brought him into contact with the stove which broke his back. I was present at the time. I had had a part to play in this because earlier in the day I had constructed a wax image, tied a label round its neck proclaiming the name of the master and stuck pins in it. Overcome with amazement at how rapidly this spell had taken effect, I went and confessed all to K.T. I was caned for indulging in witchcraft, and the school library book about witchcraft was summarily removed from the shelves.

A man of a very different ilk was Arthur Turner who arrived in the last year of the War. Tall, gangling and known from the size of his feet as 'Turntoes', he was of a gently, amiable disposition and, perhaps fortunately for him, secure in Nicholas Hodson's affection:

> He was a brilliant teacher and gave me a great deal of enthusiastic help with my Maths which was for me much the most interesting subject. He had a fund of stories invented on the spur of the moment about his pal George Not. Washington. On burberry walks he would flap along in an immense green cloak [3] with an old trilby he called his wholly, holy, holey hat with a crowd of youngsters round him hanging on his every word.

Although Maths was his main subject Arthur Turner was reputed also to have a gift for writing poetry and had even published a slim volume. Certainly he had considerable musical talent and this was welcome at this time. Since the arrival in Scotland School music had been kept going by Miss Lunn and Miss Playsted (now reduced by arthritis to a wheelchair) with their usual skill and devotion. But, no doubt, they were glad of reinforcements, and both at Blair and later at Winchester Turner took over as principal organist during chapel services.

As is usually the case in wartime there was an increased number of women on the teaching staff. On the whole West Downs was well served by these, not least by Marjorie Coombs, a ski instructor from Switzerland, who took over the department of P.T. (as it was then called). A lively, rather bouncy figure in gym tunic and plimsolls, she made a great impression on some boys. Life for her in a remote Scottish castle must have seemed rather sombre after the ski slopes of Switzerland and she made efforts to liven it up, introducing Scottish country dancing sessions not only for the boys but also for the staff (a little difficult to imagine some of these letting themselves go in an Eightsome). She even persuaded Mungo to accompany them on the bagpipes. She also found social life, so it is said, outside the Castle among the Canadian army which meant returning late after lock-up. This would not have pleased the Tindalls, but it seems she squared a member of the staff to let her in.[4]

After the retirement of Miss Squilley there came first a Miss Flint who is said to have had a difference of opinion with K.T. as to whether boys in the lowest forms should go on a run before breakfast. She was followed by Maisie Richardson who had had previous experience as a governess but not in a school. However, she proved a great success and was to remain at West Downs for almost as long as Miss Squilley. Another lady who made her mark was Miss Campbell[5] who was an ardent naturalist and enlivened many a burberry walk by turning it into an enthralling 'nature ramble'.

Domestic staff in wartime was, of course, as great a problem as teaching staff. It seems that here not much help was available locally. Cooking and catering at Blair was largely in the hands of two Jewish refugees from Germany called Lotti and Gerda. Broad of beam and with only limited guttural English, they are remembered by some boys of that time as being inseparable – one seemed incomplete without the other (rather like Gert and Daisy in a different context). An OWD remembers feeling mystified when one of them asked him to do something for her. 'Why not *us*?' he thought, expecting to see the other half of the combination lying dead nearby.

West Downs was very fortunate to retain the services of Sister Guy in Scotland – she was to be at West Downs for another twenty-five years. School nurses are sometimes envisaged as hoary old battleaxes, but this was not at all Sister Guy. With light blue eyes and golden hair she reminded one OWD at least of a ministering angel. In all matters of health she was entirely reliable. Mrs Tindall had complete confidence in her and allowed herself to be deflected by her from some of her more unorthodox ideas. Sister Guy had various assistants at this time including one lady known as 'Sourface Tiptoes' from the way she prowled through the dormitories at night looking for any kind of trouble. Occasionally she came across a cat making itself comfortable on somebody's bed, and this she would summarily dispatch through a window. But, despite a drop of 18 feet or more, the animal never failed to reappear.

One West Downs 'old timer' who for family reasons was only to come up to Scotland for a short time was May or Matron, as she was called – inappropriately one might think as she had nothing to do with health. Her job was to look after linen and laundry and everything to do with boys' clothes. In her room at Winchester, and no doubt for a time in Scotland too, she mended, darned and cleaned in a room suffused with fumes of ammonia which she used to remove ink stains from clothes. She also dispensed tie pins, clips and studs when, as very often happened, these were lost. At Blair her place was taken by Mrs Ward who had the reputation for being the life and soul of the ladies' sitting-room.

In many ways life for West Downs at Blair was idyllic. It was housed in an historic and spacious castle, surrounded with magnificent country, and as remote from the War as it was possible to be in the British Isles. There was the black-out which had to be observed and food rationing, but this did not, perhaps, impinge as severely in the Highlands as in the southern part of the country. For example the meat ration was regularly reinforced by haunches of venison, and although, after the ministrations of Lotti and Gerda, these were not universally popular, they were surely preferable to such things as whale and snoek with which some schools had to content themselves. Some boys at Blair, who remembered pre-war food at Winchester thought there was little difference. In one not unimportant way there was an improvement. It was not until sweets and chocolate were rationed that they were allowed at West Downs.

Of the trappings of war all too familiar in the South – barrage balloons, anti-aircraft guns, air raid shelters and enemy bombs – there were no signs at Blair. For some parents living in the midst of these things and seeking a respite from them, it was a welcome break to have a few days at Blair Atholl. Some parents too, whose home life had been disrupted by the War, were glad to avail themselves of the opportunity offered by the Tindalls of leaving their sons at Blair during the holidays.[6] To some schoolboys it might seem a fate worse than death to stay on at school at the end of term, but this was not the case at Blair. Boys to whom it happened remember the occasions with pleasure and, in particular, the kindness shown towards them by Mr and Mrs Tindall.

But, of course, if at Blair there were few outward and visible signs of the War, below the surface there was tension, anxiety and, sometimes, agony. Fathers and brothers might be in the firing line and mothers and other members of the family in danger from air raids. And sometimes near relations were killed. No one suffered more cruelly than the Tindalls. Early in 1943 their eldest son, Richard, a schoolmaster of outstanding promise, was killed in North Africa, and a few months later their younger son, Mark, was killed in a tragic accident in barracks at York while using a defective electric iron. Their stoicism in face of these tragedies was truly marvellous. It is reported than when news of Richard's death came through Mrs Tindall was helping with the washing up; she was called away but was back soon afterwards. For Kenneth Tindall the blow hit very hard, and for a brief time even his great strength faltered; at evening chapel that day he was unable to continue and had to withdraw. But then his strength returned and he found comfort in his religion. Soon afterwards in a letter to the present author when his brother had been killed he wrote: 'I can never bring myself to think of death as a great tragedy; certainly for those who join the great company on the other side it must be a joyous and thrilling experience. It is for us who are left behind that things seem hard; but we can rejoice in their happiness.'

Soon after the Normandy landings the Winchester building was vacated by the military who had taken it over and, with the threat of invasion of the British Isles removed, it was open to the Tindalls to go back home; but they decided to stay at Blair until the end of the War. With the coming of VE Day West Downs celebrated in traditional fashion. Nicholas Hodson was there:

> At the end of the War we had a tremendous bonfire to celebrate V-E Day. We had the day off and spent the morning and afternoon building this great pyre and anxiously watching the dark clouds scudding by. The rain held off and we shouted and cheered and sang and danced our way round and round the bonfire. There was at the time a temporary master who was thought to be a German spy, though no one could think what a German spy would be doing in the Grampian Highlands. He gave fuel to this theory by standing nearby and glowering at the scene with arms folded and speaking to no one. He departed within a day or so, so perhaps a more logical explanation would be that K.T. had given him notice and he was somewhat cheesed off about it.

West Downs was at Blair for four and a half years. During that time the School can surely be said to have flourished. Nearly all boys look back on their time there with great enthusiasm.

For a time in 1942 there had been a falling off in school numbers – down to sixty-three – but this was soon made good by an influx of Scottish boys (for the first time kilts were to be seen at West Downs)[7] and in the last years of the War the School was taking as many as it could accommodate. Nor was there any question of academic standards declining; on the contrary the number of scholarships gained increased – eight during the war years including three to Winchester. By no means all Prep Schools in the same plight as West Downs – obliged to evacuate to a new and unfamiliar location – were able to survive. That West Downs did so with its full share of setbacks and at a time when the headmaster and his wife were approaching retirement age, was a feat that should not be underestimated.

---

[1] He had been born on 29th February in a Leap Year and, like Frederick in *The Pirates of Penzance*, claimed that he was really only a teenager.

[2] He subsequently became headmaster of a Prep School in Seaford from which he had to retire when diabetes rendered him blind. He wrote later that he owed more to West Downs and the Tindalls than to any other school where he had taught.

[3] Maisie Richardson (see over p. 123) recalls that once on Edinburgh platform he asked her to hold this for him for a moment and she nearly sank beneath the weight of it.

[4] Reportedly the oldest member of staff but clearly young at heart – D. L. Rose.

[5] An unfortunate name in that part of Scotland where memories of the Massacre of Glencoe still lingered. Once, when calling at a farm to buy eggs, she revealed it and the door was slammed in her face. Also a boy in the School named MacDonald would have nothing to do with her until he was told that she was of Irish rather than Scottish ancestry.

[6] After the first term, the start of which had had to be delayed until October, some twelve boys remained behind for a twenty week term.

[7] One Scottish boy was once found in tears in the sickroom because sugar had been put on his porridge and his father had told him he would never have a kilt if he ever ate porridge with sugar on it.

Chapter 22

When the War ended in August 1945 the West Downs building in Winchester had already been derequisitioned by the Army, but any thoughts of returning for the Autumn Term were at once dispelled when Mr and Mrs Tindall paid a visit there in the summer. The condition in which the Army had left it was daunting. In the early part of the War it had been used as a divisional headquarters and had been reasonably well looked after. During this time Paul Morgan (1930–35), who was in the Rifle Brigade, remembers being sent from the Rifle Depot to mount guard on his old school:

> A guard which was more formal than real had to be produced for the front of West Downs consisting of two sentries, one at each entrance. The guard room where one rested when not on sentry duty was the senior pavilion. Some previous guard had lit a fire in the middle of the wooden floor of the pavilion – very typical of the damage soldiers did to requisitioned buildings! I rather enjoyed standing in front of West Downs as a sentry, saluting officers going in and out. It was some ten years since I had been at the School. I could not go into the building but could look around outside. The grounds were still well maintained but all moveable equipment had been removed. It was a little strange, almost ghostlike.

Later, after the Divisional Headquarters had left, the building had been used for two years as a transit camp for British and American units, and each had come and gone, leaving the place in an ever worsening condition. It was not just that everywhere was very dirty, but considerable damage had been done. Shakespeare had been used at times as an officers' mess and at times as a storage depot; and the floor had been badly damaged. The Dining Room just before D-Day had been used as a top secret room with sand tables showing the plans for the invasion of Normandy. The gym had served as a records office and N-Room as a kitchen; and at one time the changing rooms had housed horses and there were still traces of them. David Howell Griffith, a Hercules if ever there was one, undertook to organise the cleansing of this Augean Stable. All that was needed, he said, was for everyone to take a bucket and scrubbing brush and get to work. But the Tindalls saw that professional help was needed and invoked the aid of Messrs Trollope and Colls.

The Christmas holidays of 1945–46 must have been the most frenetic the Tindalls ever spent. In the first place Blair Castle had to be thoroughly cleansed and all traces of schoolboy occupation removed. Ann Bass remembers her parents spending Christmas Day washing some of the marks off the paintwork in the South Wing after all the furniture had gone in the removal vans. All hands were put to the task and, of course, David Howell Griffith was in the thick of it, heaving furniture and giving encouragement to all and sundry. But sometimes there was a slight twist to this, as Maisie Richardson recalls:

> At the end of Short Half 1945 members of staff remained behind to help with the packing and cleaning. Miss Campbell and I were asked to wash the white painted walls of the South Wing passage.
>
> Supplied with cloths, pails of water and tins of a cleansing agent called 'Gumption', we worked away and were proud of the before and after effects. D.H.G. passed us frequently, moving desks from the classrooms, and would remark each time: 'Good stuff, that Gumption!' which annoyed us as we thought it was us rather than the Gumption which had achieved such results.

Although it was hard work putting Blair Castle into a fit state to be returned to the Duke, it was not an overwhelming task – nothing like the one which awaited the Tindalls in Winchester. Later K.T. took pride in the way the boys had treated both Glenapp and Blair:

> It would be easy for a school to reduce a luxurious or historic mansion in one year to a mere shambles. But the boys showed just that consideration which was needed for other people's property and took a real pride in seeing that no harm came to it; and at the end of a year at Glenapp and over four at Blair no material damage had been done to the structure or interior decoration of either castle.

When the Tindalls went down to Winchester after clearing up at Blair they found the place still uninhabitable, and it was necessary for them to stay for the time being at the Southgate Hotel. Trollope and Colls had done their best but progress had been slower than expected mainly owing to restrictions at that time on all building works. Owing to shortages of building materials all works costing more than a certain amount required a special license and, as is often the case with government departments, this involved long delays.

Another frustration was that the electricity company refused to switch on the electricity until just before the boys came back which meant that work was only possible in hours of daylight and no electrical appliances could be used. The boys were due back at the beginning of February (about two weeks later than usual) and when Maisie Richardson arrived a few days before there was still a great deal to be done. Once again the teaching staff was called in to give a hand, but it seems that some of the jobs required a degree of cooperation to which Mr Ledgard could not always aspire. Maisie Richardson recalls:

> The pressure was on as the London 'Mush' was due to arrive at tea-time. Mrs Tindall asked Mr Ledgard and me to help sweep the floor of Shakespeare. We were equipped with large brooms, and the plan was for us to begin at the balcony end, the three of us sweeping in line down to the chapel door end. We started well, Mrs Tindall on the left, myself in the middle and Mr Ledgard on the right, but he soon

got bored and either swept ahead or, when remonstrated with, lagged behind. However, all ended well and Mr Cannings arrived just in time to remove the sweepings as we heard the boys' chatter coming from outside.

Before the beginning of term the Tindalls had had to endure yet another trauma recalled by Ann Bass in masterly understatement:

One minor disaster for them was that N-room had been broken into and much of our drawing-room furniture had been taken by the Americans to a house in Chilbolton Avenue where some great man was staying – Churchill it was rumoured. That would not necessarily have mattered, but on V-J night the Americans decided to have a bonfire, and all our sofas and chairs went up in smoke.

Despite the damage and dirt left by the military West Downs' return to the old building went reasonably smoothly. Problems were overcome and those parts of the school which had been put to unwonted use during military occupation were brought back to their former functions. The cricket pavilion, said to have been used as a butcher's shop by the army, was once again full of ancient pads and bats and permeated with the smell of linseed oil. The swimming bath, used for storage, was back in action the following summer and having to cater for a large number of non-swimmers, as no swimming had been available at Blair. The changing rooms, now rid of all traces of the equine, were once again lined with clothes pegs and shoe lockers. Shakespeare with its floor repaired and its familiar objects restored[1] was once again the scene of plays, lectures, concerts and quiet reading, as well at other times as a testing ground for mini racing cars and aeroplanes propelled by elastic bands. Restored too, exactly as it had been, was K.T.'s study: the inscribed oar above the door, the ivory chess set under a glass dome on the side table, the pipe rack on the mantlepiece, the black ebony ruler on his desk, the cane on the bookcase, and the round-backed chair with diamond shaped seat over which boys were sometimes required to bend. It did not take long to restore the dormitories; furniture there had always been simple; the iron bedsteads were once again reassembled (by now rather expertly), chamber-pots placed underneath them, and chests of drawers and stools placed beside them; wash-stands with long-serving china basins and mugs were all that were then needed to complete the picture. David Howard (1948–52) remembers the scene well:

What bleak places those dormitories were just after the War! The cream and pale green walls seemed to sweat with condensation whatever the season. No carpets or curtains to remind one of the comforts at home. The windows with their great sash cords, open to the stars and the still of the evening, sometimes broken by the chinking of mugs from our neighbours in H.M. Prison; a noise that continued far into the night prior to a hanging. We learned at an early age what that was all about. Our little washstands stood in military rows, filled in the morning with tepid water. New boys leaving the top half of their pyjamas off soon learned the error of their ways when a 'trade mark' was planted on their bare backs. If you had any sense birthdays were kept a secret until K.T. gave them away after lunch, since the ritual birthday bumps in the dormitory were designed more to let out the dealers' natural aggression than to dissolve into any good wishes for the unfortunate birthday boy.

Down at Melbury there was a lot of work to be done and not all of it could be done at once. The Lodge, never robust, had fallen further into decay, and because of the building regulations in force at that time only limited repairs could be done to it. The grounds there had become very overgrown and this presented a challenge to an élite corps of the Scouts known as the Pioneers who undertook clearance work so that the Shakespeare play was once again performed there in the summer and Scouts could foregather there on Sunday afternoons to pass tests in fire and cooking.[2]

Perhaps the greatest problem to be faced was that of the playing fields. The Army had let these go and they were now a mass of long, tufted, coarse grass and deep ruts from heavy vehicles. However, the new groundsman, Tubbs, got to work with a will and by the summer all the cricket grounds had been restored except one. The second game ground had been used as a parking place for lorries and had been covered with gravel; much of this had been removed by machinery, but the job had to be finished off by hand, and for a year or two after the return of the School boys would be dispatched to pick up stones, putting them into a 'kind of kangaroo pouch' formed by turning up the fronts of their jerseys.

It is likely that most boys found the return to Winchester welcome. School life was less cramped and more convenient, and there were proper playing fields and the opportunity once again of playing matches against other schools. Also most of them were nearer home with more frequent parental visits, although these were made difficult by petrol rationing.[3] There were, however, some boys, particularly those from the north, who found the outskirts of Winchester a poor substitute for the Highlands of Scotland. This was felt strongly in Scouting; at Blair conditions for this had been ideal, and Melbury, although not to be despised, could not be compared. Henry Beresford-Peirse felt this strongly:

> I cannot speak for my contemporaries, but for me the return to Winchester was one terrible anti-climax. It was as though one had asked the Duke of Atholl to leave Blair Castle and his vast estate in the Highlands and take up residence in a small suburban house on the outskirts of Winchester. Melbury was simply a bad joke. Many of us agreed that Scouting at Blair under Harry Ricardo was something quite special and could never be as good anywhere else and, I think, most of us decided to give up Scouting thereafter.

Soon after its return the School had a reminder of Scotland in the winter of 1946–47, one of the coldest in living memory and made worse by a breakdown in the nation's fuel supplies, resulting in frequent power cuts. During that time the School was colder than it had been ever been at Blair. Paraffin stoves were put in dormitories, but this did not prevent water freezing in the basins. Ordinary games were impossible during the Lent Term, and toboggans, last used at Blair Atholl, were brought out and put to use on the golf course on the Old Sarum Road.

The Second World War brought with it many changes in social attitudes and values. For many of these it could not be expected that the Tindalls, both Victorians at heart, would feel much sympathy. But they were no bastions of reaction, impervious to all winds of change. Their rigours in Scotland and tragic family losses had had their effect; it was a mellower and more open-minded K.T. and T.M.T. who came back to Winchester. It was not, however, to be expected of them that in their last years they would introduce fundamental changes to the character and life of the School. All the time honoured institutions, then, remained intact. Chapel, respected by the military and untarnished, was exactly as it had been left five years earlier and exactly the same services were resumed there – preceded by the ringing of a bell with exactly nine seconds between each toll;[4] an organ accompaniment sometimes by a boy, sometimes by a master; readings by K.T. from the 'Unholy Gospel';[5] on Monday mornings recitals by heart of the Scripture Verses learned on Sunday; and at the end of each morning service, after a moment of silence, the prayer for energy and purpose.[6] The special services of the school year also remained unchanged – the Carol Service, the lantern slide services in Lent, the Remembrance Day Service, and the Advent Sunday Service with the Advent Talk (or pie-jaw) which still lasted over an hour and was still concerned with the School motto – Honest, Brave, Pure, but with particular emphasis on the last of these three. The leaving talks too followed the same pattern – first the swearing to secrecy, then none too detailed explanations and warnings which in those days of innocence often caused as much bewilderment as enlightenment.[7]

Of course Scouting continued to play a central role in the life of the School. The weekend camps held at Blair were continued for a time down at Melbury, but then for one reason or another (including the prevalence of swarms of midges) had to be abandoned. But camps were held during the first week of each summer holiday on a suitable and most attractive site at Little Somborne. These were thoroughly enjoyed by the boys as Nicholas Hodson recalls:

> Here we had wide games nearly every day, cooked for ourselves and learned how to camp in the way laid down at Gilwell (the Scout training base). We would spend much of our mornings collecting firewood in the neighbouring coverts; we quickly learned how to distinguish quick burning woods from slow burners and then made fires on the tunnel pattern. In the evening we had a washing session in which everyone had to soap himself all over after which there was a colossal water fight in which everyone chucked water over anyone who still had some soap on him. After that we would have a camp fire round which we would sing songs, the last of which was always 'Goodnight Ladies'. In the dark on the way back to our bell tents we could see glow-worms, and perhaps for many of us that was the last glow-worm we ever saw as it became the fragile victim of modern farming methods.

With recent advances in medical science, so that epidemics and killer diseases were no longer the menace to boarding schools they had once been, it might have been expected that after the War there would have been some let-up in health precautions, but most of these were to remain in force. Temperatures were still taken twice a day, the rigours of Sanitary Prep were unabated, and there were still regular inspections for nits, rashes and other afflictions. But at least there were no more onion bags and the Ice Age had receded into the distant past.

At this time the anti-corporal punishment clamour was beginning to be heard more loudly and clearly. The brutal flagellations of the early Prep School days had by then all but disappeared, but corporal punishment was to remain in most Prep Schools for some time yet. In phasing this out it cannot perhaps be said that West Downs took a lead. Canings and slipperings were still not infrequent. David Howard (1948–52) remembers the anguish felt at the end of a day when trouble was brewing:

> I remember so well lying in bed up in St Cross or West dormitories and dreading the heavy measured tread as K.T. mounted the concrete steps in the evening, knowing full well that without the help of a Q.C. my inadequate excuses for a nuisance point or, worse still, an all-rounder could mean instant hell in the adjacent bathroom. You learned at an early age to guess the mood of 'Guzzer'.[8] A hymn being gently hummed as he progressed towards the dormitory meant a 2–1 chance of survival. Silence or black thundrous looks usually ensured the approaching doom of a 'smacking' as he called it with a size 13 slipper over the end of a bath. The chipped enamel of the baths bears witness over forty years of where his enthusiasm had overstretched his aim.

It would seem that most OWDs, although not all, looking back at the corporal punishment they experienced at West Downs, do so without emotion or bitterness, and it is likely they had a similar attitude when they were at the School. One boy, asked by a matron how many times he had been caned, replied tersely: 'Three. Twice deserved. Once not.'

Censorship of books brought into the School was still maintained which ensured that reading matter remained conservative; but one concession was the admission of *Eagle*, a new style weekly magazine with moral undertones and containing a character called Harris Tweed of whom David Howell Griffith was reported to have been a great fan. Otherwise comics remained banned. Illicit copies of *Beano* and *Dandy* were sometimes smuggled in, but they had to be kept well concealed.

It seems that toys at this time remained old-fashioned and simple. The days of high-tech toys – computerised, transistorised, radio-controlled – had not yet arrived. One innovation recorded was of a clockwork car with remote control steering which was achieved, crudely by modern standards, by means of a rubber bulb connected through the 'exhaust pipe' to the steering by a thin rubber pipe so that a squeeze on the bulb turned the wheels. But possibly the most popular toys were the very simple ones – the 'whizzer' made out of a button and a piece of cotton and the homemade 'tank' which required a cotton reel, elastic bands, a drawing pin or two, candle-wax and an old pencil. As always crazes came and went; one rather unsavoury one at that time was the making of a sort of butter by shaking up stale milk (provided free by a caring government) in a Parker ink bottle. Butter was certainly very scarce at that time – a weekly ration of no more than two or three ounces – but even so it is difficult to imagine that there were many takers for this home-made variety.

In the following June after the return from Scotland Founder's Day was revived on the Saturday nearest to Lionel Helbert's birthday. This was always a convivial occasion. It was usually attended by thirty or forty OWDs and there would be cricket and shooting matches against the School. In the evenings Old Boys wandered round the school, searching for themselves in group photographs of bygone years and reviving happy memories in, perhaps, Shakespeare, the swimming bath or the gym and rather more painful ones, maybe, in the bathrooms or the study. The hospitality of the Tindalls on these occasions was always warm-hearted and lavish, and it was a wonder to many how in those days of stringent food rationing such a splendid spread was provided.

One of the subjects most frequently discussed at OWDs meetings was that of a memorial to commemorate the eighty-two OWDs who had been killed in the War.[9] A pressing need at that time was for a new cricket pavilion, the old one having suffered considerably during army occupation; but the sum raised (about £2000) was inadequate for this purpose. In the end it was decided that the First World War memorial[10] should be mounted on a new base so that the eighty-two names could be added. At the same time the Memorial Garden was enlarged and re-designed.

The new Memorial was re-dedicated on 12th June 1949. The ceremony was attended by many parents and OWDs. The act of rededication was performed by the Revd Arthur Ford in these words:

> In the faith of Jesus Christ we dedicate anew this Memorial to the honour and glory of Almighty God and in sacred and perpetual memory of our Brothers who in two world wars gave their lives in the same cause.

An address was then given by Lieutenant General Sir Frederick Browning (1905–09)[11]. This was in memorable words and made a deep impression on all who were there:

> In 1921 this Memorial was dedicated to thirty-six Old West Downs boys who were killed in the 1914–18 War.
>
> It is not a dead thing this Memorial, but has been a constant spur to those who survived to play their full part for their country and fellow beings, both in peace and war. Today we are gathered here for an act of rededication in honour of the eighty-two Old West Downs boys who gave their lives in the 1939–45 War. It is a day of loving memories, pride and gratitude – not of mourning.
>
> We of West Downs have, for our numbers, sustained heavy loss. We can all remember those many boys with whom we were brought up here, all of them with such promise in their lives, with whom we had never had the opportunity of fulfilling a lifetime's friendship, and who themselves were denied a full span of years.
>
> There are few of us who have not suffered irreplaceable loss during this period with its two World Wars. Those of us who have lived through these times passed though a phase, I believe, of feeling bitter sorrow and regret when our loved ones and friends were taken away. These, I think, used to be our predominant reactions. Now I know our feelings are different. We have come to realise the meaning of these things and if our Faith had been strong we should never have doubted. But it is in our nature that only through hard lessons and suffering do we come to realise the truth. This truth is plain – that those who died for us in the firm belief that they were

fighting for the preservation of decency, honesty and the hopeful future of the world are not to be mourned in sorrow and with regret. Their sacrifice should be remembered with pride, gratitude and courage. Courage to face their loss with the joy that we who remain should be privileged and bidden to go forward to make the future worthy of their sacrifice.

Nothing could be more seemly than that we should add the names of this second generation to those of the first generation who gave their lives. It doubles the challenge to you and me. We must realise that it is a challenge. We must accept it with our heads held high and say to those whose Memorial this is:

We will not forget you. We realise that you died that we might live. We can never repay you, but we will try by the way we live our lives. We promise you that we will do our best for England and for all mankind. We will not shirk our duties in time of peace, and if ever war comes upon us again, which we pray God will never happen, we ask to have the strength and courage to play our part as you did yours.

That is what we are saying at this ceremony. We are saying it to those of West Downs to whom we are making this dedication and from whom we are only temporarily parted. May God grant to each one of us that faith and courage to meet the challenge they have thrown down.

In 1947 West Downs celebrated its golden jubilee, but apart from a special OWD dinner in London, there were no special celebrations. In the West Downs magazine there was only brief reference to it by Kenneth Tindall:

Meanwhile for three years the School has once more worshipped and worked, played and swum as of old in its traditional quarters and following upon its Jubilee in 1947 is looking forward to another fifty years and more of useful service to the country.

A hope, sadly, not to be fulfilled.

---

[1]See page 55.

[2]Owing to food rationing meat and, for a time, potatoes were not freely available for this, and at times, so it is recorded, Scouts had to resort to stewed nettles and baking cakes of flour and water in old tobacco tins.

[3]Some parents found it necessary to come by train and then take a taxi up to the School. At that time these were often very ancient and dilapidated, and one boy felt such shame at his parents arriving in such a vehicle that on the return journey he asked to be dropped off a hundred yards short of the School.

[4]On one occasion a boy got carried away and started tolling too violently, bringing down slates off the roof.

[5]See page 117.

[6]Of which one OWD once remarked that it was not, he considered in his own case, a prime example of the efficacy of prayer.

[7]That the facts of life were still a mystery to many boys of Prep School age at that time is shown by a comment of a patrol leader to K.T. after he had announced to the school the birth of a grandchild whose mother had been staying at the School for the last weeks: 'Rather unexpected, sir, wasn't it?'

[8]A new nickname for K.T. Perhaps a development of 'The Geyser' which had been in fashion in the late thirties.

[9]Casualties had been particularly heavy among OWDs of the 1927–30 intake. One-third of these had been killed.

[10]The statue by Lady Kennet (see p. 85).

[11]See p. 182.

Chapter 23

Running a Prep School is not a light task at the best of times but in the post-war years there were new factors which made it even more arduous. In the first place there were shortages of nearly all consumer goods. During the War the British people had been warned that the coming of peace would not bring with it instant plenty. But perhaps few realised that the situation was going to get worse. Clothes, petrol and all the main foodstuffs, including sweets, remained on the ration, and in most cases a very small one. And there were two items, bread and potatoes, unrationed in the War which were added to the list. The task of dealing with coupons, 'points', emergency cards and all the other components of the rationing system must have taken up many hours, to say nothing of the time spent searching for non-rationed goods to fill up the gaps. Fuel for heating (at that time mainly coal and coke) was also in short supply, especially when it was most needed, and to get any at all required the filling in of forms and endless frustrating correspondence. Time consuming too was the coping with the vagaries of Bureaucracy. During the War Bureaucracy established a tight hold over the lives of ordinary people, and afterwards it was reluctant to let this go. Officials, anxious to justify their existence, disseminated forms in all directions requiring information of all sorts; and boarding schools had their full share of these. The headmaster of Temple Grove, Mr Meston Batchelor, has recorded that one question put to him was how many hot drinks had been served in his school in the course of a year. To which, taking heed of the Book of Proverbs which bids one answer a fool according to his folly, he first rang up the Department concerned and asked in all seriousness whether he should include cups of tea grown cold while answering the telephone, and then decided that the only possible thing to do was to take the school telephone number, multiply it by three and then add two noughts.[1] No doubt the Tindalls too had to answer a barrage of similar questions.

Another problem which became no easier with the coming of peace was the finding of suitable domestic staff. Before the War this had been readily available at a moment's notice and at minimal cost. But those days had gone for ever. From now on it was a question of taking what one could get – usually foreigners – and being glad of it.[2] Often there were glaring gaps when there was no one there for urgent tasks. Such a situation found Mrs Tindall at her best; she was always ready to step in and put her hand to anything, on occasions washing up, single handed, a whole school meal.

If the coming of peace did not mean the end of domestic problems, it did bring relief in the matter of teaching staff. Some pre-war masters returned to the fold. Robert Schuster, after an exciting escape from a prisoner of war camp, came back but only stayed a year or two before going off with Harry Ricardo to become partners in a Prep School in Devon. Tragically after only one term Harry died when his diabetes took a turn for the worse. Another to return was Freddy Baleine, still a formidable figure on the games field; he stayed longer than before but then decided that life for him lay not in teaching but in boats and fishing in the Channel Islands. For H.F. Rawson it was his third return to West Downs. He had been a boy in the School in the early years, and had had a brief spell of teaching before the First World War. After the War, during which he served in the Royal Navy, he returned to West Downs where he married Thelwyn Price, one of the junior school teachers. Soon after they left to found a Prep School of their own but returned to West Downs in 1950 where Thelwyn again taught a junior form and Hugh was head of Maths and took first eleven cricket; he also had the distinction of having the new cricket field (created out of the old kitchen garden) named after him. This time he stayed for sixteen years.

There were too some new arrivals. Of these the most colourful and eccentric and most vividly remembered by the boys of that time was W.J. Tremellen. Wooden leg, Breton beret, Celtic temperament and an ancient motor cycle ridden erratically, he was to become a legend in his own lifetime. In his younger days 'Melly' had been in the Royal Flying Corps (he only ever wore an R.F.C. tie) and had tried his hand at writing including a novel, said to have been partly autobiographical, about a pilot in the First World War who had developed an ingenious device called a 'Foozle-Board', a system of mirrors which enabled him to blind other pilots before shooting them down. His methods of teaching French were, to say the least, idiosyncratic. Modern practitioners would be horrified by them, concentrating as they did on a purely grammatical approach. But several OWDs have testified that he taught them the only French they ever learned; Daniel Hodson, an Eton scholar, writes that he was 'probably the most brilliant teacher I've ever been taught by.' In some ways with his multi-coloured charts and his encouragement of all forms of artistic effort, he was ahead of his times and a forerunner of the visual aids which were to become so fashionable later on. Less avant-garde was his insistence on learning by heart, although this was always assisted by some little rhyme, mnemonic or gripping story. Anthony Duckworth-Chad (1951–55) remembers a particularly chilling one of these:

> Melly's story was that a boy died young. However, as he was being buried and his coffin was being lowered into the ground the lid of the coffin was raised and a voice was heard to recite: 'ai, as, a, ions, iez, ont.'

And from that day the future endings of French verbs has been indelibly imprinted on his memory.

David Howard (1948–52) also has vivid memories of Melly's methods and their effectiveness:

> Perhaps after a gap of over forty years to look back upon the teaching of one man must be quite unusual, but such a man was W.J. Tremellen. He had such an influence in explaining the French language that I can never forget him or very much of what he so successfully put across. The brilliance of his football team to explain the firing order of adverbs: with 'y' the stitching on the football and *lui* and *leur* the two fat dative full backs; also his 'mastam' verbs that declined with *être* and his tunes that taught the spelling of *professeur* and *yeux* the plural of *oeil*.

Giles Warrack (1953–58) remembers that his French lessons were not only colourful but forceful:

> That the French for 'never' is 'jamais' is a fact indelibly imprinted on my mind by his habit of grabbing a boy round the neck and throttling him until the boy answered 'jamais' in answer to the question 'Do you surrender?'

Inevitably, perhaps, such way-out methods were accompanied by a formidable temper as Tom Brooke (1947–51) recalls:

> He had a ferocious temper, it seemed to us, if annoyed in class. As I recall, his pet phrases when angry were: 'If you want a spot of bother, laddie, I don't mind.' Or just simply: 'Get out of the door, laddie,' shouted with a hint of Germanic intonation. If the unfortunate culprit was slow in moving, Melly would pick him up by his first and second fingers inserted twixt neck and shirt collar, shake him violently, and eject him into the passage.[3]

It was improvident too to be too persistent with one's questions:

> A boy from Thailand, normally quiet and studious, was asking an unusual number of questions. These continued as Mr Tremellen became visibly more irritated. Finally in exasperation he burst out: 'For goodness sake, I didn't invent the ------- language!' (Giles Warrack)

Out of the classroom too Melly's behaviour tended to be unconventional:

> On his blue tanked Douglas motor cycle he insisted on giving lifts to unfortunate small boys as he charged the grass bank dividing the lower playing fields from the first XI pitch. Often he would come to grief: small boy, Douglas and 'Melly' tumbling in a heap to the bottom of the hill. 'Melly', marvellously athletic despite his wooden leg. (J.F. Cornes)

With 'Melly' the most humdrum and tedious of school affairs were lightened with a touch of unorthodoxy. A burberry walk under his supervision did not mean a long trudge up the Old Sarum Road but proceeding to the nearest railway bridge to watch the old steam trains thundering past. And in fourth game cricket he was always ready to interpolate rules of his own such as an extra run for 'stopping a fizzer' and honourable mentions for good scoring and umpiring. In other spheres too his restless and volatile imagination went to work:

He was ingenious and versatile in starting crazes for small boys, for yo-yos and pogo sticks, and he enjoyed demonstrating the power of pulleys and elastic bands, as shown by the Melly tanks which he invented. He was a Celt with the enthusiasms and quick emotions of his race, with a wonderful understanding of what he called the jungle of the small boy's world. (Giles Warrack)

Another teacher who made a great impression was the P.T. instructor, Harry Risbridger ('Harry Riz'). After the war Majorie Coombs had lost no time in returning to the ski slopes of Switzerland, and she had been succeeded by one or two none too satisfactory 'sergeants'. But then came Harry Riz who transformed the P.T. scene, reintroducing shooting and boxing (in time to be replaced by Judo) and reducing the large number of non-swimmers consequent upon there having been no swimming facilities in Scotland. Harry Riz had bluffed his way into the army at the age of fifteen during the First World War. He had subsequently risen to the rank of sergeant-major, and had later been in the Prison Service where it had sometimes been his lot to administer the birch to young offenders. With this background it might have been expected that Harry Riz would be a martinet and perhaps too a sadist; but he was neither of these things. A firm disciplinarian of the old school he certainly was, but he was also gentle and kindly and full of encouragement for the less physically gifted. Beneath a stern exterior he was, as one OWD put it, 'a terrible old softy.' Tony Mullens remembers him well:

> Mr Risbridger was very much a central figure at West Downs. Small in stature but always immaculate in white jersey and blue trousers, he excelled in getting the best out of small boys. He had iron grey curly hair cut short and a small, neat moustache. In essence he was the epitome of a sergeant-major.

For his previous occupation in H.M. Prisons he had no liking at all and often used to tell how after a birching his wife's best meals had to be turned away untasted. He also told how he would sometimes mitigate the sentences passed:

> He used to tell us that the victims were fastened to a board by their hands and legs and that a leather band was put across part of their backs to protect their kidneys, prior to his beating them. He told us that if they had been awarded ten strokes he only administered eight, and kept two up his sleeve which he would add on if they were ever sent back to him again. As can be imagined this had an electrifying effect on us nine-year-olds. (Anthony Duckworth-Chad)

Harry Riz was to stay at West Downs for thirty-seven years until he was eighty-three. During his latter years he had given up P.T., but was at the School part-time teaching carpentry, basket making, raffia work, marquetry and other handicrafts. At the end of each term he personally would finish off all uncompleted items so that they could be taken home. Houses all over the British Isles must contain examples of his handiwork.

These years too saw the retirement of some faithful and long standing servants of West Downs who had devoted their lives to the school and helped to make it

Harry Riz gives instructions in carpentry. Houses all over England contain bits of furniture initiated and finished off by him.

Arts and Crafts.

what it was. Soon after the return from Scotland D.L. Rose, by then seventy-six and afflicted with increasing deafness, had to call it a day; he had been at the school for forty-eight years. When he died a year later K.T. wrote of him:

> As a teacher he had a wonderful power of making things clear either to boys of quick intelligence or of slower mentality. Though Mathematics and French were his principal teaching subjects, he was capable of taking a form in any subject at all. He was a walking encyclopaedia of general knowledge to whom his colleagues as well as boys turned for information on any doubtful point – from politics to higher mathematics and from Greek mythology to practical agriculture.

At this time too Dorothy Lunn, for long the mainstay of the School's music, suddenly had a stroke and died soon afterwards at a comparatively early age. And another West Downs stalwart to take her leave was Madame de Coutouly whose teaching of French for twenty-four years had always been vivid and sometimes dramatic.

Overhanging all other problems facing Prep Schools in the post-war years was the fundamental one of their future. Were they going to be able to exist in the new order that was unfolding? Those were the days of socialist ascendancy in Britain, and independent schools were under attack. Left wing intellectuals denounced them as giving an unfair advantage to a narrow class of children (although this did not prevent many of them from sending their own children to them). Much was heard of equality; not so much of liberty. Perhaps because they were an easy target Prep Schools came under particularly heavy fire. Their weaknesses, foibles and occasional scandals were emphasised and exaggerated. As is often the case with intellectuals they were selective in the facts they put forward. Prep Schools were presented as narrow, over-privileged and a remnant of an out of date society. Defenders of Prep Schools, it seemed to some, were a little muted in their response. But although there was much talk of abolishing independent schools, Labour government shied away from this, thinking that if they made life difficult enough for them, they would die a natural death from economic reasons. Certainly the economic climate at the time was gloomy. During the War income tax had reached an all-time high and showed little sign of coming down afterwards as Britain lurched from one economic crisis to another. In order to pay school fees which had had to be raised to meet increased running costs many parents were being forced to dip into capital, and the general belief was that this was something future generations of parents would not be able to do, as, owing to the incidence of heavy death duties, they would not have any capital into which to dip. The outlook then was sombre, and pundits shook their heads solemnly and advised aspiring teachers to go into the state system as the private sector was doomed. In which, of course, they were to be proved entirely mistaken. Independent schools, including Prep Schools, were in fact on the brink of their greatest ever boom. The bulge in the birth rate helped, but the main reason was Britain's disenchantment with socialist rule with its rationing, restrictions and apparently everlasting austerity.

[1]*Cradle of Empire*, M. Batchelor, Phillimore Press.
[2]Difficult though the situation might have been, it did not prevent Mrs Tindall from warning two maids who had gone off for their half day in trousers that if such a thing happened again they would be instantly dismissed.
[3]Known by some as the 'Mellybird Treatment'.

Chapter 24

By 1950 Kenneth Tindall was sixty-six and had been at West Downs for thirty years. There was no obligation on him to retire, and there were many precedents of Prep School headmasters who had stayed on for much longer. But this was not what K.T. wanted to do. He felt the time had come for a younger man to shoulder the problems and responsibilities of West Downs. Perhaps he felt too that in the new post-War era fundamental changes were going to be necessary and he would rather that they were carried out by somebody else. It is certain that he was also feeling the call of a rose garden in the heart of the English countryside to which he could devote his remaining energies and not inconsiderable skills. Accordingly in the early 1950s he started to put it about that he was looking for a successor. He knew that this would not be easy to find; the number of suitable candidates who had sufficient capital to buy West Downs was at that time very limited. His first thought was to set up a Charitable Trust to take over the School and appoint a salaried headmaster; and with this in mind he invited a number of parents and OWDs to form an unofficial *ad hoc* committee. Today nearly all Prep Schools are Charitable Trusts, but at that time these were only just beginning and were strongly opposed by some headmasters on the grounds that they detracted from their authority. But this was not the reason why one was not set up at West Downs. Here, after serious consideration, K.T. came to the conclusion that a sum sufficient to provide himself with a pension, the new headmaster with a salary and working capital for the School could not be raised. Also at that time the future of Prep Schools was uncertain and finances very shaky as fees had been kept low for fear of being priced out of the market so that in the post-War years many Prep Schools, including West Downs, were barely profitable. And so, when there appeared on the scene a candidate with not only distinguished qualifications but also the necessary capital, it seemed the best solution to the problem.

Both literally and metaphorically J.F. Cornes had an impressive track record. A scholar of Clifton and Corpus Christi, Oxford, he had also been President of the Oxford University Athletics Club and an Olympic Silver Medallist. Like the founder of West Downs he had begun his career as a public servant and for more than twenty years had been in colonial administration with service in Nigeria and Palestine (as it then was), and latterly as a Grade 1 Administration Officer in charge of training courses for Colonial Service officers and cadets at Oxford

University. But, like Lionel Helbert, he had a latent ambition to run his own Prep School, and the prospect of acquiring a school of West Downs' standing was the realisation of a dream. Before coming to an agreement, however, Kenneth Tindall required Jerry Cornes to present himself to one or two members of the *ad hoc* committee in order to be vetted. This done and approval gained, Jerry Cornes resigned from the Colonial Service and, while negotiations about West Downs proceeded, gained some experience of Prep School teaching at the Dragon School in Oxford. In his last year at West Downs Kenneth Tindall had to suffer another hammer blow from Fate when a boy in the School died as a result of being hit on the head by a cricket ball – the first and only time such a tragedy has struck West Downs.

In the West Downs Magazine K.T. took a brief, heartfelt farewell:

> During our long time at West Downs we tried to instil into successive generations of boys a genuine belief in Christian faith and practice, a desire to be of service to the community, the joy of effort and achievement, whether in work or games, and the satisfaction of contributing their full share to the common good. And in spite of frequent anxieties and occasional disappointments, the friendships we have formed with parents and boys have been, and still are, a source of happiness and gratitude to us both.
>
> Our earnest hope is that our successors will be as happy in their work as we were.

Kenneth Tindall had been at West Downs for 100 terms. His reign had surely been a distinguished one. He took over at a time when the School had been going through a difficult period as a result of Lionel Helbert's long illness. In the inter-war years he saw the School through hard economic times and then survived magnificently the major crises of wartime. Finally he saw the School re-established at Winchester and flourishing; the numbers at 106 were higher than they had ever been and the books were full for years to come. And, as at all times during his headmastership, the reputation of the School stood very high. In the Prep School world he himself was held in great esteem and had held office for a year as Chairman of the Council of the I.A.P.S. Here he might have come across many headmasters who had once served under him at West Downs; during his time there were no less than eleven of these. One of them, G.M. Singleton, has recorded his respect and gratitude:

> I shall always feel grateful to Kenneth Tindall. He was thorough, down-to-earth, strict when necessary, but very kindly. I had not meant to be a schoolmaster, but he persuaded me to remain in the profession. At our I.A.P.S. Conference in 1961, when I was chairman, there was a number of members, including Tindall, taking coffee together, and I told them all that I would not have been there at all if it had not been for Kenneth Tindall. I think this really pleased him and gave back to him a little of all that he had given to me.

After his retirement Kenneth Tindall was to have twenty-two years of life in rural Dorset. During that time he kept in touch with West Downs, but in no way did he 'breathe down the neck' of his successor. On leaving he had given him only one injunction – to see that the roses were pruned; otherwise to do what he liked. In 1954 the OWDs gave the Tindalls a farewell dinner at the Criterion Restaurant in London. This was liable to be a sad occasion, and at first K.T. seemed a little subdued even maudlin. However, he was rescued from this mood when during his speech there was an interruption from the floor. This roused all his schoolmaster's instincts and acted on him as a trumpet to the warhorse. The interruption was dealt with forcefully and from that moment his spirits rose markedly.

At the time of their departure everyone with West Downs connections was heartfelt in wishing that the Tindalls should have a long and happy retirement, but this was not altogether to be. By the early sixties it became clear that Theodora's health was failing, and it became necessary for her to spend her last years in a nursing home. When she died in 1968 Kenneth wrote a moving tribute to her:

> I am only too conscious that such success as we had in the School was very largely due to her. Her sympathy and kindly advice to parents in many cases led to our close personal friendships with them; her ability to be kind, and at the same time firm, to one generation of new boys after another, helped them to settle down happily to the ordinary discipline of school life; her organising ability, whether in the everyday routine of school life or in the arrangements for a big occasion, inspired confidence in everyone who was working with her.

Kenneth Tindall lived on until 1976 by which time he was ninety-two. In the West Downs Magazine Jerry Cornes wrote of him:

> He was a large man, in body, mind and spirit, and he effortlessly earned the respect and admiration of his many friends and acquaintances as well as the boys who were his constant care. His influence extended far beyond the narrow bounds of his own school. He was a natural leader and a born teacher, with an almost palpable inner strength derived from his obedience to the will of his Lord and Master, Jesus Christ.

Chapter 25

When a new headmaster appears on the scene there is usually some apprehension, particularly among older members of the teaching staff, that a new broom will be wielded and that long established practices and time honoured traditions will be swept away. On his arrival at West Downs Jerry Cornes was advised by David Howell Griffith not to make any major changes for at least five years. But there was no need for this advice as it accorded with his own judgement. In his opening talk to the boys in chapel he said:

> In cricket it is a difficult thing for anyone to go in to bat after a man who had made a century. While he was in it all looked so easy, the ball was directed effortlessly to the boundary. The new man is bound to compare unfavourably with the centurion while he plays himself in and gets accustomed to the bowling. So it is with me, succeeding Mr Tindall who completed his 101st term before retiring a month ago.
> The first thing I want to say is that I intend that things should go on very much as before here. There should not be and will not be any drastic changes. The rules will remain as before just as the Staff is unchanged except for the Headmaster.

Time-honoured institutions, then, were to remain intact, and changes in organisation were to be minimal. But inevitably there was change in the atmosphere of the School. It has already been remarked that a Prep School to a great extent reflects the personality of its headmaster, and Jerry Cornes was not the same man as Kenneth Tindall. Certain things they did have in common: both were dedicated Christians, both cared deeply for the boys in their charge and spared themselves no pains on their behalf. But in personality and style they differed. Kenneth Tindall was orthodox in his methods, a firm even severe disciplinarian and inflexible in imposing his standards and beliefs on the School. Jerry Cornes was inclined to be more compromising; he believed in a certain measure of discipline, but was less authoritarian, more tolerant of nonconformity and ready to treat with boys on more equal terms. He brought with him to West Downs a lively mind, imagination, great enthusiasm, also an element of unorthodoxy amounting, some would say, to eccentricity.

Eccentricity has been the hallmark of many Prep School headmasters, including some of the most renowned. Sometimes these eccentricities have been of a none too amiable character, but this was not the case with Jerry Cornes; although sometimes disconcerting and irksome, Jerry's were mild and harmless and caused much amusement to both masters and boys. Boys recall how he was apparently indifferent as to what and how he ate; they remember in particular an incident when he covered a helping of ice cream with a brown liquid, thinking it was chocolate, and ate it with no dissatisfaction, totally unaware that it was in fact gravy. It is recalled too how he set off to take a wasps' nest encased in a fencing helmet which was to prove far from wasp-proof. Masters too have memories of the unconventional, as when one, coming to talk about a job at West Downs and rather on his best behaviour, was surprised to be interviewed by Jerry while lunching off a hunk of cheese. And another remembers being startled when, as master in charge of football, he was visited by Jerry after a successful match against Horris Hill (he was actually in the bath at the time) and given a £40 rise in salary. Such incidents greatly enlivened the West Downs scene and continue to cause hilarity. They also had their effect on the character of the school in his charge.

If the main pillars of West Downs were to remain unchanged, it was to be expected that there would be some innovations. Many of these were welcome, indeed overdue, such as the banishment of the chamber-pots from under the beds and the replacement of wash-stands in the dormitories with running water outside. In school routine perhaps the main change was putting all the younger boys (or 'early beddites' as they were called) into dormitories of their own instead of into patrol dormitories with the older boys. In the evening before lights out Jerry and Ray Cornes would spend some time in these dormitories, talking to each boy and even on occasions providing a little light entertainment, as Andrew Selous (1970–74) recalls:

> As a special treat for the two junior dormitories Jerry would occasionally dress up in an old cloak, don a bush hat with feathers, and carry a spear. He would then prowl round the dormitory singing 'Hold him down the Swazi warrior' to the delight of all the boys, while shaking his spear. I remember the excitement I felt. It was a marvellous gesture to the sense of fun and imagination of the boys, and I do not believe there would have been many headmasters then or now who would have done such a thing for their boys.

In other ways too it could be seen that a new hand was at work. Some rules were relaxed; boys were given more freedom; they were allowed to use the private garden; they were even allowed out in the rain. There was less preoccupation with health and (not at once) the daily taking of temperatures was abandoned. Jerry was also at pains to give as many boys as possible some responsibility and two new posts were introduced – Chapel Warden and Garden Curator. Towards outsiders – those who could find no joy in Prep School life – he was sometimes (but not always) sympathetic and tried to find for them some congenial and harmless activity.[1] He showed a liberal attitude too towards those boys who had no talent or liking for ball games, and these were sometimes allowed to have other occupations, such as feeding the school hens or pushing the wheelchair of Jerry's elderly mother.

Last of the boxing. In the 1960s considered too dangerous a sport for young boys.

Fencing – a gentler sport.

There was too a considerable extension of school activities. A cinema projector with regular film shows was introduced,[2] as also was a television set, although sparingly and discerningly used. Two tennis courts were constructed and the squash court was brought back into use. Also facilities for hobbies were increased. The old glory hole underneath the gallery in Shakespeare, previously used for dressing up for plays and as a piano practice room was turned into a model room, and above it G classroom (shades of Miss Squilley) became a new and up to date library with an adult librarian and boy helpers to run it.[3] Later the swimming bath was boarded over in winter and table tennis tables put up above it. Later still further opportunities were provided for such activities as photography, computers, puppetry and pets (mainly gerbils). Boys, then, were fully occupied in their spare time, but they were not over-organised; they were often left to their own resources, perhaps to play with the latest toys such as The Rubic Cube, which was all the rage for a time, and later highly expensive electronic games (some costing £200 and more). Mention should certainly be made too of the School Christmas Party introduced at this time. For junior boys this meant mainly 'progressive games' set up in different parts of the School. But for older boys it meant a dance – and with girls. These were invited in for the occasion from a neighbouring girls' school. At first the dances were mainly old favourites – Sir Roger de Coverley, Strip the Willow, Gay Gordons and Dashing White Sergeant. But later they were 'hepped up' a bit with such items as The March of the Mods. At the end came time-honoured ceremonies when the candles on the Christmas tree were lit by the youngest boy and the Christmas cake was cut by the head boy (later jointly with the head girl). Later in the evening, just before lights out, a party of carol singers, mainly staff, would tour the dormitories and sing unaccompanied carols in four-part harmony.

It was the opinion of Jerry Cornes when he arrived at West Downs that the greatest need was for more contact with the outside world. 'No man is an island, entire of itself,' wrote John Donne; and in the Tindall years West Downs had become perhaps a little insular. This is something to which all Prep Schools are prone, and to some extent it cannot be avoided. Scope for contact with the neighbouring community is usually found to be limited. But some attempts were now made. More school matches were arranged,[4] and not only with other Prep Schools, with local primary schools too; and West Downs took part in Hampshire school music festivals and quiz competitions, and the contact there had always been through Scouting was maintained.

Another way in which West Downs was 'brought out of its shell' was the organisation of many more school visits and expeditions (seven in 1968). Concerts and plays were attended, and not only in Winchester but as far afield as Farnham, Salisbury and Chichester. And there were visits to such diverse establishments as telephone exchanges, butterfly farms and chocolate factories.[5]

All these new activities meant more work for the headmaster, but it seems that Jerry was always ready to take on new burdens. Of these surely the most arduous must have been the introduction, or rather re-introduction of a school magazine. Since the end of the *Hesperid* in 1930 there had been occasional issues (usually every seven years) of the West Downs Register which included some school news, but nothing more. The new magazine, which was to come out every term, was much more comprehensive. It included long and detailed reports of all school activities as well as literary contributions from boys and a full list of term and examination marks. In his Notes on the Term, always fluent and stylish and sometimes extending to eight or nine closely printed pages, Jerry Cornes discoursed on a number of topics, at first only West Downs affairs, but later he widened the field to including 'my very personal views about education' as well as such topics as Britain's entry into the European Community, inflation, a wages policy, computer, robots, even the Pill. The lay-out and general appearance of the magazine was formal, even severe, containing no photographs or pictures and no variations of type. But it was certainly informative, and the labour of collecting, writing and editing all the material it contained must have been very considerable, and it would seem that this was undertaken almost entirely by Jerry Cornes himself – a formidable addition to the already heavy duties of a headmaster.

If there were many gains to West Downs life at this time there were also one or two losses. Perhaps the main one was the annual Shakespeare play in Melbury. This had been a Tindall speciality, something he did supremely well, and Jerry Cornes, who had no particular taste for drama, decided not to continue with them. There were, however, still plenty of opportunities for acting, but in the form of playlets, operetta and pantomime rather than in large-scale productions. Another casualty was the Peacock Cup which had originally been a competition between pairs of performers – usually a singer accompanied on the piano. It seems that following the demise of Miss Lunn and Miss Playsted music at West Downs went into a temporary decline, and there was difficulty in finding enough competitors. And so the competition became instead an inter-patrol affair. Later there was a great revival of music under C.P. Brown and Dorothy Glover when a school orchestra was formed, and ambitious choral works performed in Chapel and musicals like *Oliver* were staged.

It might be expected that the extension of so many school activities, which came with the new headmaster, would cause a decline in academic standards; but this was not the case; to the contrary they were enhanced. In Jerry Cornes' first year three scholarships were gained and the same again in the following year; and in 1964 he celebrated his tenth year as headmaster with no less than six including four to Winchester, which was believed to be a record. Over the years an annual average of two was maintained, many to Winchester and Eton, which was no mean feat for a medium sized school. It is often the case that scholarships are gained at the expense of neglecting less gifted pupils but this was not the case at West Downs. The Common Entrance record too was most impressive. At a time when there was a great shortage of places in Public Schools – sometimes as many as thirty per cent of candidates overall were rejected – West Downs had very few failures; between 1966 and 1972 none at all. This was especially remarkable as West Downs boys aimed high; between 1954 and 1964 sixty-three boys went to Eton and fifty-seven to Winchester.[6] It might be noted that generally West Downs boys did best in Latin and French. Some features of West Downs teaching practice might also be noted. There was no streaming; boys of all abilities sat side by side; but there was no bar to the progress of a boy up the school; a bright boy might be in the scholarship form for two years or more. Also classes were small – never more than fifteen and individual coaching was given readily to those who needed it and free of charge, which was not usual in Prep Schools.

Jerry Cornes then could be well satisfied with West Downs' academic record during the first ten years of his headmastership; and a notable accolade was to come his way when the magazine *Where*, whose judgement in these matters is no doubt discerning, numbered West Downs among the hundred best schools in the country – one of only six preparatory boarding schools to be included. At the same time the number of boys in the School had risen from 103 in 1954 to 126 in 1964, and the School was completely booked for the next six years. This increase in numbers had been general in most Prep Schools for, despite gloomy post-war prognostications, the demand for Prep School places was greater than ever,[7] and this in spite of rising fees. At West Downs these had been kept within reasonable bounds (rising from £95 a term in 1954 to £120 in 1964) and were less than in sixty other boarding Prep Schools. But these could not be held down for much longer. Costs were continually escalating, notably of heating fuel and building repairs. But the main increase was in staff salaries. Assistant masters could no longer be paid a mere pittance;[8] new entrants to the teaching profession were expecting the Burnham Scale, and to pay this there had to be a revision in the economics of Prep Schools, particularly as regards numbers. Before the War Prep Schools had been able to exist on fifty or sixty pupils or even fewer, but to be viable in the 1960s over 100 were necessary and by the 1970s over 150. In order to survive, then, West Downs would have to accommodate fifty per cent more pupils than before the War; and this inevitably required more buildings which in turn required more injection of capital. There had been no new buildings at West Downs since the addition of Shakespeare and Chapel in 1913. But in the late 1960s the old sanatorium was converted into classrooms and music practice rooms and a new dormitory (known as Field) was added to it. About the same time the playing fields were extended into the old kitchen garden (to be known as Rawson's Field) and a new house was built alongside for the Second Master (Reg Severn). Writing in the West Downs Magazine at the time Jerry Cornes described this building work as 'an earnest of our confidence that the School will thrive and prosper through the 70s, 80s and 90s of this troubled century.'

---

[1]As for example when he sold a discontented boy an obsolete typewriter for a few pence and encouraged him to bring out his own school magazine which subsequently appeared as 'The OP (nought pence) Trash.'

[2]For a time economy was exercised in the matter of a screen, an old sheet being used for the purpose.

[3]Although reading matter for the library was liberalised, comics remained banned.

[4]In 1968, for example, there were altogether forty-eight.

[5]Jerry was often to be seen setting out on one of these in an ancient motor car overflowing with boys, nicknamed by one parent 'Cornucopia'.

[6]This preponderance of Etonians was something new. Until then Winchester had been the main recipient of West Downs boys.

[7]Between 1947 and 1952 numbers in Prep Schools overall increased by some 5,000.

[8]In 1954 the average salary of the teaching staff at West Downs was £315 per annum plus board and lodging during term time.

Chapter 26

The staff which Cornes inherited from Tindall was a strong one – a blend of the old and the new with a slight preponderance of the old. If among these there were some who looked askance on the changes which came with the new headmaster, they did not include the oldest member of all. In his eightieth year W.H. Ledgard had apparently no inclination to dwell on the past. It might have been expected that after the departure of the Tindalls he too would, after forty-seven years, have called it a day. But partly out of loyalty to the School and partly perhaps out of curiosity he agreed to stay on for one more term. Then at last he retired, but died soon afterwards. Jerry Cornes wrote of him:

> It was typical of his unselfishness and absolute loyalty to the School that, at the age of seventy-nine, he agreed to stay on for one term with the present Headmaster, so as to see him over the first settling-in stages .... Serving as he had, under three headmasters and with his vast experience of the life of West Downs over forty-eight years, it might have been expected that he would resent changes and hark back to the Old Days. On the contrary, he was always marching towards the future, seeing visions and not dreaming dreams. Latin and Greek were not dead languages to him and so he made them alive to us. His loyalty, toughness, resilience and kindness made him a great schoolmaster, and are qualities which are rarer now than they were in an earlier age.

A few years after he died his nephew made a gift to the School of a sum of money so that his uncle's memory might be perpetuated, and it was decided to purchase an epidiascope, at that time a very up-to-date appliance, which threw the image of any object on to a screen, the ceiling or, indeed, anywhere. At the same time, so as to make the fullest use of this, the Ledgard Society was formed for the purpose of debates, talks and general discussions. It was open only to senior boys and was run on the lines of an Oxford Club with the boys electing their own officers and conducting their own business, fortified with lemonade and biscuits. The Society proved a great success and in the following years talks were given, sometimes by boys and sometimes by outsiders, on such subjects as duck shooting, pop stars, the C.I.D., endangered species (by Sir Peter Scott) and sailing along Sinbad's reported route. No doubt these activities would have given great satisfaction as well as a little quizzical amusement to the man whose memory they commemorate.

If the end of an era came in 1954 with the departure of Kenneth Tindall, another came in 1960 when David Howell Griffith, at the age of fifty-nine and after thirty-seven years at West Downs, called it a day. This he did in his own fashion. It was announced in the School magazine that he was taking a year off to attend to personal affairs, but West Downs was not to see him again. It seems likely that he dreaded an emotional farewell with a fanfare of publicity and so took this way to leave as quietly and unobtrusively as possible. The value of his work for the School had been immeasurable. For many it was difficult to imagine West Downs without him. When he left (apparently temporarily) Jerry Cornes wrote of him: 'His presence so permeates every corner of West Downs, like a guardian angel, that he will be missed in every place at every moment of the day.' Many and heartfelt have been the tributes to him from OWDs. Typical of them is that of Tom Brooke:

> He embodied everything that was best in a schoolmaster. He had the ability to build one up or reduce one to the size of a pin-head. One who had the ability to inspire duty, loyalty, manners, conscience and a sense of responsibility.

But perhaps the best tribute to him and the greatest that can be paid to a schoolmaster was the number of ex-pupils and parents who continued to correspond with him after he left.[1] David was to have twenty-five years of retirement which he spent in Devon, for the most part in Budleigh Salterton. It was, of course, impossible for him to be idle and his great solace during these years was gardening. One gets a charming picture of his retirement years from a letter he wrote to the mother of four former pupils:

> For myself I decided early on, when I left West Downs, that I would rather wear out than rust out.
>
> I now spend my entire time gardening especially in the cultivation of roses. Gardeners round here are at a premium so I garden far and wide among friends who through age or infirmity cannot manage their own plots. I tend about a thousand roses during the year and it has become such a joke that I have not been away from my various gardens which extend from Torquay to Taunton for many years. It is really, I suppose, a form of escapism from all the troubles and standards which are so foreign to what one hoped for when one was younger. I miss sadly the young companionship of former years, but I so often hear from Old Boys and get invitations to their weddings and visits from them when they are in these parts; and all this is a great compensation and brings back such happy memories of the past, as your yearly Christmas card always does.

At this time too Roger Jacques left after fifteen years. Before the War Roger had been for a brief time, before joining the Army, a partner at Summer Fields. At West Downs he had taught mainly Geography and had kept his classes amused, and sometimes in awe, by a lively, sardonic humour. Jerry Cornes wrote of him: 'His knowledge of the traditional values and customs has been of great use to me and to all newcomers to the staff.' Also to go at this time was Gerald Potts who had been at the School for eight years. Ruddy of hue and with a somewhat tempestuous temper (he was known as 'the pressure cooker') he had, since the departure of David Howell Griffith, taken the form of Common Entrance 'doubtfuls' with considerable success, and had been in charge of Scouting. He had also greatly enlivened the social scene at West Downs and had a local reputation as a bridge player. Another master who made his mark at this time, although he was only at the School for three years, was Michael Kefford. Later he was to become headmaster of Colston's Junior School in Bristol and the Pilgrims School in Winchester.

There were other members of staff who were to serve West Downs for much longer. Foremost among these was Reg Severn who arrived at the School in 1950 and with a break of four years (1958–62) remained there for the next thirty-eight. On the retirement of Hugh Rawson in 1966 he became Second Master and from then on assumed much the same role as that previously taken by David Howell Griffith - in charge of daily routine as well as taking D.H.G.'s old form of Common Entrance 'doubtfuls'. Here he had considerable success in imparting the elements of Latin and Maths to boys who found these subjects a deep mystery, and this despite the fact that these were not Reg's specialist subjects. It must be in large measure due to him that West Downs had so few Common Entrance failures. Reg was also in charge of Scouting and cricket at which he was no mean practitioner, being a member of the Hampshire Hogs and so with many useful contacts in the county. His wife, Gill, took an active part in school life, both in teaching where she became head of History, and later in administration. For the last six years of West Downs' history Reg was the executive headmaster and during that time he and Gill were the mainstays of the School.

A member of staff who played a key role in West Downs' scholarship record was Jeremy Fisher.[2] A Latin teacher of exceptional ability and flair, he was no narrow classicist and had many other interests including meteorology, Scouting, singing and fast bowling. When he left in 1979 three teachers were needed to cover his various activities.

In scholarship exams the other subject, as well as Latin, in which West Downs boys scored heavily, was French. This was largely due to Vati Carrère who taught French at the School for thirty-seven years. Succeeding the redoubtable Madame de Coutouly in 1951, her job had been at first to teach French conversation, at that time considered of secondary importance to grammar and spelling.[3] Later, however, when Common Entrance examiners came to consider the spoken word as of greater importance, she came into her own. Untiring and selfless in giving individual tuition in her free time, she obtained some excellent results.

As well as Latin and French the other heavy scorer in scholarship and Common Entrance exams was Maths. In charge of this subject for nineteen years was Richard Austin (1967–85). As will be seen it was to him that fell the task of introducing the New Maths into West Downs which he did very successfully. Once a regular soldier, Richard Austin had been with the British Expeditionary Force in France in the first months of the Second World War and had been evacuated at Dunkirk after spending four hours in the water. Perhaps because of this he was soon afterwards invalided out of the Army. For a time then he took up writing (with four books published under the pseudonym 'Gunbuster') before going into teaching and finally coming to roost at West Downs.

Another regular soldier, who spent thirteen years at West Downs (1970–83), was Robert Moss. Like Richard Austin a member of the B.E.F. he was unfortunate enough to be captured and for five years was a prisoner of war. During his time at West Downs he was in charge of Geography and greatly enlivened the teaching of the subject.

It is always a compliment to a school when teachers remained there for a long time, and there were, indeed, many of these during the Cornes era. Mention has already been made of Maisie Richardson who joined the School in 1944 when it was still in Scotland and remained until her retirement in 1981. For much of that time she was senior lady teacher and took a lead in introducing into the junior forms some of the many new methods and ideas which became prevalent. Jerry Cornes has written that she was the most modern minded of all the ladies on his staff. Her achievement of 110 terms is not quite a record, but is surpassed only by D.L. Rose and W.H. Ledgard. A close colleague of Maisie Richardson's for eighteen years was Barbara Spibey, remembered by many OWDs not only for her teaching ability but also for her Great Dane, said to have once saved her life when there was a fire.

There were yet more 'long-timers' at West Downs. Guy Eddis (twenty-one years), ex-Royal Navy, who, as will be seen later, set up the teaching of Science at the School and was also in charge of Hockey. Colin Morrison (eighteen) who, like Jerry Cornes, came direct from the Colonial Service to West Downs where he was instrumental in setting up French exchanges and tried to communicate to boys his own great love of Opera. Jim Fitzgerald (sixteen years), one of the more youthful members of staff, was in charge of Soccer and Tennis and a keen producer of plays. Mention should too be made of Christopher Maxse (a mere nine years), an ebullient Etonian who made a great impression as a History teacher.

It might be noted that, apart from Jim Fitzgerald, none of the teachers mentioned above had had a formal teacher training. West Downs' splendid academic record was achieved almost entirely by 'unqualified' teachers.

If there had been some relaxation of discipline among the boys under Jerry Cornes, this was even more the case among the staff. Both Mr and Mrs Tindall kept a close eye on those they employed and held them on a tight rein. In the school the sexes were segregated and only brief and formal conversations between them permitted. Romance was not encouraged. One master, wishing to court the school secretary with the most honourable of intentions, found his way firmly barred and had to resort to clandestine methods. Outside the school too members of staff found themselves under surveillance. Entry into pubs was forbidden. And the company they kept was noticed; one master was taken aback on one occasion to be summoned to the study and warned against an association he had formed in the city. And another remembers arriving back at West Downs with a colleague after a night on the town, only just in time for first period, and finding Mr and Mrs Tindall with baleful and disapproving looks surveying them from the study window. The Masters' Lodge then was a strictly masculine preserve and no lady was allowed to cross the threshold. On one occasion Maisie Richardson, needing to make contact with a master on some urgent matter, did so through a window, but even this was considered rather *risqué*. With the coming of the Corneses all this was changed and masters were allowed more latitude.[5] It was not long before ladies were not only entering the Masters' Lodge but even being boarded there, and one master was complaining that he could not get into the bathroom for all the female garments hanging on the line.

Like Kenneth Tindall before him Jerry Cornes had the inestimable advantage of being supported by a capable and very hard-working wife. Ray Cornes took on herself all the usual duties of a headmaster's wife – organising the domestic side, supervising health arrangements, assuaging anxious and vociferous parents and taking under her wing new boys and anyone who seemed to be in distress. In addition to all this (to say nothing of caring for a young family of her own) Ray also undertook a certain amount of classroom teaching of English. To this formidable array of tasks Ray brought a level head, great organising ability, sense of humour, on most occasions kindness and sympathy but on others a steely eye which boys knew instinctively would always get to the truth of any matter. Jerry's achievements at West Downs would surely have not been possible without her.

In many Prep Schools finding suitable domestic staff has long been a major problem, but it seems that at West Downs Ray made light of the task. When she took over from Mrs Tindall school meals were provided by an outside caterer, but she put an end to this arrangement and employed her own staff. Rather remarkably during the next thirty-four years there were only three head cooks.[6] Usually Winchester yielded a ready supply of daily help, but for resident help West Downs, like most institutions, had to rely on people from abroad. Domestic posts were sometimes filled by improbable personnel as, for example, when an ex-squadron leader took over as head gardener.

In health matters Ray had the great advantage at first of the skill and experience of Sister Guy. At the time Sister Guy had been at the School for nearly twenty-five years and was to stay another ten, and only left then because she felt bound to go and look after an invalid aunt. During her time at West Downs she had the complete confidence of both Mrs Tindall and Mrs Cornes. She had seen West Downs through numerous epidemics and, quite possibly, had saved the lives of boys. She also had an uncanny eye for spotting a boy who was really ill as opposed to one who was just fussing or malingering. Many OWDs will have memories of being dosed by her with such medicaments as Cod Liver Oil, Metatone, Cascara Sagrada and (more disagreeably) Syrup of Figs. When she left Jerry Cornes wrote of her: 'My wife will be losing a close personal friend to whom she can never be sufficiently grateful.' At the time of writing (October 1991) Sister

New boys relax in the drawing room under the eye of Ray Cornes who, not unusually for a headmaster's wife, is trying to do more than one thing at once.

The Dining Hall. In the Second World War a top secret map room.

Guy is very much alive at the age of ninety-two, living in a Bournemouth rest home, looking much as she did forty years ago and with her memory surprisingly intact.

Under Sister Guy and after her a succession of young or youngish ladies arrived at West Downs as assistant matrons; it seems these came and went fairly frequently, some filling in time before becoming interior decorators or beauticians. Some were solid citizens – one believed to weigh more than twenty stone – but others much less so, some even a little flighty. One caused undue interest by her sunbathing; another is reported to have held parties in her room after lights out with television, coca-cola and even a whiff of a cigarette, but no more. On one occasion, when one had to leave rather suddenly, it was discovered at what time she would be driving away, and the fire escapes on the front of the building were lined with well-wishers to give her a send-off.

---

[1]An exceptional tribute was paid by S.F. Macdonald-Lockhart (1925–29) who dedicated a book he wrote 'To D.H.G. With memories of C classroom.'

[2]He once translated the Beatrix Potter book of his name into Latin. The opening sentence was: 'Olim erat rana nomine dominus ieremias piscator.'

[3]Referred to contemptuously by W.J. Tremellen (see p. 135) as 'all that parlez-vous stuff'.

[4]He seems to have lived rather dangerously at West Downs where he lost a toe as a result of an accident with a mowing machine.

[5]But not entirely. One young master, returning from the holdiays with a moustache, was told firmly by Ray Cornes to remove it.

[6]The readiness of the kitchen staff to cope with all contingencies was summed up in their motto hung on the wall: 'We do the impossible at once. Miracles take a little longer.'

Chapter 27

In the nineteen-sixties and seventies the I.A.P.S. was very concerned to improve the public image of Prep Schools. Already many of these, including West Downs, had done much to put their houses in order; but still in some quarters the mental picture of a Prep School was that portrayed in the pages of Evelyn Waugh and George Orwell. Although at that time independent schools were flourishing as never before, its opponents were ever more vociferous and shadow Labour Ministers of Education were uttering dire threats that they would abolish them when the Party next came to office. The danger of abolition, then, had to be taken seriously so that the strongest possible case against it could be made if the need were to arise. And so in 1959 the I.A.P.S. issued a pamphlet called *Foundations* which asserted the right of Prep Schools to exist and stated their objectives. This stressed that Prep Schools provided more than just classroom learning. Three points were laid down as being fundamental: boys should be taught that the individual was less important than the group; boys should learn to work hard at tasks which might be uncongenial; and boys should be taught to develop their abilities to use them for the good of others.

At the same time Prep Schools were anxious not to be seen lagging behind as regards new educational ideas and techniques. And of these at that time there were a great many. There was much talk of 'child-centred' education and 'relevance'. In the public sector courses were being introduced in such subjects as Peace Studies, Life Skills and Social Awareness. Teachers were being exhorted to abandon old-fashioned ways ('talk and chalk') and to adopt new and more enlightened methods with the emphasis on creativity and self-expression. The basic skills[1] were not to be neglected but were to be less pre-eminent than before; and testing and examinations were to be kept to a minimum. It was also urged that children should not be taught sitting in serried ranks in a classroom but in groups in a large 'open plan' room with as much freedom and informality as possible.[2]

Although some Prep Schools might be sceptical of the new ideas they could not afford to ignore them; they must not appear to be outdated establishments impervious to change. And to avoid this it would be necessary to make basic changes in the curriculum: more time must be given to English; Science must be introduced, and more prominence given to music and art. Many Prep Schools had been wanting to make changes of this kind for a long time, but had been prevented by the demands of the Common Entrance Exam. It was all very well to be expected to bring in new subjects and expand others when Common Entrance results depended almost entirely on Latin, Maths and French. But relief in this matter was at hand. Latin was at last toppled from its predominant position and by 1968 it was no longer a compulsory subject for Common Entrance; and schools were urged to teach it only to those academically able to benefit from it.

Although the merits of these new methods and ideas have not been universally acclaimed, most would agree that they have been stimulating and on the whole beneficial. As a result of them pupils have found education more congenial and more rewarding. But winds of change have their dangers: as well as being exhilarating they can also be intoxicating, and there were some schools at the time who were rather carried away by them, introducing the new all too eagerly and letting go the old simply because it was old. But this did not happen at West Downs. Here Jerry Cornes regarded the new methods with interest but also with caution. In one of the editions of the West Downs magazine he wrote that he was not prepared to jettison old and tried ways of encouraging boys to work such as competition through marks and examinations.

Nevertheless, significant changes were made. The number of periods for each subject was altered to take account of the new priorities in Common Entrance. In the revised timetable seven periods were allotted to Maths, six each to French, Latin and English, three to Science and two each to History and Geography. The main change was, of course, the introduction of Science.

The need for the teaching of Science in Prep Schools had long been acknowledged but had been put off partly because of the difficulty of finding room for it in the timetable and partly because of the considerable cost of providing a science laboratory. But in the early 1960s the matter could be put off no longer, and at West Downs Commander Eddis was charged with establishing the subject in the School. He has since described his early efforts and tribulations:

> I had the doubtful privilege of being detailed off to start Science at West Downs. Before my first term (August 1961) Winchester College had agreed that its head of Science would allow half a dozen boys from West Downs, the Pilgrims' School and Twyford with accompanying master to attend once a week at the College laboratory. The subject was 'Soil', and we examined earth, weighed its moisture content, tested its pH level; and no one was very excited.
>
> The next step was provided by Esso Petroleum Company which supplied a number of boxes, each containing one term's work on a scientific subject – Pond Life, Astronomy, Heat, Sound, Light, eleven in all – and at the end of each term the box was packed up and sent to the next school on the distribution list. We passed through two cycles of this before the next step financed by Nuffield which, with modifications, is the basis of the present C.E. Science syllabus. I was sent to attend holiday courses at Malvern where the emphasis, certainly at first, was on the DIY construction of apparatus and the cheapest suppliers of materials. For a year I was allowed two extra 'free periods' a week to fit up the lab (in the old 'N' Room) and make the required apparatus from the cheapest possible sources.

> So West Downs boys learned their Science through Heath Robinson style
> equipment and were, no doubt, highly impressed, on arrival at their Public Schools,
> by the marvels of modern technology. I have not yet heard of any OWDs of this
> vintage achieving any dizzy scientific heights!

Another major change, which West Downs could not afford to ignore, was the
new approach to the teaching of Mathematics which arrived at the same time. Up
till then Maths had been basically a matter of 'sums'; calculations had been made
according to certain rules and the only object was to get the right answer. In
modern times (especially with the invention of calculating machines) this was
found to be inadequate, and the New Maths attempted to do much more. In the
words of Captain Austin, who was in charge of the subject at West Downs, the
object was 'to acquaint boys with a deeper knowledge of the nature of
mathematics and its uses in the modern world.' This meant working on such
aspects of the subject as the geometry of motion, statistics, probability and linear
programming. In practical and simple terms it meant that pupils spent less time
labouring at long multiplication and division sums and more on measuring,
weighing, experimenting and, of course, using computers. In some quarters these
changes were greeted with reserve but in others with great enthusiasm, some
teachers 'going over the top' and maintaining that even the learning of tables was
no longer necessary – a viewpoint they were not able to maintain for long. At
West Downs it seems that a sensible, pragmatic view was taken and great interest
and enthusiasm were generated. A Maths Library was established as also was a
Maths Workshop in which 'surgeries' were held for any boy who cared to come
along.

In the teaching of French too new ideas were abroad. Hitherto the approach
had been basically grammatical with emphasis on spelling, accents and verb
endings, the object being to produce written work of a high standard. But now it
was being maintained that the spoken word was of greater importance; it was,
after all, more likely that in later life pupils would want to speak the language
rather than to write it; and it had been noticed that those who were able to
produce impeccable proses and translations from the printed word were unable to
carry on even quite simple conversations in French.[3] The reformers also attached
great importance to creating French atmosphere in the classrooms, and these
were hung about with such items as bottles of cognac (empty), packets of
Gaulloises, pictures of the Eiffel Tower and maybe even, among the avant-garde,
a scene or two from *The Folies Bergères*. In French periods from now on pupils
were to spend less time learning irregular verbs and the feminine forms of
adjectives and more carrying on animated conversations while pretending to be,
perhaps, fishmongers, bus conductors, policemen or air hostesses.

In Common Entrance a French oral exam was introduced,[4] and to cope with
this some schools at great expense set up 'language laboratories' containing tape
recorders and earphones for each member of the class. At West Downs this was
not done, but the School found itself in a strong position to cope with the new

exam because of the presence on the staff of a gifted and highly dedicated French lady, Mlle Carrère (see p.153) who was of more value than any tape recorder. French results in examinations were always good.

Other subjects too were to feel the winds of change. In English prime importance was attached to creative writing, and because correct spelling and grammar were thought to impede this, they were treated as of minor importance. Not everyone agreed with this, but few disputed the emphasis being put on the spoken word. Lord Duncan-Sandys once told Jerry Cornes that the only complaint he had of his teaching at West Downs was that he had not been taught how to speak. This was something that Jerry had already taken steps to put right, having, at the instigation of his wife, introduced an event known as Standing Up in which boys from all forms of the School gave recitations of poetry and prose.

It was unlikely that Latin would escape the attention of reformers. For many years this had been taught grammatically, based on Kennedy's *Shorter Latin Primer*[5] and Caesar's *Gallic Wars*, graduating in due course to Hillard and Botting *Latin Proses* and the verses of *Ovid*. In the 1970s a new and imaginative course was evolved by a group of classicists at Cambridge. They urged that the subject be renamed Classical Studies and that it should be concerned more with the 'glories of Rome' and the Roman way of life. An exact knowledge of such matters as the genitive plural of *mensa* or the future perfect of *utor* was de-emphasised. The Cambridge Latin was adopted by many schools but not by West Downs. However, the School's examination record in Latin continued to be of a very high order.

---

[1]Often referred to as the three Rs: reading, writing and arithmetic.

[2]An interesting example of the wheel going full circle. In the early days of Prep Schools, and of other schools too, classes would often be held in one large room, but for reasons of economy rather than ideology.

[3]It was discovered with some surprise that French boys, coming to West Downs on exchange, were not all that strong in written work, particularly verb endings. In one class a French boy came near to bottom in a grammar test.

[4]Not easy to evaluate or to administer and very time consuming especially if, as suggested, there were two examiners to each candidate, one to carry on a conversation, the other to operate a tape recorder, out of sight if possible so as not to cause tension.

[5]All too often and too easily changed on the title page by frivolous schoolboys to Shorter Eating Primer.

Chapter 28

At the time of change of headmasters, in spite of their differing styles, it seems that boys in the School noticed little difference in everyday life. As has been seen Jerry Cornes made no great changes at first and, as a newcomer to the Prep School scene, paid heed to advice from old timers on the staff. But this situation would not last. Jerry had ideas of his own and struck at least one of his pupils as being 'a man with a mission'. Increasingly then his ideas and ways of doing things would be coming to the surface; and increasingly too, as some of these ideas were unorthodox, even idiosyncratic, they would be liable to stir up opposition from those whose attitudes tended to be inflexible. With the retirement of David Howell Griffith in 1960 and of W.J. Tremellen and R.A.K. Jacques soon after, the way for change lay more open.

At that time too forces for change were abroad outside West Downs. For this was the age of the so-called 'Swinging Sixties' when young people, and some not so young, flocked to London to listen to the new pop music of the Beatles, to dance wildly at discotheques and to deck themselves out in exotic dress from Carnaby Street. The era also saw the coming of the so-called Permissive Society – with the *Wolfenden Report*, the unexpurgated *Lady Chatterley* and *Oh Calcutta!*[1] Time-honoured values were being questioned and derided. In some quarters, notably the universities, there was unrest and sometimes uproar. Here students were proclaiming that they were finding the pressures of life in the Affluent Society intolerable, and in noisy demos and sit-ins were protesting against 'the rat race', middle class values and a harsh, oppressive discipline. The cry went up for more student participation in management, and there were many angry and turbulent scenes.

In the event this ebullition of 'student power' proved short-lived, and it was not long before students resumed a more quiescent way of life. But the movement had lasting consequences on all places of education, including West Downs.

During the turmoil there had been some activists who had attempted to bring student power into primary schools, but not, it seems, West Downs. Here life went on much as before – no sit-ins or demands for power-sharing with the headmaster, and it might seem that the School had been completely unaffected. But this was not quite the case. In many homes a new attitude was developing as to the relationship between adults and children – less formal and less authoritarian. Respect and obedience were no longer *de rigueur*. Where before parents had told children what to do and (usually) seen that they did it, now the tendency was to 'negotiate' with them and seek compromises. In such matters as dress, reading matter, language and hair-style children were being given much more latitude. And this new atmosphere in the home was bound to have its effect on school life. Authority would be less unquestioned and children would express themselves with more freedom. Some teachers struggled bravely to maintain old-fashioned standards, but they must often have felt that they were swimming against the tide.

It would be a mistake to think that in this new climate West Downs, or indeed most other Prep Schools, became something of a free-for-all. Generally authority was maintained, so too were academic standards – it has been seen that it was in the sixties that West Downs had its greatest successes. But concessions did have to be made to a new life-style. Uniform was relaxed, hair was allowed to grow, pocket radios and cassette players were allowed into the dormitories. Also boys were allowed to spend more time away from school – two weekends a term which meant that Sunday morning chapel was often sparsely attended.

It was the opinion of Jerry Cornes that discipline at West Downs under Tindall had been severe, even repressive. Writing in later years in the School magazine he talked with some hyperbole of finding that he had 'inadvertently become a prison governor.' And in a letter to a parent in the late seventies he wrote:

> The atmosphere is, of course, utterly different from that when you were at the School. I will never forget my first evening as headmaster in April 1954 with the whole school herded like sheep into Shakespeare and even a patrol leader crying, to join all the new boys who were in tears. Thank God the School is nothing like that now. It is, and always has been, my policy to make West Downs a happy school because I do not think that children can work or make the best use of their talents unless they are happy. So there is a strict discipline in the classrooms, but a very relaxed atmosphere outside it.

Jerry is surely exaggerating here; few OWDs of the Tindall era will recall these orgies of tears. And Jerry himself, at least in the first part of his headmastership, was no mean disciplinarian. Boys remember a formidable temper; and although some of his punishments may have been mild and unorthodox,[2] he was also quite prepared to use the cane and the slipper.[3] In particular he came down hard on slackness in school work. He carried on from Tindall's day the system of weekly marks, but these were no longer read out in front of the whole school assembled in Shakespeare; instead Jerry came round to each form where he would go over the marks, commenting on them and taking action where necessary.

By the mid-seventies it became apparent that outside the classroom boys were being allowed considerably more freedom. But it must be doubtful if this always achieved the 'very relaxed atmosphere' of which Jerry wrote. For freedom is all too readily abused. It has been portrayed graphically in *The Lord of the Flies* how boys of Prep School age can do terrible things to each other if left to themselves.

The bully will thrive and the weak and helpless will suffer. And it does seem that for a time at West Downs there was a certain amount of unpleasant, even vicious, bullying – more, it seems to the author, than when he was at the School some forty years before. One OWD of that time, no doubt with a certain measure of hyperbole, has told in graphic terms of his ordeals – of being tied to a tree and lashed with stinging nettles, and being 'buried alive' (with leaves) and 'thrown from precipices' down at Melbury. Others have described the ritual of 'running the gauntlet' after lights out. For this they were made to strip naked and run up and down the dormitory while the remainder of the patrol pitched into them with dressing gown cords, knotted towels and anything else that came to hand. It should be said that this was not always as brutal as it sounds and was taken by some of the victims with good humour and afterwards it was a source of pride that they had endured it. It seems too that some patrol leaders at this time took the law into their own hands. Left to cope in the dormitories on their own without interference they inflicted distinctly unorthodox punishments.[4] And some masters too, perhaps despairing of effective punishment at the top, acted on their own initiative. It had always been, and still was, a rule at West Downs that only the headmaster could inflict corporal punishment, but it seems that at this time the rule was not always heeded.[5]

Another consequence of greater freedom is that boys are liable to run wild on daring escapades, sometimes running into danger. Many tales, often no doubt embellished, have been told of such exploits at this time. It seems that these usually happened after lights out. It had always been the custom at West Downs that masters did not go into the dormitories, so responsibility for maintaining discipline there rested almost entirely with the patrol leaders and the matrons, some of whom, as has been seen, took this duty rather lightly. It seems that nocturnal excursions were not uncommon. Some of these were comparatively harmless – creeping round the school, perhaps helping oneself to a few tit-bits from the kitchen or even from the headmaster's wine and cigarette supply. Modernists will, no doubt, say that such things are all part of the growing up process; but consequences could be serious, as when the Science cupboard was raided and a chemical removed which, when flushed down the lavatory, caused a minor explosion. More dangerous still was the custom of 'roof ragging' – clambering round the roof, perhaps coming in the window of another dormitory, perhaps forcing an entry through the window of the room where the sweets were stored, perhaps even, as one OWD has claimed, climbing to the top of the bell tower and carving his initials on the lead flashing round Chapel bell. As was to be expected these practices led eventually to a serious injury when a boy fell through a skylight and needed a great many stitches to sew him up.

As in many Prep Schools the last night of term was often the occasion of riotous behaviour, notably of 'dormitory raids' when one dormitory invaded another and was vigorously repelled. Sometimes the patrol leader would be drawn into battle on a rug pulled by four 'charioteers'. In the pitched battle that followed weapons might be something comparatively innocuous like a pillow, a knotted towel or a sockball; but the latter were not always filled with other socks; sometimes they contained hair brushes, shoes, boxes or some other hard, jagged object. Remarkably it appears that no one was ever seriously hurt. Remarkably too these occasions often went undetected, although they can have been far from soundless. But on at least one occasion Jerry appeared on the scene and the offenders were marched off to Chapel where they were made to sit penitentially into the watches of the night. On the last night of the Summer Term with many boys leaving and excitement running particularly high there were even wilder scenes including sometimes wilful damage.[6]

It must not be thought that West Downs was ever an anarchic society. Such incidents as those recorded above were sporadic and usually involved only a small number of boys. For most of the time the great majority of boys led reasonably peaceful, profitable, law-abiding lives. But it does seem that for a period of time, perhaps about six or seven years, boys were able to avail themselves of a certain amount of licence. And it may have been the case that this was not wholly detrimental. More than one OWD have recorded positive advantages. Philip Colfox (1971–75), who today runs a rapidly expanding construction business has described how his entrepreneurial skills were first developed at West Downs on a neglected piece of ground used for a time as a rubbish dump:

> The dump between Chapel and the Waterworks depot beyond the Masters' Lodge became about 1973–74 the biggest building site at West Downs. Approximately half the boys at the School[7] spent most of their time there turning it into a fortress of huts, barricades, tree houses and tunnels. I and about four others were more or less in charge. Jerry Cornes could not believe what was going on. We rented out freehouses and other 'dens' that we had had made by 'slaves' for money every week, and at the end had accumulated about £5 which was embezzled by one of us and spent at The Sweet Content by Westgate in Winchester. This was one reason why the culprit was beaten twice in the same day. The other was for stealing the communion wine and drinking it in the area of the Waterworks where he left evidence of smashed bottles. During breaks and some games periods there would be pitched battles with the usual paraphernalia of dustbin lids and anything else that lay to hand. In the end during one holiday Jerry sold all the scrap, and the site had to be abandoned. It was a mark of Jerry's gift of developing characters of problem boys that this situation had been allowed to develop without undue interference and has had such a major effect on some young boys' lives.

This freebooting style of life was not to last long. It almost entirely disappeared when Reg Severn took charge of the School in 1982. But there is evidence that it did impart to West Downs boys an independence of mind and a toughness which was noticeable when they went on to their Public Schools (very different from the old 'cotton wool shop' image of years ago).

It should be noted that it was not only the 'upper dogs' who enjoyed their time at West Downs. Several who had little success there and who came in for some vicious bullying, have recorded that it was the happiest time of their school careers, notably more so than at the famous Public Schools to which they subsequently went.

---

[1]The first all-nude production on the London stage.

[2]As for example when a boy stole a prayer book of another and tore out the title page with his name on it and threw it away. For this the boy, together with Jerry, was made to spend some time raking through the rubbish tip to try to find it.

[3]It seems that Jerry was not a skilled practitioner with the cane. One OWD remembers that on one occasion he missed him completely and the cane was shattered when it hit the back of the chair over which he was bending. Another OWD remembers a totally painless caning being administered to him when wearing a kilt.

[4]Such as being made to stand for a period of time with legs apart on two stools with a cup of water on one's head, while the patrol leader bombarded the stool with slippers and other missiles.

[5]Prep School masters' tempers are, of course, often under pressure, and not only with the boys. It is reported how on one occasion a master nearly came to blows with the pantry boy for making a great clatter of knives and forks during the saying of grace at the end of a meal.

[6]Such as mutilating West Downs' justifiably famous cricket square, or letting loose pet gerbils.

[7]This proportion is disputed by other boys of that time.

Chapter 29

It must be evident by now that running a Prep School in modern times is very different from what it had been fifty years ago. Then a headmaster would set his own course with unquestioned authority and was little beset by outside trends. And in the home moral standards were firm and religious faith strong. Today many of these moral standards have lapsed and religious faith in most homes has disappeared. At school the headmaster is no longer the autocrat he once was and he has to keep abreast with the everchanging educational scene.

This must at times have left Jerry Cornes somewhat breathless; but he was no reactionary caught in a time capsule. It has been seen that he introduced many new features into West Downs life and this he continued to do. A particular interest of his was that Britain should take part fully in the European Community,[1] and he was eager to give West Downs a more European flavour. In furtherance of this he organised exchanges with French schools. Here it seems that West Downs boys had the better deal; they stayed in French homes, spent little time in the classroom and were taken on a round of exciting visits to such places as Versailles, the Eiffel Tower, the Circus and other places of entertainment. The French boys on the other hand found themselves living in a boarding school with a routine to which it cannot have been easy for them to adapt.[2] This resulted sometimes in them being 'cliquish' and uncooperative. Later on, however, great efforts were made to entertain them with visits to Stonehenge, the Beaulieu Motor Museum, the *Victory* (perhaps rather tactlessly) and a tour of London which included the food department of Harrods.

It was not only with France that contact was made. Football matches were arranged with German schools and there were ski trips to the Alps.

Calls on a headmaster's time come from many directions, and usually Jerry was unsparing of time and effort in responding to these, but there was one area in which he held back: he seldom allowed himself to be drawn into Prep School affairs on a national level. Although a member of the I.A.P.S. he took little part in their affairs and thought many of them a waste of time. He was not by nature a committee man, and had little inclination to attend seminars on such matters as 'how a headmaster can produce leadership in creating and maintaining a group of motivated teachers whose energy should be harnessed for the good of their pupils and the school.' And who can blame him?

To his credit too Jerry kept free of the fearsome jargon with which modern educationists find it necessary to clothe their thoughts. He would never have sent out to all parents, as one famous Prep School did recently, a circular urging them to support an organisation known as The English Speaking Board (International) Ltd whose aims are to 'support all teachers and trainers who set high standards in the use of language by providing a carefully graded structure of assessments which motivate the pupils or students to progress constructively in oral communication. And to provide a meeting point of craft, trade, commerce, science, arts and leisure activities through oral, manual and visual presentation to a participating group. And to give young people confidence and skill in self-learning, stimulated, controlled and guided by teachers who are also seekers and learners, and to give overt recognition of progress in oral and life-skills through a system which 'measures' rather than 'marks' effort, ingenuity, clarity of thought and word and the subsequent growth of language.'

Parents should be grateful to Jerry for sparing them gobbledygook of this sort.

In the changing world of the seventies and eighties it was to be expected that some West Downs institutions would disappear – the Advent Talk, Scripture Verses learned by heart on Sunday and repeated tremulously in Chapel on Monday mornings, the Harvest Festival procession bearing fruit and vegetables down to the Hospital, even Sanitary Prep – all had gone. Others were still in place but much modified. Prize giving was now a rather low-key affair compared to some schools. No array of masters in academic dress, no serried ranks of dutiful parents, no guest of honour, speeches and an interminable succession of prize winners. Instead a modest gathering strictly confined to masters and boys with a few announcements, reading of results, some prizes and good wishes for the holidays and it was all over.

Also considerably modified was the leaving talk. Partly owing to explicit Biology classes, often taken by a woman, and partly to modern openness boys of this era were much more fully informed than their predecessors of forty years before. It seems that they knew what was coming to them in the talk and that in order to avoid long explanations of matters already familiar to them it was only necessary for them to say that they had lived or had spent long periods on a farm. But although this curtailed the talk it did not replace it, it being considered that not all matters concerning life in a Public School could be picked up in a farmyard.

One pillar of West Downs life remained in place: Scouting continued to the very end.[3] In the late 1960s the whole Scouting movement had been overhauled to give it a more modern slant with a new uniform, new activities,[4] and to some extent a new ethos. But certain time-honoured events remained. The annual Baker-Wilbraham competition between all the Winchester Scout troops continued to take place at West Downs. So too did Investiture. In Helbert's and Tindall's day this had been a very solemn affair with the recruits who had come of

Scouts (new style) attempt to get a fire going. Headmaster gives moral support.

Keen competition for Garden Prize.

age being formally invested after the taking of sacred oaths and the recital by heart by one of their number of the Scout Law.[5] These had now been dispensed with as also had the prayer for divine guidance in the election of patrol leaders – there was even a suspicion that sometimes patrol leaders were elected not so much for their strength as for their weakness, of which advantage would in due course be taken. Tindall used to appear for the occasion in Scout uniform of the time – large, baggy shorts and wide brimmed hat, but in latter days Jerry sported a vaguely nautical outfit. The atmosphere was generally more informal and secular. From 1982 Scouting had to be carried on without the use of Melbury (see below p. 173). Perhaps for this reason it was noted by some OWDs that Scouting became more 'academic' with plenty of lectures, talks and demonstrations but little action in the great outside.

A major event which remained on the calendar but in a different form was Parents Weekend (Pater's Day in Helbert's and Tindall's time). On Fridays, instead of the Melbury Shakespeare play, there were the cricket and shooting matches against the School and sometimes a rounders match against the mothers and sisters (no longer a cricket match against maters and sorors). And in the evening there was a display of gymnastics and maybe too of Judo and fencing. Then on Saturdays there was Sports Day; this had been transferred from the Easter Term and greatly expanded. As well as the usual athletic events there were more informal items like an obstacle race (with the same maze used in Tindall's day), a Visitors' Race and even a Dog Race. And for several years proceedings were inaugurated by the release of a flight of homing pigeons.

An event which remained almost entirely unaltered was Founder's Day – the special service in Chapel, the meeting of the OWD Society, cricket and shooting matches – all remained in place. Regrettably on one or two occasions the day was marred by some OWDs from Public Schools arriving in outlandish garb and behaving like hooligans, rampaging through the dormitories and even starting fires. Because of this consideration was given to discontinuing the occasion, but in the end it went on and the yobbery subsided.

On the final Founder's Day in 1988, attended by a large group of OWDs some of whom had not visited the School for twenty years or more, there was still plenty to remind them of their years at West Downs. Chapel looking exactly as it had always done and the traditional service with 'Jerusalem', the reading from *Isaiah*, the founder's prayer and finally, after a pause, the prayer for energy and purpose. Then wandering through the building, looking for oneself in the school photographs, still on the walls after fifty years and more, and perhaps too for one's name on the panels in the Dining Hall and, for the more distinguished, on the Honours Boards, still occupying the same place behind top table. Readily memories came flooding back – games successes and failures, anxious waits outside the study, temperature queues, the none too salubrious *foricas*, the eager peering out of the classroom windows for the arrival of the family car to take one out. *Plus ça change, plus c'est la même chose*, or words to that effect, must have occurred to more than one OWD on that occasion just before the final curtain came down.

[1]At least one parent, who felt differently on this subject, was dismayed when prayers for this country's entry into the Common Market were offered in Chapel.

[2]One concession to the French visitors was that in Chapel the Lord's Prayer was said in French.

[3]At the end of the last term the Sixth Winchester Troop was formally disbanded in a ceremony presided over by the County Commissioner and an impressive array of Scouting notables.

[4]Badges could now be obtained in such skills as Car Maintenance, Practical Electricity, Making Radios and Computers.

[5]Which the present author remembers doing impeccably.

Chapter 30

In 1964 Jerry Cornes made West Downs into a private company owned by him and his wife and their four sons. In the West Downs magazine of that year Jerry wrote: 'The object is simply to minimise the Death Duties risk, should the Headmaster unexpectedly die.' At the time this development seems to have attracted little attention; but eventually it was to seal the fate of West Downs. It meant in effect that Jerry and Ray lost control of the School. No doubt they hoped at the time that one of their sons would take over as headmaster and West Downs would be carried on into the next generation. But in the years that followed the value of the West Downs property increased rapidly as Winchester spread westwards. At the same time the profitability of the School was lagging. So long as Jerry was alive and fit there was no immediate threat to the future of the School. It was recognised by his family that West Downs was his life and that he should carry on there for as long as he was able. By 1981 Jerry was seventy, and after twenty-six years, during which he had never spared himself, he knew that the time had come to appoint a successor and 'to take a permanent back-seat.' By then he was aware that none of his sons was interested in becoming headmaster. But at that stage there appeared to be another solution to the problem: a godson of Jerry's, Andrew Morrison, had won a great reputation for himself at Charterhouse, and he and his wife, Liz, were delighted at the idea that he should take over at West Downs. Andrew at the time was thirty-eight, Liz was a State Registered Nurse, and they had a family of three. It all seemed ideal. In the West Downs magazine Jerry wrote: 'I can't think of any pair more ideally suited to carry on our traditions. We hope and believe that the School will go on well into the twenty-first century.'

Andrew Morrison was given a ten-year contract and shares in West Downs Ltd and he accepted that Jerry would stay on as bursar. For this Jerry had to maintain a presence in the School and it soon became clear that his idea of 'a permanent back-seat' did not concur with Andrew Morrison's, and there were some disagreements. The crunch came in March 1982. Andrew became convinced that there was no long-term future for the School unless it was made into a Charitable Trust. He realised that on the death of Jerry or on the expiry of his contract the future of the School would be in the melting pot; it would be in the hands of the Cornes family who might or might not be interested in keeping the

School going. So after two terms at West Downs he made it a condition of his staying on that it should be made into a Charitable Trust at once. To this the Cornes family would not agree, and so Andrew left at the end of the year to become headmaster of Mowden Hall in Northumberland. Although their stay at West Downs had been a brief one Andrew and Liz were insistent later that it had been a memorable time for them with much that they had learned and enjoyed.

The departure of Andrew Morrison, inevitably, caused much unease to West Downs parents and boys in the School; and rumours proliferated about impending closure which had increasingly serious effect on school numbers. But at that time (1982) it seems there was no intention of closing the School on site. Advertisements were placed for a new headmaster and a number of candidates were interviewed, but with the future of the School in doubt no one suitable could be found. And so Reg Severn, who had been second master for a number of years, became acting headmaster, a post which he was to occupy until the closure of the School six years later.[1]

For some years it had been evident that extensive repairs and improvements were needed to the fabric of the school building. These would require a large injection of capital and to provide this the decision had been taken in 1979 to sell Melbury. This must have been done with reluctance as Melbury had been an integral part of West Downs life since the First World War. Many OWDs have memories of open air Shakespeare plays, firework displays, efforts to light fires with damp unburnable wood and then cooking on them a hardly eatable substance known as 'dampers'.[2] Melbury Lodge with its Tyrolean aspect had charm and had been used partly as classrooms, partly as staff quarters, and sometimes as extra dormitories – always much sought after by boys as discipline in them was less vigilant and opportunities for extra-mural activities greater. But there were strong reasons for selling. Like the main school the value of Melbury as a building site had soared in recent years, and the amount it was used hardly justified keeping it. Also the Romsey Road had become extremely busy and some parents were put off sending their boys to West Downs because of the crossing. Over the years the Lodge had fallen into decay and recently had had some very rough treatment from squatters and vandals. Finally it was burned to the ground. The northern part of Melbury was sold to a developer in 1979 and a number of up-market houses were built there. Later further parts were sold for more houses, and the Dell was sold to the Wessex Regional Health Authority for the building of a mental unit.

In the 1970s many I.A.P.S. boarding schools were less than full. Nearly fifty had had to close. Overall the number of pupils in I.A.P.S. schools continued to rise, but more and more of these were day pupils including girls.[3] This trend could not be ignored and in the middle of the decade West Downs started taking day-boys on a regular basis. In the years that followed these grew rapidly in number, and inevitably the nature of the School changed. For some of the day-boys came from a different home background to the boarders, so that there was a greater social mix at West Downs.

At the same time with the trend for pupils at boarding schools to spend more time at home during the term, parents were increasingly looking for boarding schools near at hand. More and more then West Downs was becoming a local school catering for the citizens of Winchester and the surrounding district – as had been the case in the days of the Winchester Modern School before the arrival of West Downs (see p. 7). An exception to this was that more foreign boys were coming to the School. For the most part these were of Indian or Chinese origins. Some of them were extremely gifted pupils. One Chinese boy, starting from scratch, learned enough French in two terms to take the Winchester entrance; and an Indian boy gained a scholarship after only two years at West Downs.

It was at this time too that West Downs started taking girls on a regular basis. It was not, of course, the first time girls had been to the School. Tindall's daughters and granddaughters had been there, as from time to time had those of members of the staff. But now girls became a permanent part of the establishment and not only on a day basis but also as boarders. It seems that this was achieved quite painlessly. Sleeping accommodation was found for them first on the private side, then in Field Dormitory (next to the old San.) and finally in the former domestic quarters. Their welcome by the boys may at first have been rather tepid, but they were soon accepted and joined in all school activities apart from Scouting and games, although they did take part in house cricket and hockey matches. All leisure pursuits were open to them and one or two of mainly feminine interest (ballet and needlework) were added for their benefit. Girls also played an important part in the annual opera and in form plays, and in Chapel Choir and all musical activities.

It is probable that at West Downs, as in most other schools which went co-educational at this time, the reasons were economic rather than ideological, but it was noted how they had a civilising effect on the School and Jerry and Ray were keen on recruiting them for this reason.

Until the mid-1970s the numbers at West Downs had kept up well, and in 1978, following the sudden closure of a neighbouring Prep School, they had reached a new peak – 165 of which twenty-one were day pupils. But in 1980 there had been fifty-eight leavers, and from then on numbers began to decline. There may have been several reasons for this, but the main one must have been the uncertainty about the future of the School. As Andrew Morrison had found and as Jerry himself once admitted, the only way of ensuring the long-term future of the School was to make it a Charitable Trust.

In the early 1980s some boys and girls already had the feeling that they were at a school in decline. It is true that Reg Severn gave a strong lead so that the School was always well organised and the high academic standard was maintained with scholarships being won right to the end. The standard of games too remained high and in 1986, only two years before the closure, West Downs had an outstanding success when it won the Hampshire Prep School Cricket Championship.[4] But at the same time the fabric of the building continued to deteriorate and the numbers to fall. To offset this a pre-preparatory school for children aged 5–8 was started in the old Sanatorium in 1983, as also in the following year was a kindergarten for 3–5 year olds. Certainly many changes came to West Downs in its latter years. And yet something basic remained the same. The special character imparted on the School by three headmasters, each outstanding in his way, was not lost.

But nothing could stem the mounting losses and early in 1987 Jerry decided that at the end of the Summer Term 1988 the School would be closed and the property sold for redevelopment. Reg Severn was informed of this at once and the rest of the staff at the end of the Easter Term. Although this information was given in confidence, rumours of it were spread abroad and more parents took their children away from the School, and losses for the last year were very large indeed.

Although still not officially announced, closure of the School seemed to most people to be imminent and inevitable. But already for some time efforts had been under way to save West Downs. In the summer of 1986 David Denison, Vice-Chairman of the West Downs Parents Committee,[5] had a meeting with Daniel Hodson, Hon. Treasurer of the OWD Society and at that time financial director of Unigate. As a result of this a campaign was started to form a Charitable Trust with the aim of ensuring the future of West Downs. In the following months this gained considerable support not only from parents and OWDs (including Lord Duncan-Sandys, Sir Jeremy Morse, Admiral of the Fleet Sir William Staveley and the Marquess of Bute who agreed to act as patrons),[6] but also from a number of local interests. The chief executive of the Hampshire County Council gave assurances that the Council was strongly in favour of the continuation of West Downs as a school; and Sir Basil Ferranti, the local M.E.P., gave his support and agreed to join the patrons. In addition local firms of solicitors, accountants and stockbrokers, although not necessarily having any direct contacts with the School, offered their services free of charge.

In April 1987 Andrew Foster, chairman of the West Downs Parents Committee, wrote to Jerry Cornes, expressing the anxiety of parents about rumours of impending closure. In reply Jerry said he could not guarantee the future of the School on site after June 1988. Later at a meeting of the OWD Society on Founder's Day (June 6th) he said he was unable to add anything to this because the matter would be settled finally at a meeting of the directors and shareholders of West Downs School Ltd (the Cornes family) later in the summer. It was now virtually certain that West Downs would be closed unless urgent action was taken to save it. Already schemes were afoot. A committee had been formed to look into the possibilities of purchasing a large country house near Winchester, Worthy Park, to which West Downs could be transferred. The property was owned by Dixons Ltd whose chairman, Mr Kalms, was interested in education and sympathetic to the idea of the building becoming a school. But the scheme depended on the purchase of land for playing fields from a neighbouring farmer, and here it foundered. For although the farmer was offered three times the current price of agricultural land, he refused to sell.

Following this setback the Committee turned to another scheme – to form a company, to be known as Handhaven Ltd, which would make an offer for the purchase of the shares in West Downs School Ltd. A substantial sum would be needed for this and quickly – outside the range, it was thought, of a Prep School. But incredibly during the next six weeks pledges were received, almost entirely from OWDs, of such size and from such trustworthy sources that the Royal Bank of Scotland was prepared to underwrite an immediate and unconditional offer of £2½m. This was dispatched by Messrs Cobbold Roach on 17th July 1987 and was considered by the shareholders when they met two weeks later. During this time there had been little contact between the Committee and the Cornes family and it seems that the latter was taken aback. They could not believe that such a large sum had been raised and thought that it must depend on a subsequent sale of parts of the West Downs estate for building purposes. But this would have needed planning permission, and it was made clear that the offer was not conditional on this being obtained. The offer was, however, far short of what was believed could be obtained on the open market if redevelopment was allowed. And so the shareholders decided to reject the offer and put the West Downs property up for tender. At the same time it was formally announced that the School would close in June 1988.

Although unsuccessful, the Handhaven offer was an extraordinary achievement and a remarkable tribute to West Downs in its last days. It is sometimes assumed that in the field of education Prep Schools are the poor relation; that people will give generously to their Public Schools and universities, but will be much less open-handed to their Prep Schools. But West Downs showed that this is not necessarily the case. To have raised sufficient pledges to make such an offer possible was a feat any educational establishment would have envied. In the past old members of the School had not always been very outward in their support; they had seemed reluctant to attend Founder's Day and other reunions and rarely sent their sons to the School. But faced with the prospect of West Downs being closed, they reacted strongly. It seems they had a stronger affection for the School than they thought they had and the idea of Shakespeare, Chapel and other sacred places being turned into flats or offices and the playing fields being bulldozed for a housing estate appalled them and they dug deeply into their pockets to avoid it.

The rejection of the Handhaven offer was not the end of the road. In the following months further efforts were made by Andrew Foster and David Howard to find alternative accommodation in the Winchester area. A disused army camp near Oliver's Battery was inspected as also was Bramdean, a property lying between Winchester and Petersfield; this might have fitted the bill, but then the Highway Department made difficulties about access. The final attempt came at the end of 1987 when discussions took place with the headmaster and governors of Northcliffe School near Southampton about a possible merger. Some progress was made in these, but there were difficulties. Northcliffe was a much smaller school than West Downs and not so well known, and a merger on the terms required by West Downs would mean that it would be swallowed up; its name would be changed and it might be impossible for its headmaster to remain. However, the governors of Northcliffe were interested in the idea, and it seemed at one time that agreement might be in sight, but the negotiations had been carried on without the participation of Jerry Cornes, and when he realised the implications of the matter, he somewhat abruptly brought it to a close. It seems he could not accept the idea of West Downs in alien premises under another name.

And so on 19 November 1987 Andrew Foster sent a letter to West Downs parents in which he wrote: 'We regret to inform you that all our efforts to secure the future of the School have now failed.' At the same time he resigned as chairman of the W.D.P.A. But still for some time hope lingered on. David Howard did not give up and remained on the look-out for suitable properties. But finally it had to be accepted that West Downs would close at the end of the Summer Term 1988.

The closure of a school can never be painless; it will inevitably cause distress to parents who have to find a new school, for their children who have to settle into new surroundings, and to staff who have to find new jobs. Other Prep Schools in this predicament have minimised their losses by closing down suddenly within a few weeks. This did not happen at West Downs where over a year's notice was given and help was provided to find new schools. Many went to the Pilgrims School where the headmaster, Michael Kefford, once a teacher at West Downs, did all he could to help. Others went to West Downs' old rival, Horris Hill, where, perhaps not unexpectedly, they came in for a certain amount of ribbing.[7] As regards the staff the younger members had little difficulty in finding new places, but for the older ones, notably Reg Severn, this was impossible.

It was predictable that the closing of West Downs would cause bad feeling. The rescue attempt had been a magnificent effort and had come very near to success. Many felt that it was worthy of a better fate. Jerry Cornes always realised what would be the consequences of closure. He wrote later: 'The decision was made rationally, knowing that there would be a lot of pressure, threats and abuse against it.' The case of the Cornes family was that the School had long since ceased to be profitable and that the demand for boarding places was declining. At the same time the value of the property had increased out of all proportion and no commensurate return could be obtained while it was a school. It must be said on Jerry Cornes' behalf that he took full responsibility on himself, even though he was only one of several who took the decision and, as a minority shareholder, may have been powerless to prevent it. In answer to his critics he took the line that he had been obliged to do what he had done in the interest of his large and growing family. He personally should certainly be defended against the charge of cupidity. Although he had invested a large sum (by the standards of the time) in West Downs and had worked night and day on its behalf, he had during the years of his headmastership never taken much in the way of remuneration; and it was noted by several people during that time that his life-style was simple, not to say frugal.

Whatever may be one's feelings about the events of 1987 and 1988 it will be agreed by most that with the passing of West Downs there went a notable piece of history. West Downs was no run-of-the-mill Prep School. It had a character and ethos which were unique. No one will claim that during its life of ninety-one years everything about it was admirable, but surely at different times and in different ways it had epitomised all that is best in English education.

Few can feel any satisfaction in what has happened since 1988. Planning permission to redevelop has not been forthcoming and for four years West Downs has stood bleak and empty. A Protection Order has been placed on the building so that it must be preserved for posterity in some form or other – not easily imaginable except as a school, and the Highways Department is raising objections about access. In the meanwhile the grounds are becoming ever more overgrown and everywhere there is a somewhat spectral atmosphere. It is not perhaps far different from what it was like ninety-four years ago when Lionel Helbert first arrived on the scene and its future then was as uncertain as it is now.

---

[1]To comply with the rules of the I.A.P.S. it was necessary for Jerry to be the official headmaster. Reg was 'executive headmaster'.

[2]A concoction of flour, water and salt.

[3]In I.A.P.S. schools in 1967 boarders were 50.5 per cent of the total. In 1977 the percentage was 38.4. The total number of pupils in 1975 was 73,555, in 1981 it was 79,682.

[4]The final of this on the Hampshire County Cricket Ground was almost unbearably exciting. Mungo Denison, who made the winning hit, said that at the end he felt as if he could walk on water.

[5]This had been formed in 1982 after the departure of Andrew Morrison and had been concerned at first mainly with peripheral matters for the most part of a domestic nature. But, as will be seen, it later became involved with the future of the School.

[6]Inevitably such a galaxy of names caught the attention of the media, and the *Evening Standard* in a splurge of journalese described them as having been 'sucked into the fray to save the place where they first learned to play conkers.'

[7]It seems that the old mutual insults of 'Horrid Hill' and 'Wet Downs' had not lapsed.

Postscript

During West Downs' ninety years' history there were about 2,200 pupils in the School, including 100 girls. Most of these came from similar social backgrounds and, when they left, went on to similar schools. What happened to them later varied considerably and might make an interesting study, but in the present work it is only possible to record those fields in which OWDs have been prominent and the successes and distinctions they have gained.

In the political arena West Downs has been well represented – ten members of the House of Commons and forty-four of the House of Lords. Of these three have been senior cabinet ministers, one has been Prime Minister of Northern Ireland, and seven have been junior ministers.

Duncan Sandys (1917–20),[1] a son-in-law of Winston Churchill, held many of the top offices of state including Housing and Local Government, Defence, Aviation, and Colonial and Commonwealth Relations. He was regarded by some as a Tory 'hatchet man', often being given assignments which required a degree of toughness; he was reputed to be particularly uncompromising with his civil servants. Throughout his political career he was a strong European and founded the European Movement in 1947 and Europa Nostra in 1969. Outside politics he was a Member of the Magic Circle and was founder and President of the Civic Trust. At West Downs he made no great name for himself, but it is remembered of him that, unusually, he had special lessons in Russian. Christopher Soames (1929–32),[2] another Churchill son-in-law, also held several senior portfolios including War and Agriculture. He was later Ambassador in Paris and senior British E.E.C. Commissioner, in both of which posts he was noted for his fluency in French (learned at the knee of Madame de Coutouly ?). Later he played a key role in the transfer of power in Zimbabwe, and his political career might have gone further but, as was remarked by John Colville (also an OWD), he and Mrs Thatcher 'were not birds of a feather.' He too attained no great prominence at West Downs and is remembered by his contemporaries, rather strangely, for his extreme thinness. Lack of rapport with Mrs Thatcher is not a trait of Nicholas Ridley (1940–41).[3] He was said to have been the cabinet minister closest to her in outlook, particularly as regards Britain's integration into Europe. Before his resignation on this matter he had been at the Ministries of Transport, Local Government, and Trade and Industry where he had a reputation for

179

independence of mind and outspokenness with occasional abrasiveness. He was only at West Downs for a short time during the Scottish period and seems to have no clear memories of the School, at least none that he wishes to resurrect. Terence O'Neill (1923–27)[4] was a member of the House of Commons for a number of years and was a junior minister before becoming Prime Minister of Northern Ireland from 1963 to 1969.

Other politicians include Victor Montagu (1915–19),[5] at one time Private Secretary to the Prime Minister, Stanley Baldwin, and later during the last years of the Second World War one of the leaders of the Tory Reform Movement; and Malcolm McCorquodale (1910–13)[6] who was Parliamentary Secretary to the Ministry of Labour during the Second World War (under Ernest Bevin). At the time of writing (1991) there are two OWDs currently in office: Robert Ferrers (1938–42)[7] is Deputy Leader of the House of Lords and Minister of State at the Home Office; and Nicholas Ullswater (1950–54)[8] is Parliamentary Under-Secretary of State at the Ministry of Employment in charge of Tourism.

It is not only in Conservative governments that OWDs have found a place. Wayland Kennet (1933–35)[9] was a junior minister in Harold Wilson's first Labour administration. Later he joined the S.D.P. of whom he was a spokesman in the House of Lords on foreign affairs and defence. He also became a member of the European Parliament.

At this point one might mention another OWD who has been described, among other things, as 'the stormy petrel of British politics', and who might have attained greater heights than any of those mentioned above. It is generally agreed that Oswald Mosley (1906–09)[10] had brilliant gifts – a first-rate mind, imagination, powerful oratory and considerable presence (what is today called 'charisma'). But these were not balanced by patience and judgement. At first a member of the Conservative Party where his prospects were bright (especially after marrying the daughter of the Tory grandee Lord Curzon), he crossed the floor and joined the Labour Party and was a minister in the first Labour government under Ramsay MacDonald. His prospects here were outstanding. Harold Macmillan has written that he only had to bide his time and he must have become leader of the Party. Instead he broke away and in 1931 formed The New Party which at first attracted much attention among MP's of all parties, including Harold Macmillan; but then it deteriorated into a pseudo-Fascist movement, and Mosley and his supporters took to holding noisy public demonstrations and marching through the streets in black shirts and jackboots. It was never to become more than a strident fringe movement. During the War Mosley and his second wife (one of the Mitford sisters) were interned as they were considered (surely wrongly) a danger to public safety.

Another political eccentric from West Downs was Hugh Rhys Rankin (1910–14),[11] who describes himself in *Who's Who* as having 'extreme political views'. Apparently on behalf of many different causes, having been at various times a member of the Labour Party, the Scottish Nationalist Party, the Scottish

Communist Party and the Welsh Republican Nationalist Party. Outside politics he was, among many other things, a champion sheep shearer, Broadsword Champion of the British Army, a Buddhist and the Hereditary Piper of the Clan Maclaine.

In the Civil Service West Downs is not, perhaps, as well represented as one might expect. But there is one towering figure. Roger Sherfield (1913–17)[12] joined the Diplomatic Service where he rose to be Ambassador in Washington. Then, most unusually, he was invited by the Prime Minister of the day to become one of the Permanent Under-Secretaries at the Treasury, John Colville has written of him: 'There are not many diplomats or civil servants to rival Roger Makins in distinction and intelligence.' He also had the reputation, according to Colville, of being a superb ballroom dancer. Makins' success began at West Downs where he was head of the school and captain of football and cricket. John (Jock) Colville (1923–27)[13] was also a member of the Diplomatic Service but was somewhat side-tracked when he became Private Secretary to three prime ministers – Chamberlain, Churchill (for most of the War years) and Attlee. During the Second World War he kept (illegally) a fascinating diary which gave a unique account of Churchill and his entourage and the conduct of the war from Downing Street; it has since been published as *The Fringes of Power*. Other distinguished members of the Diplomatic Service were David Scott-Fox (1919–23),[14] Ambassador to Chile, Finland and Turkey, George Warr (1924–28),[15] Ambassador to Nicaragua and Samuel Hood (1920–24),[16] who, after five years as HM Minister in Washington became Deputy Under-Secretary at the Foreign Office.

In the home Civil Service West Downs is sparsely represented; only Ronald Harris (1922–26),[17] who was for several years in the Treasury, and then successively Secretary to the Church Commissioners and First Church Estates Commissioner attained any eminence. In a different field Peter Thorne (1923–27)[18] was Serjeant-at-Arms in the House of Commons.

It used to be maintained that one of the main purposes of the Public Schools, and therefore of Prep Schools too, was to provide a steady stream of young men of high character and ability to govern the British Empire. Of course, for much of West Downs' history the British Empire has been in decline, but not for the first half, and during this time the School's contribution to colonial administrators was minimal, although Malcolm Barclay-Harvey (1901–05)[19] was Governor of South Australia.

The field in which West Downs has been mostly fully represented, it seems, is the armed services. In the Army and Navy, although not the Air Force, one finds a galaxy of senior officers. In the Army are to be found one Field Marshal, five Lieutenant-Generals and no less than twelve Major-Generals. Francis Festing (1911–15)[20] gained a reputation in the Second World War as a general who led from the front with outstanding qualities of leadership. After the War he was appointed Chief of the Imperial General Staff, a post in which he is said to have found the administration and routine of Whitehall much less congenial. The

Lieutenant-Generals include Gerard Bucknall (1903–07)[21] who commanded a corps at D-day, and Frederick ('Boy') Browning (1905–09)[22] who commanded the First Airborne Corps at Arnhem and later became Chief of Staff at South East Asia Command under Lord Louis Mountbatten; he also had the reputation of being the best turned-out officer in the British Army. George Collingwood (1913–17)[23] became G.O.C. Scottish Command and Governor of Edinburgh Castle, posts in which he was followed in a later generation by Norman Arthur (1940–44).[24] Still serving (in 1991) is Tony Mullens (1945–49)[25] as Deputy Chief of Defence Staff. Of West Downs' Major-Generals John Nelson (1921–25)[26] was G.O.C. British sector of Berlin and then G.O.C. London District and Major-General commanding the Household Brigade. John Sinclair (1906–10)[27] was Director of Military Intelligence; David Dawnay (1912–16)[28] commanded The 56th Armoured Division and was then Commandant of the R.M.A. Sandhurst; E.A.W. Williams (1920–24)[29] was G.O.C. Singapore; and Giles Mills (1931–35)[30] was Major-General and Resident Governor H.M. Tower of London and Keeper of Jewel House.

Although a larger number of boys from West Downs joined the Royal Navy, not so many, it seems, reached senior rank – one Admiral of the Fleet, one Admiral, two Vice-Admirals and two Rear-Admirals. As in the Army an OWD became professional head of the Service. William Staveley (1937–41)[31] was First Sea Lord and Chief of Naval Staff; previously he had been Allied Commander-in-Chief Channel and East Atlantic. Another OWD who had an outstandingly successful career was Deric Holland-Martin (1915–19).[32] A brilliant destroyer captain during the Second World War, he later became Commander-in-Chief Allied forces Mediterranean and the youngest ever Second Sea Lord. He would almost certainly have become First Sea Lord but for too great public outspokenness which upset his political masters. Two other senior officers of considerable eminence were Edward Evans-Lombe (1910–14)[33] who was commander of Allied Forces in Northern Europe and Deputy Chief of Naval Staff; and Peter Dawnay (1913–17)[34] who was Deputy Controller of the Navy and Flag Officer Royal Yachts.

It might be noted at this point how many of the OWDs mentioned above and others have been members of the Royal Household. Edward Ford (1919–23)[35] was Assistant Private Secretary to King George VI and to the present Queen. Subsequently he became Secretary of the Pilgrim Trust and Registrar of the Order of Merit. Of other royal servants Frederick Browning was Controller of the Household of Princess Elizabeth and the Duke of Edinburgh after their marriage. John Colville was the first Private Secretary to the Queen before she came to the throne. Oliver Dawnay (1929–33)[36] was Private Secretary and Equerry to Queen Elizabeth the Queen Mother. Joseph Henley (1918–22)[37] was Flag Officer Royal Yachts. William Staveley, Edward Evans-Lombe and Philip Tillard (1931–35)[38] were ADCs. Robert Boscawen (1931–35)[39] has been Comptroller of H.M. Household and Julian Loyd (1935–39)[40] has lately retired as land agent at

Sandringham.

It might be mentioned too that five OWDs have been Lords Lieutenant and seven have been High Sheriffs. These latter include George (Toby) Marten (1927–31)[41] who in the early fifties took a firm and successful stand against a government department about its failure to de-requisition his land at Crichel Down in Dorset; this led to the resignation of a cabinet minister and was regarded at the time as a notable victory of the individual citizen over ever-encroaching Bureaucracy.

An organisation well served by West Downs is the National Trust. Randal Antrim (1920–23)[42] was Chairman from 1966 to 1976 and Jack Boles (1934–38)[43] was Director General from 1975 to 1983. Also Mark Norman (1919–22)[44] was Deputy Chairman and Treasurer; Edward Holland-Martin (1909–12) was Hon. Treasurer; and John Bute (1942–46)[45] was Chairman of the Scottish National Trust.

It might be appropriate at this stage to note those fields in which West Downs has not been strongly represented. As far as can be ascertained no OWD has achieved eminence in Science, although Edward Collingwood (1909–12)[46] was Vice-President of the London Mathematical Society and a member of the Medical Research Council. Surprisingly, considering the strong Christian ethos of West Downs, very few OWDs (perhaps no more than six) have entered the Church, and of these only one has become a bishop – Keith Arnold (1936–40).[47] Outside the Church of England Henry Coombe-Tennant (1916–19), after a varied career as a soldier and diplomat and having made one of the few successful escapes from a prisoner of war camp, became a Dominican monk and taught at Downside. In the Law three judges can be found: John Stephenson (1919–22)[48] was a Lord Justice of Appeal; Oliver Wrightson (1929–32) was a Circuit Judge and W.H.R. Crawford (1945–50) is one at the present time; and John Phipps (1919–23) was a Metropolitan Magistrate. In Education West Downs has produced only one headmaster, A.O.H. Quick (1933–37) of Bradfield, and in the academic world only two professors – Patrick Nowell-Smith (1923–27) and I.G. MacDonald (1939–41). On the Stage only Nicholas Phipps (1922–25) and Peter Howell (1928–32) have made careers for themselves. (Although it is reported that one OWD did have aspirations as a ballet dancer but had to abandon them when his weight passed fifteen stone!).

In the world of Business there are more names to conjure with, but in the City rather than in Industry. Jeremy Morse (1937–42),[49] once a director of the Bank of England, is at present Chairman of Lloyds Bank as well as being Warden of Winchester College, Chancellor of Bristol University and President of the British Chess Problem Society. Edward Holland-Martin (1909–13) was a director of the Bank of England; Christopher Glenconner (1909–13)[50] was Chairman of Charles Tennant, Son and Co. and a director of I.C.I. and Hambro's Bank. John Simon (1912–15)[51] was Deputy Chairman of P & O and President of the Chamber of Shipping. William Harcourt (1917–21)[52] was Chairman of Legal and General

Assurance (also of the Rhodes Trust and the Oxford Preservation Trust). Mark Norman (1919–23) was Chairman of Gallaher and Managing Director of Lazards. Alexander Hood (1923–27)[53] is Chairman of Petrofina and a director of Schroder Wragg. James Spooner (1940–44)[54] is Chairman of Morgan Crucible and a director of J. Sainsbury. Peter Wilmot-Sitwell (1943–47) is Joint Chairman of S. G. Warburg. James Harvie-Watt (1948–52) has been Managing Director of Wembley Stadium.

In the field of literature West Downs is moderately well represented – no household names but several authors of distinction. Perhaps the best known, although not so much for his literary works, is Peter Scott (1918–22),[55] a man of infinite variety if ever there was one. Today he is remembered chiefly for his pioneering work in preserving wildlife, notably in the setting up of his wildfowl sanctuaries at Slimbridge and Arundel and as Chairman of the World Wildlife Fund. But he was also an artist, explorer, a president of the British Gliding Association, an intrepid and highly successful commander of coastal craft during the Second World War, and an Olympic Bronze Medallist in single-handed dinghy sailing. Among many honorary posts he was Chancellor of Birmingham University and Admiral of the Manx Fishing Fleet. His books were almost entirely on wildfowl. At West Downs his love of wildlife was much in evidence; his pockets were always full of living creatures and his desk was a positive zoo. He is also remembered by his contemporaries for the extreme rigour of his personal regime: the son of the Antarctic explorer, Captain Robert Falcon Scott, he seemed to be preparing to follow in his father's footsteps. Peter Scott's half-brother, Wayland Kennet (see p. 180) has had a number of books published on a diversity of topics including The Italian Left, Old London Churches, The Profumo Affair and Erotica Denied (much of this in language he surely did not learn at West Downs).

Mention has already been made of John Colville's wartime diary, *The Fringes of Power*, in reviewing which Anthony Sampson described him as 'a diarist of genius.' Tom Pocock (see p. 61–63) is mainly known as a distinguished journalist but he has also written several books on Nelson and naval history. The most widely read of OWD writers is likely to be Richard Ingrams (1947–51), for twenty-three years editor of *Private Eye* and founder of *The Oldie* magazine. At West Downs, it seems, he was a relatively orthodox citizen with no reputation for rebelliousness; he was a keen cricketer and won the fielding prize. But the most distinguished OWD in the field of journalism is, surely, David Astor (1921–24)[56] who was proprietor and editor of *The Observer* from 1948 to 1975. Run on idiosyncratic, some say amateurish, lines, it was regarded by Sir Peregrine Worsthorne as being 'by far the best Sunday newspaper in the world, a pre-eminence which it swiftly lost when he ceased to own and edit it.' Several well known writers today look back on their time on *The Observer* under Astor as having been a unique experience.

Finally note should be taken of those OWDs who have had success in the world of sport. It was said of David Milford (1915–19) that at West Downs he never missed a chance of hitting a ball against a wall with whatever weapon came to hand. Later he became an outstanding ball games player – once world and seven times British rackets champion and an international hockey player.[57] Other sportsmen of national standing include A.N. Henniker-Gotley (1899–1903) who was an England rugby captain; Richard Rawson (1901–04) was amateur heavyweight boxing champion; Thomas Brocklebank (1917–20) was an England oarsman who had previously stroked Cambridge to victory in the Boat Race three years running, and who also went on one of the pre-war Everest expeditions; John Lakin (1920–24) was an England polo player. On the cricket field Neville Ford (1916–18) played for Derbyshire, Giles Baring (1920–24) for Hampshire, A.R. Legard (1920–24) for Sussex, and Arthur Hazlerigg (1919–23)[58] was captain of Leicestershire in his early twenties and played against the first Australian team to be captained by Don Bradman, also in his early twenties. West Downs is well represented too in Equestrianism. Derek Allhusen (1922–26)[59] was a member of the Gold Medal Team at the Mexico Olympics of 1968; and Mark Darley (1935–39) and Norman Arthur were also members of successful Olympic teams. On the subject of horses J.E. Oxley (1939–42) was a popular and successful Newmarket trainer.

Of the OWDs mentioned above it is notable that the majority of them made no great name for themselves at West Downs; for the most part they were solid middle-of-the-roaders. It is also notable that all of them were at the School during the first sixty years of its history, and most of them during the Helbert and early Tindall years when West Downs had a reputation in some quarters as being a 'snob school' and when its academic record was unimpressive. When it is considered that during this time there were only about 500 boys at West Downs, the success rate must be outstanding. For whatever reason no OWD who was at the School since the mid-fifties (when academic success was much greater) has as yet attained eminence (or not enough to gain admittance to the pages of *Who's Who*), but there is, of course, still time.

---

[1]The Right Hon. Lord Duncan-Sandys, C.H.
[2]The Right Hon. Lord Soames, G.C.M.G., G.C.V.O., C.B.E.
[3]The Right Hon. Nicholas Ridley.
[4]The Right Hon. Lord O'Neill of the Maine D.L.
[5]Better known as Viscount Hinchingbrooke, under which honorary title he sat in the House of Commons for twenty-one years before succeeding his father as 10th Earl of Sandwich, a title he disclaimed two years later.
[6]The Right Hon. Lord McCorquodale of Newton-le-Willows, K.C.V.O.
[7]The Right Hon. Earl Ferrers. Previously Viscount Tamworth.
[8]The Viscount Ullswater.
[9]Lord Kennet. Previously Wayland Hilton Young.
[10]The Right Hon. Sir Oswald Mosley, Bt.
[11]Sir Hugh C. Rhys Rankin, Bt., F.S.A.
[12]The Right Hon. Lord Sherfield, G.C.B., G.C.M.G., F.R.S., D.L. Previously Roger Makins.
[13]Sir John Colville, C.B., C.V.O.

[14]Sir David Scott-Fox, K.C.M.G.
[15]G.M. Warr, C.B.E.
[16]The 6th Viscount Hood, K.C.M.G.
[17]Sir Ronald Harris, K.C.V.O., C.B.
[18]Sir Peter Thorne, K.C.V.O., C.B.E
[19]Sir Malcolm Barclay-Harvey, K.C.M.G.
[20]Field Marshal Sir Francis Festing, G.C.B., K.B.E., D.S.O.
[21]Lieutenant-General G.C. Bucknall, C.B., M.C., D.L.
[22]Lieutenant-General Sir Frederick Browning, K.C.V.O., K.B.E., C.B., D.S.O.
[23]Lieutenant-General Sir George Collingwood, K.B.E., C.B., D.S.O.
[24]Lieutenant-General Sir Norman Arthur, K.C.B.
[25]Lieutenant-General Sir Anthony Mullens, K.C.B., O.B.E.
[26]Major-General Sir John Nelson, K.C.V.O., C.B., O.B.E., D.S.O., M.C.
[27]Major-General Sir John Sinclair, K.C.M.G., C.B., O.B.E.
[28]Major-General Sir David Dawnay, K.C.V.O., C.B., D.S.C., D.L.
[29]Major-General E.A.W. Williams, C.B., C.B.E., M.C.
[30]Major-General, G.H. Mills, O.B.E.
[31]Admiral of the Fleet Sir William Staveley, G.C.B.
[32]Admiral Sir Deric Holland-Martin, G.C.B., D.S.O., D.S.C.
[33]Vice-Admiral Sir Edward Evans-Lombe, K.C.B.
[34]Vice-Admiral Sir Peter Dawnay, K.C.V.O., C.B., D.S.C.
[35]Sir Edward Ford, K.C.B., K.C.V.O., E.R.D., D.L.
[36]Captain Oliver Dawnay, C.V.O.
[37]Rear Admiral Sir Joseph Henley, K.C.V.O., C.B.
[38]Major-General P.B. Tillard, O.B.E.
[39]The Hon R.T. Boscawen, M.C., M.P.
[40]Sir Julian Loyd, K.C.V.O.
[41]Lieutenant-Commander G.G. Marten, M.V.O., D.S.C.
[42]The Earl of Antrim, K.B.E.
[43]Sir Jack Boles, M.B.E., D.L.
[44]Mark R. Norman, C.B.E.
[45]The Marquess of Bute.
[46]Sir Edward Collingwood, C.B.E., F.R.S., Ph.D.
[47]The Right Revd K.A. Arnold, D.D., Bishop of Warwick
[48]The Right Hon. Sir John Stephenson
[49]Sir Jeremy Morse, K.C.M.G.
[50]Lord Glenconner
[51]Viscount Simon, C.M.G.
[52]Viscount Harcourt, K.C.M.G., O.B.E.
[53]The 7th Viscount Hood
[54]Sir James Spooner, Bt.
[55]Sir Peter Scott, C.B.E., D.S.C. (and bar), F.R.S.
[56]The Hon. David Astor
[57]Of slight and wiry build he was once recommended by an osteopath he visited to take up some sport to develop his frame.
[58]Major the Lord Hazlerigg, M.C.
[59]Major D.S. Allhusen, C.V.O., D.L.

APPENDIX

The prayers used in West Downs chapel made a great impression on all who heard them. Of exceptional beauty and simplicity they are a great testimonial to the genius of Lionel Helbert, and should surely be preserved.

At Morning Prayer

Into thy hands, O Lord, we commend ourselves this day: bestow, we pray Thee, Thy merciful blessing upon our School. Teach us to remember that as without Thee we cannot live, so with Thy help we cannot fail. Give us strength to carry out our appointed tasks in work and in play with all our might. Help us to do unto others as we would that they should do unto us; and in all our thoughts, words and actions keep us honest, brave and pure. Through Jesus Christ our Lord.

At Evening Prayer

O God, who didst bid children to be brought unto Thee, take us to Thyself this night. Forgive us the sins we have committed this day. Accept our thanks for all the happiness and blessings which we have enjoyed by Thy good mercy. Guard us through the hours of darkness, bless and keep our dear ones at home, and teach us all to love one another for the sake of him who so tenderly loves all of us, even Thy Son, our Lord Jesus Christ.

The Founder's Act of Thanksgiving and Prayer

Let us praise God in gladness and humility for all the great and simple joys; and for the weak things of the earth which have confounded the strong.

Glory be to thee, O Lord.

For the gift of wonder and the joy of discovery; for the everlasting freshness of experience; for the newness of life each day as we grow older; for the fireside and the intimate talks of friendship; for the little traditions and customs of the home; for meals eaten there in fellowship; for all the sanctities of family life; for games and holidays in the open air; for books and pictures and all our small possessions.

Glory be to thee, O Lord.

For birds and beasts and all God's creatures; for children and the joy of innocency; for the joy of work attempted and achieved; for the joy of harvest and the wedding feast; for the beech trees and the bluebell woods in spring; for the smell of the country after rain; for the green grass and for flowers; for clouds and sun; for hills and mountain streams, and for the joy which is born of sympathy and sorrow.

Glory be to thee, O Lord.

For all pure comedy and laughter; for the gift of humour and gaiety of heart, and for all who have consecrated mirth with the love of Christ; for all singers and musicians; for all who work in form and colour to increase the joy of life; and for all who rejoice in their work and make things well.

Glory be to thee, O Lord.

For all who have loved the poor and borne their sorrows in their hearts; for all obscure and humble saints and for poor village priests and ministering women, and for all ignorant disciples who have misunderstood the Christian doctrine and yet lived in the fellowship of Christ.

Glory be to thee, O Lord.

For the image of Christ in ordinary people; for their forbearance and generosity, their courage and their kindness; for the glory of God shining in commonplace lives; for holy and humble men of heart in whom the loveliness of Our Saviour Christ has been made manifest to the world, and for great saints who have been true followers of most perfect and holy poverty.

Glory be to thee, O Lord.

A Boy of my Time's Prayer

Lord, give us strength today to live as you would like us to live, without fear, joyfully and lovingly.

Help us not to get flustered when things go wrong, and when there's confusion and tension give us your deep peace so that we can remain calm whatever happens and so help others to turn to you for strength and support.

Help us also, Lord, not to be led into temptation to sin, and if we sin and if we fail, to repent at once, without any hesitation, as that sinner did when he was hung on the Cross all those years ago, through Jesus Christ Our Lord.

Index